WHY
WE LOVE
PIRATES

WHY WE LOVE PIRATES

The Hunt for Captain Kidd and How He Changed Piracy Forever

REBECCA SIMON, PHD

Mango Publishing
Coral Gables

Cover Design: Gabrielle Mechaber
Cover illustrations: paseven/Adobe Stock
Layout & Design: <Designer name>
Interior Illustrations: kuco/Adobe Stock

For permission requests, please contact the publisher at:
Mango Publishing Group
2850 S Douglas Road, 2nd Floor
Coral Gables, FL 33134 USA
info@mango.bz

For special orders, quantity sales, course adoptions and corporate sales, please email the publisher at sales@mango.bz. For trade and wholesale sales, please contact Ingram Publisher Services at customer.service@ingramcontent.com or +1.800.509.4887.

Why We Love Pirates: The Hunt for Captain Kidd and How He Changed Piracy Forever

Library of Congress Cataloging-in-Publication number: 2020940961
ISBN: (print) 978-1-64250-337-1, (ebook) 978-1-64250-338-8
BISAC category code HIS057000—HISTORY / Maritime History & Piracy

Printed in the United States of America

Dedicated with all my love to my grandpa, Bernie Jack Shapiro, who, sadly, will never be able to read this book. Thank you for your endless love, support, and interest, reminding me often that you read a book about Jewish pirates.

TABLE OF CONTENTS

TIMELINE OF THE GOLDEN AGE OF PIRACY

- **1536:** King Henry VIII passes Offences of the Sea Act

- **1650–1680:** First Pirate Round: English, French, and Dutch Protestants known as "buccaneers"

- **1651:** Navigation Acts passed

- **1654:** England takes Jamaica from Spain

- **1654–1660:** Anglo-Spanish War

- **1670:** Treaty of Madrid between England and Spain; recognizes English ownership of Jamaica

- **1690s:** Second Pirate Round: Indian Ocean piracy

- **1692:** Pirate stronghold of Port Royal, Jamaica, collapses in an earthquake; pirates scatter

- **1695:** Pirate Henry Avery robs Mughal ships

- **1699:** Pirate Captain Kidd arrested

- **1700:** Act for the Effectual Suppression of Piracy passes to modify Offences of the Sea Act

- **May 23, 1701:** Pirate Captain Kidd executed

- **May 24, 1701:** Captain Kidd's trial transcript published

- **May 25, 1701:** Captain Kidd's trial transcript sells out

◆ **May 26, 1701:** Captain Kidd's trial transcript gets second printing

◆ **1706:** Pirates begin to establish unofficial "Pirate Republic" in Nassau, Bahamas

◆ **1713:** Pirate Captain Benjamin Hornigold establishes official Pirate Republic in Nassau, Bahamas

◆ **1701–1714:** War of Spanish Succession

◆ **1716–1726:** Third Round of Piracy: Post-war Atlantic piracy

◆ **1718:** Woodes Rogers becomes Governor of Bahamas

◆ **1717:** Act for the Effectual Suppression of Piracy repassed

◆ **1718:** Blackbeard killed in battle

◆ **1720:** Captain Jack Rackham, Anne Bonny, and Mary Read terrorize the Caribbean and are found guilty of piracy

◆ **1721:** The Act for the Effectual Suppression of Piracy repassed

◆ **1723:** Cotton Mather's *Useful Remarks* published in London

◆ **1724:** Captain Charles Johnson publishes the first volume of *A General History of the Pyrates*

◆ **1726:** Pirate William Fly executed in Boston, Massachusetts. Last public execution "spectacle." Considered the end of the Golden Age of Piracy

◆ **1728:** Captain Charles Johnson publishes the second volume of *A General History of the Pyrates*

● **1730s:** European wars break out and Atlantic piracy is officially over

CAST OF CHARACTERS

Henry Avery (August 20, 1659–unknown): English pirate who operated in the Atlantic and Indian Oceans. Known as the "King of the Pirates." Famous for robbing Indian merchants and escaping persecution.

Captain William Kidd (January 22, 1645–May 23, 1701): Scottish sailor who worked for the British East India Company until he was arrested and executed for crimes of piracy.

Captain Benjamin Hornigold (1680–1719): English privateer during the War of Spanish Succession who later became pirate. Established the "pirate kingdom" in Nassau, New Providence (Bahamas).

Captain Edward Teach (Blackbeard) (c. 1680–November 22, 1718): English pirate who operated between 1716 and 1718. Killed in battle.

Captain "Calico" Jack Rackham (December 26, 1682–November 18, 1720): Pirate captain who once sailed with Charles Vane. Married to Anne Bonny. Captured off the coast of Jamaica and executed for crimes of piracy. Known as "Calico Jack" because of his penchant for fine clothing.

Mary Read: (1685–April 28, 1721): Female pirate who occasionally sailed under the name Mark Read. Sailed under Jack Rackham with Anne Bonny. Found guilty as a pirate but not executed because of her pregnancy. Died in a Jamaican prison of childbed fever.

Charles Vane (1680–March 29, 1721): English pirate who mostly operated in and around the Bahamas, known for his cruelty. Executed for piracy in Jamaica.

Anne Bonny (c. 1697–April 1782): Irish pirate who sailed with Captain Jack Rackham with Mary Read.

Edward "Ned" Low (1690–1724): English pirate known for his brutality.

Woodes Rogers (c. 1679–July 15, 1732): English privateer who later became governor of the Bahamas.

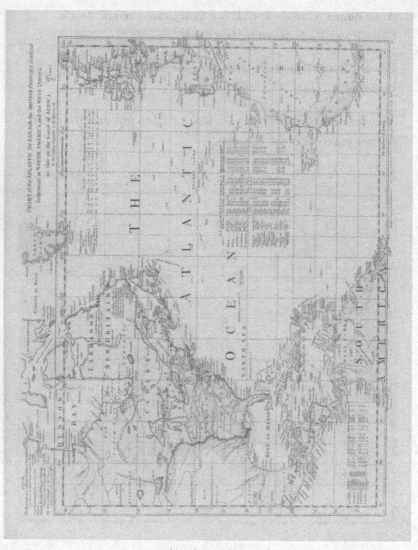

Map of the Atlantic World, c. 1757
Courtesy of the John Carter Brown Library

Map of the West Indies
Courtesy of the John Carter Brown Library

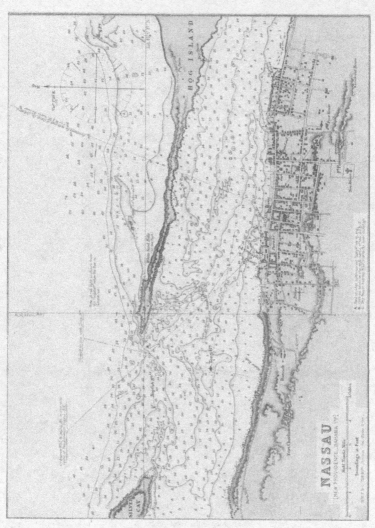

Map of Nassau, c. 1800
Wiki Commons

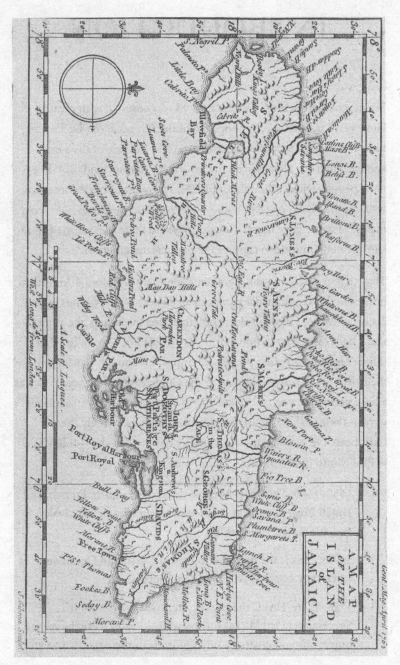

Map of the Island of Jamaica, c. 1760
Courtesy of the John Carter Brown Library

INTRODUCTION

Before graduate school, I wouldn't say I was *obsessed* with pirates. However, I was definitely a huge fan of the *Pirates of the Caribbean* films (still am…except for the fifth one) and the ride of the same name (which has always been my favorite) at Disneyland. But, like most people, when I thought of pirates, I thought of buried treasure, walking the plank, peg legs and eye patches, and the phrase "Arrrrrr, matey!" I never gave much thought to where these ideas came from or why pirates continue to capture the popular imagination.

That changed when I took a graduate seminar on Colonial American history and was assigned a book called *Villains of All Nations* by the historian Marcus Rediker. His book upended the beliefs about pirates that I had learned from pop culture my whole life. One of the first things I learned was that pirates are important enough figures to have their own era of history, known as the Golden Age of Piracy. This was a time period between 1650 and 1726 when piracy and persecutions were at their peak in the British Atlantic colonies, namely the Caribbean and North America. Rediker has divided the Golden Age of Piracy into three rounds:

1. 1650–1680: The buccaneers were mostly English, French, and Dutch Protestants who hunted wild game on deserted islands and attacked Spanish ships.

2. 1690s: This is the period of piracy in the Indian Ocean and when they established a haven in Madagascar.

3. 1716–1726: This is the period after the War of Spanish Succession (1701–1714) during which pirates were the most numerous and created a crisis of trade in the Atlantic Ocean.[1]

The most famous period of the Golden Age is between 1716 and 1726. These ten years were when the most famous pirates in history sailed together, such as Blackbeard, Anne Bonny, and Mary Read (more on these legends later). All of what we think we know about pirates is inspired by those who lived during that decade. The Golden Age of Piracy is said to have ended in 1726 with the death of the pirate William Fly, who had the last "dramatic" public execution in Boston.[2]

In his book, Rediker said pirates were seventeenth- and eighteenth-century terrorists hell-bent on forcing Caribbean and North American trade to its knees. In response, the British authorities pursued them…behaving as terrorists themselves. Manhunts were staged to end piracy at all costs. Pirates were brutalized and tried. They were publicly hanged for all to see. The pirates retaliated by specifically targeting British ships. This dance, referred to as a dialectic of terror, continued back and forth until piracy was practically eradicated by 1730.

If pirates were such terrorists, how on earth did we come to see them as cool, swashbuckling sailors? I wanted to find out, so this became the subject of my master's thesis. To my surprise, I found that no source made any mention of eye patches, peg legs, walking the plank, or anything else of the sort. There *was* one rumor about buried treasure, but that turned out to be false. These tropes did not appear until the 1880s, when a man named Robert Louis Stevenson wrote a little book called *Treasure Island*.

But it couldn't just be *Treasure Island* that created popular interest in pirates…right? Pirates were common subjects in newspapers and other written pieces in the 1700s and early 1800s. So, what did people think about pirates at the height of their notoriety? In the early stages of my PhD research, I found that public executions of pirates were meticulously recorded and published with a wide readership. Newspapers published numerous articles about gruesome attacks

from pirates throughout British America. Initially, it made logical
sense that pirates were seen as evil and that people attended their
executions to feel smug self-satisfaction.

Soon I discovered the story was much more complicated than that.
In the beginning of my research, I came upon a series of documents
that completely blew my mind—the *Calendar of State Papers*. This
nineteen-volume collection contains letters and correspondence
between plantation owners, merchants and traders, governors,
Admiralty officers, and parliamentary officials about pirates in the
colonies. Many of these letters complained that the American colonies
were harboring pirates and encouraging their plunder. The Carolinas,
Rhode Island, and Pennsylvania were especially hot topics because
they had the strongest comradery with pirates. Letters from the
Caribbean show that many people begged officials to let jailed pirates
go because they were valuable members of their communities. They
brought in goods and money that helped many cities thrive. Killing
pirates would kill their communities.

This contradiction is fascinating. On the one hand, newspapers
worked to make people see the worst of pirates. On the other hand,
many American colonists and governors were happy to trade with
pirates, much to the ire of the British authorities. These actions
upended the colonists' relationship with the Crown, allowing them
to create their own laws, separate from Britain's, and to support
themselves. In fact, pirates brought so many valuable goods into
the colonies that they ended up playing an important role in their
development and success. The Crown did not see it this way, however.
Pirates were destroying trade and corrupting their colonial subjects!
As the British would discover, interfering with the colonies' dealings
with pirates could permanently damage Britain's relationships with
its colonies.

Pirates were more than criminals. They were more than swashbuckling sailors. They were instrumental to the early development of the British Empire, and even played a role in planting the seeds for American independence. They have been painted as one of two extremes for too long: the terrorist or the cool hero. Some were, for a lack of a better term, evil (such as Ned Low or Charles Vane). Others were flashy and mostly interested in attracting attention (such as Jack Rackham or Blackbeard). But the reality is that the vast majority of pirates fell somewhere in between. Some were sailors who wanted to make money quickly so they could settle down and give their families nice lives. Others considered piracy legitimate employment. They chose to rob ships because they believed picking and choosing their victims ultimately benefitted the greater good.

One pirate that fits all of the above descriptions is Captain William Kidd, who only operated as a pirate from 1698 to 1699. While this was before the infamous decade from 1716 to 1726, he was a huge character in the Golden Age of Piracy and inspired the next generation of pirates. He had long been a privateer (a sailor paid to rob enemy ships) for the British government. However, he was known to be troublesome and too often bent the rules of his "letter of marque," a legal document issued by the government that allowed him to rob enemy ships. (Remember this—letters of marque will be very important!) After he angered Indian emperors, known as Mughals, by stealing too many of their ships, India threatened to stop all trade with Britain, and even declared war. To add insult to injury, Britain was also in a stalemate with its European competitors about who was the most powerful nation in the world. In order to protect their trade, prove themselves the dominant world power, and keep control over their sailors and their people, they had to destroy Captain Kidd.

Kidd embodied everything that we associate with pirates. He was ruthless to his crew if they stood against him. He even killed a crew member who argued against him. He dressed in only the finest clothing, and made grandiose claims about stealing a huge amount of goods, which included a hoard of gold, silver, and jewels. And to top this off, he considered himself a legitimately-employed privateer working on behalf of the British government who had simply gotten trapped in an unjust system.

Captain Kidd provides us with the most well-rounded view of the history of pirates. He was, for instance, the first pirate to become the subject of an ongoing worldwide manhunt. The timing was fortuitous—the printing industry had just taken off in the 1690s, and news about his actions and the hunt was printed on both sides of the Atlantic Ocean, making him an international sensation. At a time when society was obsessed with the good manners and behavior necessary to be considered a well-respected gentleperson, Kidd broke all the rules. Legends of buried treasure also exist thanks to Kidd and a letter he wrote to a well-connected friend, promising to tell him the location of all of his wealth if he would help set Kidd free. Once captured, Kidd's trial was transcribed verbatim and then published at a cheap price for mass consumption. When the day came for him to receive his fatal punishment, he had an audience of thousands.

Kidd exemplifies all of the reasons we are fascinated with pirates to this day: rebelling against social norms, angering the British government, violence, rumors of buried treasure, a large public presence, and a theatrical public execution. I dare say Captain William Kidd is responsible for pirates' eternal fame in popular culture.

To top it off, Kidd's life also shows us how Britain sought to control the oceans to make itself the most powerful nation in the world.

Kidd's widespread fame caused people to start seeing pirates in a new light. For the first time, pirates were not just nuisances or dangerous foes out to destroy those who came across their path. They were not boogeymen of the sea. Rather, they could be respected employees of the Crown. They could be well-to-do captains and high-ranking officials who organized their methods of plunder in a surprisingly civil manner. Perhaps most strikingly of all to the classist upper crust, pirates could also be lowly sailors from poor backgrounds who rose in up in their ranks and earned a lot of money very, very quickly.

It is no coincidence that Britain had to start a massive crackdown on piracy just a few years after Kidd's death. There were many factors that led to an increase in piracy during the early 1700s, including a prolonged period of peace. Peacetime meant less employment at sea, so adventurous people drawn to the ocean had to find other means to make a living without the constraints of merchant or naval ships, both of which had extremely strict and harshly enforced rules. Pirating was an excellent choice. Shipping lanes were crowded and the ships were ripe for the picking.

Of course, the reality was much more complicated than this idealist fantasy. Kidd did not intend to become so famous. He was a privateer who became too rash for his own good out of desperation. Unfortunately, his final voyage was rife with mistakes and missteps that ultimately cost him his life. Even though Kidd ultimately suffered a brutal hanging, he symbolized how anyone could cast off their loyalty to authority and make their own way in life.

This book explores piracy through the lens of Captain Kidd's pirate life, but he is only the outer shell. His life opens up the deeper history of pirates and how society truly reacted to them. From here, we will discover exactly who pirates were and why people chose this profession. We will uncover the true story of Captain Kidd, and of how and why the British government sought to exterminate pirates at all costs. Also, we'll unbury how the exploding print industry influenced public opinion about pirates, and how the cultural and social norms of the era made us love pirates so much. And, ultimately, how their deaths gave them permanent infamy.

There is one area that this book not does cover, save for a discussion in the first chapter, which is enslaved people. That is a subject that is a very unfortunate gap in my research because their roles on the pirate ship were no less important than others. Both freed and escaped, formerly enslaved Africans were known to work these vessels because they were places where one could live away from the law. Freed, formerly enslaved people often had difficulty finding work and escaped enslaved people were at risk of capture and/or death. A pirate ship would be a haven for them. The pirates' role in the slave trade is also a subject that deserves more attention. There is debate among historians about whether pirates engaged in the slave trade. Some say yes because enslaved people could be sold for profit, while other historians argue that pirates would not abet the persecution of marginalized people. This is a subject that goes beyond the scope of this book, but more importantly, deserves an entire volume unto itself.[3]

This book includes several pieces of dialogue that sound like they could be from a work of fiction. I assure you, they are all true. For the sake of making them as accessible as possible, I added some emotion and modernized the wording. But everything is taken directly from the actual source. Some of it is so wild that I could not make it up if I tried.

So, pour yourself a glass of rum, hitch up your sails, and travel with me over the horizon and back in time!

CHAPTER 1

WHO WERE
PIRATES?

E veryone knows what a pirate is. We all think of a man who
sails the high seas with his brethren to pillage and plunder
any ships that cross their path. After burying gold coins
and jewels in a secret location, they sell the rest of their goods and
immediately spend that money in taverns on alcohol and women.
They sing into the night, start fights, attack towns, and escape right
under the noses of the most highly trained officers. After a short
period of time, the sea calls them back, and they return to their ship
to continue their plundering. Their unlucky hostages walk the plank
and are cast into Davy Jones's Locker (the origins of this legend
are mysterious even to this day). They swagger and radiate sex.
Pirates are *cool*.

The truth is a bit more complicated than that. But one thing that is
for sure is that pirates have always been and continue to be deliciously
illicit. We have always been morbidly fascinated by pirates. Who were
these people who chose to sail under such risky conditions? If capture
meant a certain death sentence, why undertake such an endeavor?

Essentially, pirates were people who rejected society and created their
own little world on their ships. Their community was multicultural
and everyone got an equal share of the prize. They answered to
nobody but themselves. Their deeds were reported in newspapers
and other publications, which flew off the shelves, for the common
people to consume. In Britain and Colonial America, when people
gathered around in taverns to hear someone read the news, pirates
were always a subject that came up. They read about pirates who
brutally murdered their hostages, stole large ships with huge caches of
supplies, were captured and put on trial, and were sentenced to harsh
public deaths at the gallows. Reading between the lines, they learned
about how pirates brought desired forbidden items into the colonies.
These stories were gulped down like the tastiest of rums.

What really made pirates seem so cool was that they were able to cast off all of their social obligations and roles. During the seventeenth and eighteenth centuries, your status was pretty much fixed from birth. If you were born poor, you would stay poor. If you were fortunate enough to be born wealthy, you would stay rich. If you were born into a skilled middle-class family, you would follow in your father's footsteps. Sailors often came from either poor or middle-class families. If they were less fortunate, they were put onto ships at a very young age and, over time, could work their way up a bit. If they were middle-class and educated, they could become a First Mate or Quartermaster before long. Pay was based on position and was often withheld for various reasons.

Pirates, on the other hand, only needed to know how to sail (or to be able to learn quickly) and to be brave in a fight. They were assigned duties based on their skills, and money or prizes were doled out equally so that everyone had a fair share. A destitute man could become extremely wealthy after just a year or two on a pirate ship.

One way to avoid the risk of capture and hanging while still enjoying the benefits of piracy was to become employed as a privateer. During wartime, sailors were called upon to fight against specific enemy ships, depending on the country that hired them. These sailors were given letters of marque, which, again, were official documents that gave them permission to attack and rob enemy ships. They would be paid in whatever loot they could steal. A letter of marque, however, was like a contract. It had an expiration date that was usually at the end of whatever conflict was taking place. At that point, the sailors were required to stop their privateering and return to a legitimate line of work. Many privateers enjoyed being able to rob ships and steal anything they could carry because it guaranteed a much higher income than they would have earned as a merchant or naval seaman. Plus, it was a lot more fun and adventurous to travel the world as one wished in search of new things to steal. Be honest—what would you choose to do?

Captain William Kidd was one of the most well-known pirates during the Golden Age of Piracy, the years from 1650 to 1730, in which pirates were most active and organized throughout the Caribbean and North American colonies. Pirates may have existed since the day people figured out how to make a boat float, but this time period was different because it was the first time history saw a pattern of large, organized societies made up of hefty pirate fleets. During this era, ownership of the colonies and Caribbean islands was constantly fought over by various European powers. Britain managed to secure Jamaica from Spain around 1670 with the Treaty of Madrid, but one of the requirements of this treaty was to rid the seas of pirates. With the uptick in persecution, pirates who already lived in the Caribbean began to scatter, but then formed their own squadrons. This persisted for the next fifty-odd years. Piracy also flourished during the early eighteenth century because peacetime had returned, and many people who worked as privateers in wartime (as in the War for Spanish Succession, a fourteen-year conflict about who would succeed to the Spanish throne after King Charles II's death) were suddenly unemployed. The number of pirates shot up to the point where Britain had to begin an extermination campaign to get rid of them all.

Pirate...or Criminal?

Captain Kidd became the prime scapegoat. His exploits created the first concurrently-documented manhunt in history, rendering him one of the most famous pirates that ever lived. Newspapers were constantly publishing articles with the latest news of his exploits until he was finally captured in Boston. His life and death captured the public's attention, forever changing our perception of pirates.

But were pirates criminals? And who was in charge of capturing
them? The definition of piracy has always been debated. Official
definitions of piracy were written into English law in 1536 when King
Henry VIII signed the *Offences at Sea Act 1536* (28 Hen 8, c.15),
which was later modified in 1700 to create the *Act for the Effectual
Suppression of Piracy*. (This would be reissued twice, in 1717 and
1721, in continued efforts to curb piracy.) However, both laws
essentially used the same definition. Pirates were legally defined as
"*hostis humanis generis*": enemies of all mankind. In essence, a pirate
was anyone who robbed, plundered,
and murdered on any type of body of
water.[4] As for their pursuers,
England had a special court—the
High Court of Admiralty—for all
things related to the sea and
exploration. The Admiralty was
created in 1260 to ward off potential
Viking invaders, but their authority
did not grow until Henry VIII passed
the above-mentioned act. This law officially declared England an
empire and made piracy punishable by England no matter where in
the world the pirates were. The High Court of Admiralty was ordered
to put its complete focus on pirates. Admiralty Officials then had the
power to arrest pirates just for being accused of piracy.[5]

If Britain was attacked for any reason, or even just harassed, the
deliberately vague wording of this definition became very convenient.
If the government wanted a certain group of sailors punished or
killed, it could easily twist the definition of piracy to serve its purpose.
Anyone who committed any sort of crime could be considered
a pirate. Even if the person did not murder anyone, it could be
suggested that their robbery was an intent to harm their own nation.
Bam. Pirate.

This legal ambiguity meant that it was sometimes hard to decide who really was a pirate, which presented a major problem. What if a man killed someone or stole something on his own ship? What if someone killed another person at sea without taking anything?

Many "pirates" did not consider themselves pirates. For instance, Captain William Kidd had specific orders from the British government to rob French ships while sailing the Indian Ocean. His fatal mistake was robbing a big and powerful Armenian ship. In his defense, he *thought* it was a French ship, or so he claimed. Throughout his trial, he maintained that he was absolutely most definitely not a pirate. He had legal orders to rob enemy ships in the East Indies.

"Then produce proof," Admiralty officials told him. "Bring us your letter of marque."

Kidd, unfortunately, could not produce the letter of marque, because it had conveniently disappeared.

Another example is Richard Coyle, a sailor accused of murdering his captain. Was this piracy? Or—just as bad, if not worse—was this mutiny? Naturally, at his trial, Coyle claimed that he was innocent.

"I had no choice but to murder him!" he declared. "That man was not really our captain. The ship's carpenter killed our captain and then forced me to sail under him. I had no choice but to avenge my real captain!"

The judge was no doubt exasperated by this claim. There was always a reason. "Very well," the judge said, calling his bluff. "Produce some witnesses, or someone who can vouch for your character, and we will look more closely at these charges." Coyle was never able to produce any witnesses, and so he was sentenced to hang.[6]

Coyle was not unique. There were other cases like his. The Admiralty never actually called him a pirate, but others were, just for the sake of semantics. This was the case for Captain James Lowrey, who was found guilty of the murder of Kenneth Hossack, a prisoner on his ship. Lowrey's chief mate, James Godderar, was the star witness of this case. He claimed to have watched Lowrey beat Hossack to death. The circumstances of how Hossack came to be a prisoner, however, were murky, and it seemed no one could provide any specific details about this.

"Did the captain accuse any of the crew of acts of piracy?" the prosecutor asked.

"No, he did not," Godderar responded.

The context of the murder was also tricky. Did Lowrey intend to beat the prisoner to death, or just give him a routine beating? Did the prisoner do something to antagonize him? The details were too unclear. Finally, out of sheer frustration, the British argued that, by taking Hossack a prisoner, Lowrey had stolen a man. Since Lowrey beat him to death, he had killed a man. Therefore, Lowrey *must* be a pirate. So they declared him one and hanged him for it.[7]

This is why many pirates did not believe they were pirates. The rules were so fluid and constantly changing that they often did not *know* they had committed a serious crime. Murder on the high seas? Meh. It happened. Sometimes ships had to battle, and in battles there were deaths. Robbery? This also happened. During battles, people took advantage of the takings if they had the opportunity.

Sometimes these actions were also a necessity. What if there was a crew member who began threatening the lives of everyone on board? The crew member could be marooned. But what if they were not anywhere close to a spit of land? It is very unlikely that a dangerous crew member would be killed in cold blood. Instead, they would be locked up or chained belowdecks. However, if a fight broke out, death was always a possibility due to the available weapons and the harsh realities of living on a ship. There could also be an accident. What if someone caused someone's death unintentionally? Perhaps there was a fall due to human error or an emergency situation that would cause panic, such as a ship threatening to capsize during a storm. Not every case could be defined as murder in the way that the Admiralty wanted to consider it.

It is a similar case for robbery, although, yes, it would be harder to justify. Sometimes robbery happened out of necessity rather than for the sake of stealing goods for monetary gain. Medicine and foodstuffs would be the items most needed on ships, especially if an illness broke out or extenuating circumstances caused a food or water shortage. These times would be desperate and, unfortunately, one side would have to suffer as a result. But could desperate needs be taken into consideration? This is a question that no doubt would come up.

It is also important to consider that many people were forced into piracy. These people were usually hostages taken on after a battle to replace members of the crew who were killed. The hostages were either kept in custody or forced to swear their fealty and join the crew. In the eventuality that the pirates were captured, the hostage would plead innocence. This was a complicated situation because it was difficult to prove that the person was forced into piracy against their will. There would have to be witnesses to speak for him, but pirates generally did not betray each other.

The law boiled down to what was written on paper. If murder and robbery were committed on the high seas, it was piracy, punishable by death. After the turn of the eighteenth century, the law became even more strict. In efforts to stop piracy, colonists and governors were explicitly forbidden to deal with pirates. If they did, they would be considered pirates as well, and therefore subject to the law. After all, in the end, how is helping a pirate different from actually being one?

Here Be Pirates

When Britain was trying to prove its might over its European competitors, the country used pirates to prove itself the most powerful nation in the world. European countries were constantly trying to outdo and outrace each other to become larger and more powerful. That is why American colonization happened so quickly during the seventeenth and eighteenth centuries. Spain, France, Portugal, and England haphazardly chopped the American continents and Caribbean Sea into chunks that they constantly fought over. Imagine all the sailors this sort of conquest required. They would require a lot of goods and reinforcement, right? This helped create major trade routes and sea lanes that stretched from Europe to the Americas, which were filled with ships swollen with goods. What prizes for the picking! Anyone who was inclined to become a pirate found themselves in the right place at the right time.

Pirates were a menace to opposing powers from the get-go. At first, they were mostly just annoying and frustrating, but not seen as a huge problem. Over time, as competition became fiercer, especially between Britain and Spain, pirates became downright threatening. British pirates attacked Spanish ships and vice versa, which practically called for all-out war. The British in particular were intent on grabbing Spain's plantation islands, such as Jamaica, and in order to do this they would have to prove themselves the most powerful colonizers out there. Britain had to make itself look like the only nation that could possibly rule the ocean and enforce the law against all threats. Therefore, pirates *had* to stand out against all other types of defined criminals. As we've discovered, these people were considered enemies of all mankind. Their crimes against the British crown and growing empire were considered the worst crimes against humanity.[8] If a British pirate attacked a British ship, this meant he was attacking his own nation, therefore the Crown, and therefore God. Nothing—absolutely nothing—was worse than piracy.

As the number of British subjects who moved overseas to colonize the Caribbean islands and North American continent increased, more people came into property ownership and trade agreements. As a result, there were more people ready to be robbed of their goods and other forms of cash. By the 1600s, the number of criminal convictions and public executions skyrocketed.[9] The balance between the violation of the law and the all-powerful majesty had to be reestablished. Publicly killing pirates, therefore, gave the Crown the perfect chance to reclaim its dominance.

Public executions were not just punishments, though; they were ceremonies intended to return the injured party (in this case, the king) to its dignity.[10] Therefore, it was the king, country, and finally God who became the real victims.[11] The public execution was the most effective way to demonstrate the power of the state against other states and over its people.[12] While pirates did not actually "wrong" people on land, their murders and robberies at sea were viewed as wronging their colonial neighbors. They insulted the Crown on both sides of the Atlantic![13] The repeated efforts to control the problem involved many loopholes in interpreting the laws.

An example of this loophole interpretation concerns the Boston Tea Party. In case you slept through your high school history class, on December 16, 1773, a group of two hundred men aboard three ships in Boston Harbor stole and destroyed an entire shipment of East India Company tea by dumping all of it into the water. This was done to protest the Tea Act, which charged a 10 percent tax on all tea imported into the colonies. Many unfair taxes had been passed before, but this was the straw that broke the camel's back. Don't mess with Brits and their tea! The King was absolutely furious. England had now lost a huge amount of revenue that could not be recovered. In retaliation, the actions of the Boston Tea Party members were described as "acts of riot and piracy."[14]

Here is another way the definition of piracy gets twisted to serve a certain purpose. Technically, the two hundred men were on a body of water and stole a huge amount of goods. But that's only half of the official definition of piracy, so how was the rest justified? Well, if they were stealing and destroying several ships' worth of revenue, then it could be assumed that they were trying to destroy the British economy. Therefore, they were trying to destroy the King. Thus, they were trying to kill Britain. Boom. Pirates. This sort of logic lasted throughout the eighteenth century.

Who Were Those Who Betrayed Their Nation?

The majority of known pirates during the seventeenth and eighteenth centuries in and around the Atlantic world were British white men, a little over 50 percent. They would likely be from port towns where they met many sailors passing through. Stories about the sailors' destinations and adventures would always be floating around the town, which held them in an almost reverent awe. Residents of port towns were usually employed in some line of work related to shipping and sailing. It is likely that most families with young boys would send them to work on ships as cabin boys from a very young age. Their lives at sea would begin at ages as young as five or seven.

Many sailors were also former officers of the Royal Navy. In order to be a successful pirate, one had to be an experienced, strong sailor, and either a skilled fighter or unafraid of fighting. A naval officer would likely have both of those qualities. It is not too farfetched to say that a pirate who had been a naval officer might have contacts and protection in locations all around the American colonies.

Other pirates had mercantile origins. Former merchants knew about the value and costs of goods and were helpful members of the crew when deciding which goods to plunder. They would also know the best places to go to sell these items for the largest amount of money. Merchants sailed all over the world, so a pirate with this background would have specific knowledge of ports and smaller places to sail into.

Escaping the Toxic Work Environment

Why would these types of sailors jump ship, so to speak, and leave a life of legitimate and solid employment to go onto a pirate ship?

First, naval and merchant ships were not always pleasant places to be, to say the least. These professions were known to be extremely rough. High-ranking Navy officers were often cruel and divvied out harsh punishments for the smallest infractions. Everything was regimented and highly controlled. A cruel captain stayed captain. If someone was disliked on a Navy ship, their life could be hell.

These ships could also be disgusting places. They were highly populated, and the quarters were cramped. Illness would sweep through the berths, and medicine at the time did more harm than good. Bloodletting was still common and often made the person sicker or even killed them. Besides, with so many people in such close quarters, illnesses would often spread too quickly to be treated properly. One sick person could wipe out a whole ship.

Then there was the issue of food and water. Ships had to carry enough of each for a six-month journey in addition to everything else they required: supplies, goods, weapons, etc. Fresh food, particularly fruit, vegetables, and meat, ran out within the first few weeks due to spoilage. After that, sailors subsisted on a diet of dried legumes, salted and dried meat (that may or may not have been preserved properly), and bread baked several times over until it could only be eaten after a long soak in soup, ale, or whatever liquid was available. They got their calories, but nutrients were scarce. Scurvy, a condition caused by a long-term lack of vitamin C, was rampant on ships. Gums would bleed, teeth would come loose, and wounds would constantly reopen, just to name a few of the symptoms. Life was also dangerous and guaranteed injuries, many of which were fatal due to infections. There was little compensation to a sailor's family if he became too injured to work or if he died.

Payment was also an issue. Pay was not distributed equally, and wages could also be garnished for a number of reasons, such as breaking or losing equipment. No one entered this type of life with expectations of becoming rich unless they were guaranteed a high rank or captainship. Indeed, life at sea was no picnic.

What made pirate ships so different? The most important thing was that pirates elected their captains. Those elected were usually the bravest, most knowledgeable, and most skilled fighters. Once elected by a majority, they could captain the ship. If the crew felt they were doing too bad a job, they could vote them out and make someone else captain. This sort of representation did not exist on any other ships at this time.

Pirate ships were also not usually as populated as merchant or Navy
ships. The crew had to be large enough to run the ship properly, but
overcrowding was not an issue. As a result, pirates did not get sick
as often. Even so, pirate ships were known to have a large stock of
medical supplies. Robbing allowed them to keep a consistent fresh
stock of materials.

Food was also of much better quality. Like every ship, they had
limited fresh food and mostly dried goods, but raiding other ships
allowed them to replenish their stores. Since pirates did not care
which ships they attacked, they were able to keep their food varied.
Pirate ships were laden with British, American, French, Spanish, and
other items from around the world. They had a varied and healthier
diet. This kept them in better health and more fit. One would have to
look hard to find cases of scurvy on a pirate ship.

Alcohol was also *very* popular on pirate ships. Pirates did not get
a reputation for drinking without reason. Their ships had large
stores of ales, wines, and rum thanks to the sugar trade. Ale and
wine were considered nutritious, so these drinks accompanied most
meals. Alcoholic drinks also kept pirates free of scurvy because of a
concoction called "grog." Yes, that drink is real and it was the pirates'
favorite! In fact, it was considered so important that it was an essential
part of their daily diet. The main ingredients, rum, water, and lime,
kept them hydrated and full of vitamin C. Rewards were often an
extra portion of grog. No one had to worry about going thirsty while
sailing under the black flag.

What made pirate ships really unique was that their crew were
generously compensated for injuries. Skilled fighters were what
kept pirate ships afloat, so these sailors were their most valuable
commodity in a sense. If a pirate lost a right hand, arm, or leg in a
fight, he could expect something between £400 and £600.[15] A left
hand, arm, or leg yielded between £200 and £300.[16] Losing a finger or

an eye got them about £100.[17] If the pirate died, his earnings would go directly back to his family without fear that the money would get "lost."

The best part was that the money they got from selling their plunder was distributed evenly among the pirates. If there were gold and jewels on the ship, those were divided up as well. Every person was a vital member of the ship and therefore earned every piece that was their due.

Fair captains, solid medical treatment, a healthy diet, health insurance, and equal pay? Who would *not* want to be a pirate?

Outlaws of the Sea

Work benefits aside, pirates also needed to escape.

Pirates were likely unwelcome at home for various reasons. They could be convicted criminals who could no longer find work, or people on the run who needed to disappear or escape their personal situation. Some were mistreated on other ships, and others simply wanted an adventure where they did not have to answer to anyone.

The varied backgrounds of the sailors meant that pirate ships were diverse places to be. The crew was often made up of a medley of seamen from Spain, France, the Netherlands, Germany, Wales, Scotland, Ireland, Colonial America, India, and sometimes even China.

A huge number of sailors on pirate ships were also from African nations. Those sailors were either freed, formerly enslaved people who could not find employment, or escaped enslaved people. Black sailors were prevalent in the maritime world both legally and illegally. We have no exact numbers of Africans or those of African descent who worked as sailors, but it is likely that there were more black sailors on pirate ships than in the merchant or naval service during the eighteenth century.[18] The infamous pirate Edward Teach (Blackbeard) employed five black pirates in his crew of eighteen during his last battle in 1718.[19]

Pirate historians (there's a hearty crew of us) have debated whether escaped or freed enslaved people could find a better life on a pirate ship. Some say that African pirates were tasked with hard and menial jobs, such as working the pumps, going on shore for food and water, washing and cleaning, and acting as servant to the pirate captain.[20] However, it would not make sense to send an African pirate on shore on his own to find food and water, so this might not have been true. Once off the ship, African pirates would be risking their lives. Africans could only walk around freely if they were not enslaved. They always had to carry a pass or papers to prove they were free. A pirate would of course not have these papers if he had escaped slavery. Even if he had them, the Royal Navy and other members of the Admiralty were always on the hunt for anyone who might be a pirate. As for the other duties, everyone on board the ship had their part in cleaning and maintaining the ship's condition. And even if an African member of the crew was a servant for the captain, he still received his fair share of the prizes. Pirates practiced "equal pay for equal work," or "equal pay for equal prey," and they extended this suffrage to all members of their crew, regardless of their origins. They were not abolitionists, but it was in the interest of the ship to have equality among the crew.[21]

Christians, Catholics, Jews, Muslims, and those without religion found their place under the black flag. This was in a time when Jews and Muslims did not have a place in the British world, and even Catholics could sometimes be in a precarious situation. Protestantism took over Britain when Elizabeth I ascended to the throne, Catholicism came back under James I, and then Protestantism returned again. The return to Protestantism meant Catholics were heavily discriminated against in England. Jews were never welcome in any part of Europe, save the Netherlands for a period of time. They were cast out of England several times throughout history and many other European countries followed suit. Muslims, or Moors (a slur they were sometimes referred to) also lost their place throughout Europe. A pirate ship offered refuge for these marginalized groups. Ships were not very religious places in any case. Pirate ships only had two qualifications: be a brave sailor and be a brave fighter. Pirate ships were some of the few places in the world where people could find some semblance of equality.[22]

Sirens of the Sea

So what about women? There is a common misconception that women were not allowed on ships because they were bad luck, a stigma that likely stems from folklore dating back to ancient Rome. Old tales spoke of "sirens of the sea," dangerous and beautiful women who came out of the water to seduce sailors before dragging them to the bottom of the ocean. In the *Odyssey*, sirens sang a seductive song that bewitched sailors into diving into the sea. Odysseus had to be tied to the mast with wax in his ears to avoid this deadly fate.[23] Since the sirens were women, over time, the legends devolved into superstition until women in general came to be seen as unlucky.

This line of reasoning contradicts history, however. There has been a long-held belief dating back to Ancient

Greece that water is a female element, and that women have powers from the sea denied to men. The Great Goddess of the Cretans, according to legend, not only symbolized fertility, but also protected sailors during their voyages. When the Greeks took the Egyptian goddess Isis as their own, they made her the goddess of seafarers.

The mermaid has also almost always been presented as female in folklore. Myth shows us the mermaid as a beautiful symbol of death and of men's ambivalence toward women. She was a temptress, like Eve, and her tail was said to represent the serpent in the Garden of Eden. Her long flowing hair indicated an insatiable sexual appetite. In medieval times, the mermaid was said to represent a harlot who tempted men with forbidden pleasures.[24]

Sirens and mermaids were creatures that could lure men to their deaths or drive them to such distraction that they would abandon their duties. These are female representations of beings that would destroy a ship. The most interesting part of this is that no one knows where these tales came from. Their origins are lost in the depths of time, but over the centuries, these myths have been diluted down to the belief that women were simply bad luck on ships.

In reality, females as harbingers of misfortune could not be further from the truth. Women sailed on ships, and not just as passengers. The wives of captains (the Royal Navy would turn a blind eye to officers' wives on board), diplomats, and colonial governors often traveled overseas without bringing any harm to themselves or their fellow passengers.

Women also had their own important roles on ships. Crewmen employed women as healers, tailors, and kitchen managers. Sometimes pirates brought sex workers on ships for morale purposes or to prevent homosexual activity.[25] Close quarters and intimate male company sometimes developed into sexual or even romantic relationships, and the idea was that prostitutes could prevent "buggery." But women didn't just function as sex workers. For instance, a woman named Mary Read started her sailing career disguised as a man (more on her later). There is no reason not to believe that many other women did the same during this time period. It is likely that there were many female pirates who are simply unaccounted for. They might have disguised their gender, or the writers of history might have simply neglected them. Society left women with very few options. Disguising themselves as men was extremely risky, but it also provided a freedom they could not experience elsewhere.

Did every ship allow women? No, of course not. There were many ship captains who felt that women either would have no purpose on a ship, or would be a distraction and a cause of fighting among the sailors. Some pirate captains felt the same. Blackbeard was known not to allow any women on board for this very reason. Pirates ran a risky enough life, and they could not afford fights caused by petty jealousy.[26] Other pirates, such as Captain Jack Rackham, allowed their wives to sail and even fight with them.

Hooks, Peg Legs, and Scars—Oh My!

If women could disguise themselves as pirates, then there must have been a pretty common look among them. Physically, pirates looked similar to most sailors, but they were healthier. The novel *Treasure Island* provides a vivid and accurate description of how a typical pirate might have looked through the character Captain Flint, a.k.a. the "old sea-dog": "a tall, strong, heavy, nut-brown man, his tarry pigtail falling over the shoulders of his soiled blue coat, his hands ragged and scarred, with black, broken nails, and the saber cut across one cheek, a dirty, livid white."[27] This description makes sense. Life at sea was rough. Other pirates were also described as brown-skinned, with excessive swearing habits, and often drunk. They would wear red kerchiefs to protect from the sun, and they had impressive athletic abilities.[28] Extreme sun exposure darkened everyone's skin to the point where, at a glance, one might think each pirate had a similar racial background. They were strong because of hard work and varied diet. Tar was common in hair and on clothes because it provided protection against wind, salt, rain, and the sun. Of course, a dirty jacket, ripped nails, and a facial scar is telling of the harsh physical toll on their bodies.

The stereotypical pirate that people think of is likely to feature an eye patch, a peg leg, and even a parrot on his shoulder. Much of this also comes from *Treasure Island*, but the descriptions were based on fact. All types of sailing involved risks that were often destructive to the body.[29] Injuries were guaranteed at sea. Wounds could lead to infection, which might have required amputation. The presence of parrots has truth in history as well. They were popular pets on ships because they were colorful, could be taught to speak, and were easy to look after on a ship.[30] They also provided much-needed morale. (People have always needed companionship, no matter their trade.) However, one might be disappointed to find that pirates never made anyone "walk the plank"—a punishment in which victims were forced to walk to the end of a board and jump off a ship. This story came to fruition due to some instances of punishers throwing mutineers overboard as punishment during the late eighteenth century. The punishers were not pirates, who preferred to maroon or shoot their betrayers. The idea of "walking the plank" became popular when Stevenson used it in his novel *Treasure Island*.[31] (If you haven't guessed by now, most popular ideas about pirates come from that book.)

Fun with Flags

For a pirate ship to be fully operational, all members had to be completely loyal to each other. No one could afford a rat in their midst. Since pirates didn't just attack merchant and naval ships, but also their own countrymen, one whisper could be their downfall. It was imperative that pirates be at one with their crew. The crew were brethren. The high stakes and tight-knit community meant pirates did not consider themselves to belong to any country. Rather, they were only loyal to themselves and each other. Their ship was their country and they pledged loyalty to only one flag. With this nation came their emblem—the black flag with the skull and crossbones, known as the Jolly Roger.[32]

History of Sea Rovers, 1725
Courtesy of the John Carter Brown Library

The Jolly Roger seems like something television producers might have fabricated for the screen, but it was as real as any other flag. By law, ships had to sail flying the flag of their country of origin. This sustained peace and agreement between countries, especially during peacetime. Many ships fared from European countries which had colonized multiple lands. These ships often sailed between the west coast of Africa and the Caribbean and North American eastern seaboard. To avoid conflict, they had to make sure that other ships knew who they were. Flags were also a useful way to signal for help if they needed a doctor, water, or some other form of assistance. If a ship hailed another in this manner, the other would sail over to offer help. Naturally, pirates exploited this custom.

You might be asking, "If pirates had their own recognizable flag, then how were they able to attack anyone? Couldn't the other ships simply sail away or attack from afar?" You underestimate the pirates! During the seventeenth and eighteenth centuries, all ships had to identify themselves to maintain the peace and make sure that ships were sailing within their own boundaries. Ships had to hoist the flag of their country to make themselves visible to other ships from a distance. Pirates, of course, knew this. And that's why pirate ships often had a whole collection of flags from plundered ships!

Here's how one of their schemes might play out. A pirate ship is sailing toward the Caribbean islands when they see another ship in the distance. Upon a closer look through their spyglass, they are able to determine that it is a Portuguese ship, based on the colors and pattern of the flag flapping in the air. Excellent. A Portuguese ship would most likely have a huge cache of Madeira wine on board, which was extremely valuable, not to mention delicious. The pirates hoist a flag signaling that they're in distress. Now the Portuguese ship is obligated to come help them. The Portuguese turn and sail toward the pirates, completely ignorant of the trickery. Once the Portuguese are too close to turn back, the pirates take down their flag and replace it with the Jolly Roger. As the black flag with the skull and crossbones flaps in the wind, the Portuguese know they were tricked. It is too late to turn back, and they must scramble to prepare for a fight.

That said, pirates were not all that violent. It was in their best interest to be more frightening, less deadly. In order to successfully rob a ship, they had to attack, get on board, threaten, and steal. In and out. If they fought, they would lose members of their crew. Therefore, it was more efficient to curtail their physical attacks.

However, I would be remiss to neglect the fact that there were some very deadly pirates. The most infamous were Charles Vane and Edward Low. Both of these men were known to injure and even maim their victims. Today we would refer to them as sadistic.

Charles Vane was born in England around 1680. His first forays into piracy are a bit murky, but we do know that he became active as a pirate captain in 1717. In February of 1718, he and his men were captured while sailing in the West Indies. He decided to take a pardon, but just a few months later, he ended up back on the sea as a pirate. At this point in his career, he became notorious for his cruelty. He and his men often beat, tortured, and killed sailors from the ships he captured. This ended in November of 1719, when he was caught in a hurricane and wrecked on a deserted island. After the storm, English ships had stopped by the island to collect fresh water from the springs when they encountered the infamous pirate. The English crew arrested him and sent Vane to Spanish Town, Jamaica, where he stayed in prison for over two years. On March 22, 1721, the Admiralty tried Vane for piracy and found him guilty. A week later, he was hanged for his crimes at Gallows Point in Port Royal. The British government made sure his corpse hung in chains nearby at Gun Cay, as a warning to fellow and would-be pirates.[33]

Captain Charles Vane, A General History of the Pyrates, 1725
Wiki Commons

Edward Low was known for similar but even worse behavior, though
he had one of the strictest sets of behavioral codes on any pirate
ship. Low was born in Westminster, England, in 1690. Not much
is known about his early life, save for information in the collection
of pirate biographies, *The General History of the Pyrates* (more on
this book later). What we do know is that Low was sadistic and
that his penchant for cruelty and thievery showed up as early as
childhood. He eventually took to the sea life and worked in the West
Indies. In 1721, he led a mutiny and took his ship, thus starting his
career as a pirate. Low immediately became a famous and feared for
attacking ships all up and down the North American coast and taking

numerous prisoners, whom he tortured, much to his enjoyment. He notoriously forced a victim to eat his own lips before murdering him.[34] He also took a Spanish ship and killed everyone on board— except for two boys. Low plundered other ships and cut off the ears and noses of several victims.[35] This was a man to be reckoned with; a man who many felt had been born from the depths of hell. Eventually his terror caught up with him and he was captured in late 1723. Though he managed to escape, this is where his story died.[36] To this day his ultimate fate is unknown.

Captain Edward Low in ye. Hurricane which he and all the Crew had Like to perish'd, Joseph Nicholls, 1736
Courtesy of the John Carter Brown Library

Vane and Low were the exception, not the rule. Even so, all pirates, like these two men, were on the lookout for merchant ships, which would be ripe for the picking. Merchant ships would also be less heavily armed than, say, a warship, for example. They wanted to board a ship and scare the hell out of everyone so they could rob the place and get out of there as fast as they could. Fighting would lead to injuries and death, and it would not do to lose crew members. In order to replace lost crewmembers, pirates would have to abduct members of the merchant's crew. The kidnapped sailors would be too risky to manage and would likely be the first to try to escape and betray them. Fighting, then, was an inconvenience many felt it best to avoid.

In Pirate Territory

So where did pirates live and operate? According to Alexander Exquemelin, author of *The History of the Buccaneers of America*, published in 1678, the pirates chose to make the West Indies their main base of operations for three reasons.

First, there were a lot of uninhabited islands and quays, which were great places for pirates to take shelter and hide their loot. The numerous islands, cliff faces, and intricate coastlines provided natural security from pirate hunters.[37] The islands were dotted all over the place with craggy coasts and tiny inlets that were almost impossible to sail into…unless you knew the way. Pirates needed to sail quickly and efficiently, so they often would hide their large ship in favor of a smaller one that could zig-zag among the islands to find refuge. The British, however, needed to make sure everyone knew they had the most powerful navy in the world. To display British power, they sailed on massive ships called Man-o-Wars. These ships were much too big to get into and around those small islands. Pirates knew that size mattered.

Second, the Caribbean had very active trade routes for Spanish, French, Portuguese, Dutch, and English ships. This gave pirates ample opportunity for raiding. The best places for pirates to hide were also near the best locations to rob. Nassau, the famed pirate colony in the Bahamas, was smack-dab in the center of one of the busiest sea lines in the eighteenth century. For any ship from Europe to get into the Caribbean and vice versa, it had to sail through the Bahamas, directly off the coast of Florida. Any ship that wanted to sail from the Caribbean up the North American eastern seaboard had to sail through the Bahamas as well. Pirates were able to sneak out of their enclaves disguised as fellow merchant ships and dive into their attacks.

Finally, the Caribbean was a highly contested space between the major European powers during the seventeenth century. Constant wars and rivalries caused many treaties and truces to be passed, rescinded, and rewritten. Basically, the area was really politically unstable. The British were scrambling to keep control of their Caribbean plantation islands, especially Jamaica, which kept falling alternately under Spanish and English control. The European powers were so distracted by their conflicts with each other that they could not effectively deal with pirates as well. Pirates knew this and took advantage of it. They sailed openly throughout the sea lanes and in and out of major port cities. The instability also allowed governors to work with pirates to bring in excellent booty.

Sodom of the Sea

Jamaica was the key location for pirates in the Caribbean. During the seventeenth century, the island of Port Royal was so well known as the major pirate haven that the city was known as the Sodom of the Sea. Today, Kingston is Jamaica's bustling capital city, and Port Royal is a small fishing town about a half an hour away by bus on a narrow highway that connects the town to the mainland. Jamaica was also a major hub for the slave trade, and today that legacy is still very apparent. When I did my research there, everyone—archivists, cab drivers, my Airbnb host—asked if I was there to research slavery, only to be confused when I said, "No, I'm here to research pirates." That said, the main research hub, Jamaica's National Archives, sits about a half-hour or forty-five minutes' drive inland in Spanish Town, a fitting location because that is where the legendary trials and executions of pirates took place.

Even though pirates aren't thought of very much in Jamaica today, Kingston still bears many similarities to what these sailors would have found on sailing into port. Today the downtown streets bustle with markets and music while people gather to socialize, eat, and sell their wares. It is easy to imagine how this scene would have played out in the eighteenth century. Music plays loudly and people laugh, talk, and shout everywhere. In the eighteenth century, merchant ships would be docked instead of modern-day cargo ships. The streets would be loud and bustling with people under the hot sun. The main market square would be packed with people selling their wares and goods to people eager to buy them.

On the other hand, today one would never know that Port Royal was once populated by pirates and overrun with drinking establishments and brothels. Now it is a sleepy fishing village. In fact, the legacy of piracy seems to be almost gone. Rather than remnants of "vice" establishments, the ruins of Fort Charles, the Royal Navy stronghold, still stand along with late eighteenth- and early nineteenth-century cannons.

Situated right in the heart of the Caribbean Sea, Jamaica has a hot, tropical climate. It is extremely humid and the air can be thick with mosquitos (depending on the weather). Just because the island is tropical, however, that does not guarantee rain. Drought can happen there as easily as anywhere. One can only imagine the physical shock an eighteenth-century officer or plantation owner fresh off the boat from England would have experienced. Woolen clothing would be stifling. Skin probably itched something terrible from mosquito bites, and of course there was high risk of diseases like malaria. However, the people would not experience the cold damp of Europe and this would raise spirits, leading to a raucous atmosphere. Kingston would be especially lively as the port city. With people coming and going every day to either settle permanently or sell their goods—including human beings—the area never lacked for company.

The island changed ownership several times between the Spanish and the English throughout the seventeenth century. The area was so politically unstable that authorities literally did not have time or energy to hunt down pirates. Jamaica deserves credit for the large role it played in piracy. Before outright war could break out, Spain had to relent and was practically forced to sign the aforementioned Treaty of Madrid to cooperate with Britain in 1670. This was a humiliating blow for Spain. The two countries had been at odds with each other for centuries, each always trying to outdo the other. For the most part, Spain had been in the lead against Britain, save a pesky incident involving the Spanish Armada in 1588. With Spain weakened by losing its most lucrative island, there were no promises that its interests elsewhere could be protected. The solution was a condition in the treaty—in exchange for Jamaica, the English would rid the Caribbean of piracy. The idea was that the treaty would end all arguments between Spain and England. One key sentence read: "Peace in Europe should also mean peace in the West Indies."[38] The British agreed, and the deal was done.

The Spanish were really bitter about the treaty, however, and felt they got the raw end of the deal. They were forced to stand back and trust Britain's word, which was a tall order. Britain had never exactly acted as a trustworthy nation. Though the Spanish did not fight to get Jamaica back, they got their satisfaction in another way. They decided to steal any British ship that got too close to their islands, such as Puerto Rico and especially Cuba, using security as an excuse.[39] They reasoned, why should we not defend ourselves if an unfamiliar foreign ship gets too close to our shores? So, let the games begin!

The British decided to fight back by hunting Spanish ships. When they caught a ship, the British used loopholes in the laws to declare the Spanish sailors pirates. Once they were able to justify their claims, Britain made efforts to execute the said "pirates" in Jamaica, a really low blow. Infuriated, the Spanish tried to lodge complaints against the British government, but this just made the British more determined to win. On May 18, 1722, a Spanish pirate ship commanded by a pirate named Matthew Luke (a British-sounding name meant he was likely a free-agent privateer) was captured. Luke and all fifty-three members of his crew were charged with stealing two English ships. The Spanish had ordered Luke's ship to protect the shores of Puerto Rico, a common occurrence. Of the total fifty-four accused pirates, forty-two were hanged, including Luke. Those who were not hanged were "sold among different merchant ships in order to be sent to Europe in shame."[40]

If you have seen any of the *Pirates of the Caribbean* films, you'll be familiar with one of the many favored pirate hideaways, Tortuga. This island and Jamaica became the famous pirate havens that exist in pirate lore today. The pirates took a risk with Jamaica, since the English decree was formally declared there twice: in 1664 and again in 1674.[41] Despite the laws, the area was still known as a hotbed of criminal activity. The isolation and difficult terrain made it hard to enforce English laws. This also made it an attractive place for drifters, escaped enslaved people, indentured servants, criminals, prostitutes, religious radicals, and political prisoners, who gained newfound freedom. Pirates enjoyed the comforts of Jamaica until an earthquake sank the city of Port Royal, their main hub, in 1692. After the tremor, the Royal Navy stepped in to set up a permanent base and establish order. Pirates then scattered and roamed the Caribbean seeking a new home base until they settled for the city of Nassau, located on the island of New Providence in the Bahamas.

The Pirate King and His Kingdom

The establishment of a pirate city in the Bahamas was absolutely infuriating to the British. Being so close to Florida, these islands were the gateway to the Caribbean and southern colonies of North America. Just as in Jamaica, the Spanish and the British often fought over the Bahamian islands. The Spanish could use the islands to outfit pirates to attack British ships, while the British could use them as a defensive base to protect the North American colonies. This fighting absorbed the two rival countries until 1702, when pirates were able to swoop in under their noses and basically claim the islands for themselves. For the next fourteen years, the Commissions of the Board of Trade and Plantations in Nassau made complaint after complaint to the English Crown about the miserable conditions of the Bahamas. They wrote that, if things did not improve, the island would permanently fall to the Spanish, pirates, or worse, the French.[42]  Before the Commissions of the Board of Trade and Plantations could do anything, however, a pirate captain named Benjamin Hornigold took up residence in the Bahamas in 1713, and became the so-called "pirate king."

Hornigold was born in England in 1680 and fought in the War of Spanish Succession in the early eighteenth century as a privateer. When the war ended, he found himself out of work and, like many others in his position, he decided to keep raiding ships and occasionally murdering sailors if he had to. Thus began his career as a pirate.

He spent a few years operating in and out of the area, attacking merchant ships. This was not good enough, however. He wanted to organize a large band of pirates and, to do so, he had to create a base where pirates could congregate safely. The Bahamas was a contender. The island nation was difficult to sail through and was conveniently close to both North America and the Caribbean. But many said the capital was violent, dirty, full of disease, and populated by the absolute dregs of society. In short, Nassau had a terrible reputation and people tried to avoid it.

Naturally, this was the perfect place for a pirate city.

Hornigold came into Nassau and saw that the city, though known as a pirate republic, had no real leadership. Perfect. He had a great air of authority, having been a captain for years, so he immediately set out to establish order. Within weeks, the streets began to clean up, establishments became more orderly, and he had created a local government of sorts. Word went around that pirates could come to Nassau and not just hide out, but trade their goods, restock their ships, and have families without fear of attack or betrayal. Now that the pirates had an official base, they could find some sort of order and safety. The people of Nassau hailed Hornigold as the Pirate King.[43] Over the next few years, the city attracted some of history's most famous pirates to have ever lived: Hornigold's protégé Edward Teach (a.k.a. Blackbeard), Sam Bellamy, Stede Bonnet, Charles Vane, Jack Rackham, Anne Bonny, and Mary Read, just to name a few.

Pirates were people from all walks of life, and none fit perfectly into any specific legal definition. They sought a new life and were respected citizens, family members looking to get rich quick, and adventure-seekers. While they knew the risks of their chosen career, they still had no idea that they would become the most hunted people to sail the seas. Nor could these pirates have ever guessed that their lives would become some of the most lucrative fodder for entertainment in history.

CHAPTER 2

THE HUNT
FOR CAPTAIN
WILLIAM KIDD

One of the most famous and hunted pirates who ever lived was Captain William Kidd, who met his end in London in 1701. His name might not have instant recognition today, but his life and death were the catalyst that set off the war against piracy. He became a martyr for the pirate community, inspiring generations of literature, including *Treasure Island*, and his exploits gave us the myth of buried treasure. (Spoiler alert—yes, buried treasure is a myth. Sorry.)

Portrait of Captain William Kidd by Sir James Thornhill, Eighteenth Century
Wiki Commons

Let's look at a brief roadmap of this pirate captain's life before we go into detail. Kidd was born in Dundee, Scotland, in 1645, and worked as a privateer for the East India Company. He married a socialite and eventually owned property in New York. After an eventful pirate career, he became a wanted man and the authorities caught up with him in the West Indies. From there, they sent him to Stone Prison in Boston before shipping him off to London for his trial and execution. Kidd may have led a troubled life, but he was able to rise above his station and marry into a wealthy family before his downfall.[44] All the while, he constantly bent and pushed the rules in his job, which made him a huge annoyance to his employers. Even more aggravating was that he was too good at his job to get fired. Gaining wealth and power for the English Crown while also making the King of England furious? What a hero.

In 1689, Kidd began his career as a sailor in an English-French pirate crew under Captain Jean Fantin, after which he worked as a privateer for the British East India Company for several years. Fellow sailors knew Kidd to be brash, and they often spoke of how he always walked the line between privateering and piracy. Kidd and the rest of the crew grew tired of Fantin's leadership, claiming that they were not receiving as much in stolen goods as before. (This avarice would be Kidd's downfall later.) What followed was Kidd's first act of mutiny. He and his crew ousted Fantin and declared the ship theirs—with Kidd at the helm.[45]

Normally, since mutiny was a high crime, this alone would have led British officials to pursue and arrest Kidd, but England was busy with the Nine Years' War against France. Most of the war was fought at sea, so England needed skilled sailors to help fight it. During wartime, convicted pirates were often given a quick pardon if they agreed to sail as privateers. Kidd was one of them.

The government granted him a pardon since he had mutinied against a French ship, so they hired him as a privateer with commissions from New York and Massachusetts colonies. Kidd became a privateer celebrity when he captured an enemy ship off the coast of New England. This newfound reputation earned him Richard Coote's attention. (Coote was the First Earl of Bellomont—or Lord Bellomont, as we'll refer to him—who governed Massachusetts, New York, and New Hampshire.) Lord Bellomont made Kidd his most trusted privateer. This association tied Kidd to England, and the English Crown now gave Kidd letters of marque (with *zero* leeway) to pursue and capture French ships. Kidd could still essentially practice piratical activities, which, having an independent streak, he preferred. Unfortunately, now he was bound to king and country. He did not want to risk angering Bellomont, who he considered a dear friend. It also helped that Bellomont generously financed Kidd's expeditions.

This amicable relationship would end in just five years. Kidd was sailing toward the Indian Ocean under commission to rob French ships accused of disrupting England's trade with the Mughal Empire in and around modern-day India. Britain's East India Company's trading relationship with Indian Mughals (powerful merchants) grew quickly and became a huge source of income for the English crown. The stakes were high. Unfortunately, Kidd ended up robbing the wrong ship, completely disrupting the relationship between the English and their Mughal trading partners. This gaffe not only nearly destroyed Bellomont's reputation and leadership role—he nearly lost his title and lands.

Kidd put the relationship between the East India Company and the Mughals on eggshells in 1698. For the Crown to keep its trade partners and continue making heaps of cash through overseas trade, the British would have to make sure that everyone in the world knew they were more powerful than lowly sailors. Kidd's actions as a pirate were like sledgehammers on a brick. His doings were but one

of many blows that finally shattered the tolerance of officials. The
Crown decided that Kidd was to become the ultimate example of
what happened when one turned pirate. But more importantly, Kidd
would turn into the unwilling symbol of Britain's power over all of
its competitors.

The sad reality is that the British used Captain Kidd as a scapegoat.
Adversaries had angered the Mughals too many times, and it was time
for the British to take action.

However, the Crown might never have hung Kidd as a pirate had
it not been for one pesky pirate about five years earlier: Captain
Henry Avery.

The First Manhunt

Henry Avery was an English pirate who mostly operated in the
Atlantic and Indian Ocean in the early to mid-1690s. Although his
career as a pirate only lasted for two years, he became famous because
he wrought havoc on the English.

Avery started his maritime career when he joined the Royal Navy in
1690. His foray into piracy came about a few years later while working
on a ship called *Dove* as a first mate. All was not smooth sailing—the
captain of the *Dove* was an abusive drunkard who made life miserable
and dangerous for the crew. Avery began to secretly brainstorm a way
to oust the captain once and for all.

His opportunity came when a longboat called the *Duchess* hailed the
ship. Sixteen sailors boarded the *Dove* and began to attack. Avery
saw this as a perfect opportunity. He joined forces with the *Duchess*'s
sixteen sailors to fight against his captain, sparking a full-blown
revolt. After winning the ship, Avery declared himself the new captain

of the *Duchess*. Under his command, they all headed to Madagascar to commence their pirating.

Avery's fortunes peaked in 1695 when he joined forces with other pirates and unified a fleet of twenty-five ships. Together they sailed east and attacked an Indian ship, the *Ganj-I-sawai*, and its escort, the *Fateh Muhammed*, taking their vast wealth and treasure. Avery and his squadron captured upwards of £600,000 in coins and jewels, which would be worth nearly £90 million today.[46] In just one day, Avery and his men became the richest pirates in the entire world.

Meanwhile, the relationship between Britain's East India Company and the Mughals approached collapse. Simply put, trade competition in the region was fierce. The East India Company was just one of several European companies looking to establish official trading systems in and around India to easily access items such as tea, silk, and spices. Several wars broke out between the British and the Dutch, their major competitor in the Indian Ocean. Fighting made the region unstable and caused trade to slow, which left the Mughals in dire straits. Britain was able to come to an agreement with the Mughals by offering an official Royal Charter, which would put India under Britain's protection. The agreement was shaky, however. The Mughals would not tolerate any more trouble.

So, naturally, when the Mughal Emperor realized that he had been robbed by an English captain, he was furious.

He vowed to send a mighty army "with fire and sword to extirpate the English from all their settlements on the Indian coast."[47]

He also threatened to cut off all trade, which would ruin the East India Company and therefore England's economy—unless they could stop Avery.

To protect their trade, the East India Company launched a manhunt for Avery and his crew. Once Avery discovered the English were on

their tail, he decided they had to head for America. Philadelphia had
a reputation for protecting pirates, so his goal was to reach the port
city as soon as possible. Once they arrived, he and his men scattered
throughout the colonies. Avery was never captured, and the last days
of his life remain a mystery. Some say he was captured and killed.
Others suspect he went back to India and married an Indian princess.
Or perhaps he went back to England and died a penniless beggar in
Bristol, wandering the ports, remembering his glory days. We will
never know.[48]

Several of Avery's crew, on the other hand, were not lost to history.
There were rumors that local governors and colonists sheltered them,
helped them escape, or helped them establish new identities.[49] The
Admiralty forced Rhode Island to send out arrest warrants for Avery's
crew to prevent them from corrupting any other colonies.[50] This did
not work. In fact, the people of Philadelphia were more than happy
to help out two crew members, Robert Clinton and Edward Lassells.
Several unnamed colonists helped the two men escape from prison.
No one was too eager to bring them to justice. The sheriffs even
refused to write a new warrant for their arrests.[51] Clinton and Lassells
even begged the governor for help. They gave the governor, his
wife, and his children a large sum of money to buy their protection
and, lo and behold, it worked. The two pirates guaranteed that they
would continue to bring money and goods in to Philadelphia to help
the great colony of Pennsylvania. How could the governor refuse?[52]
Authorities eventually spotted some of Avery's other men in Rhode
Island and New York, where they attempted to go back to piracy by
taking a New York merchant ship.[53] Over the next year, several more
members of Avery's crew were captured in New York, New Jersey,
Rhode Island, and the Carolinas.

In the meantime, the helpful North American cities gained a
reputation as the best unofficial pirate havens beyond the Caribbean.

Despite this—or perhaps because of this—the Crown ordered all governors to prevent more piracy.

"There are too many mentions of New England in the trial of Avery's crew. It appears this is the place where pirates are supplied and entertained. It appears that all pirates come out of New England, especially Boston,"[54] wrote the Council of Trade and Plantations to Lieutenant Stoughton.

Ah…the overbearing parent was growing wise to the chummy relationship between the pirates and colonists.

Avery was, ultimately, never captured. This failure was a massive embarrassment for the British, making them look seriously weak. Failing to capture Avery nearly plundered any hopes of British alliance with the Mughals. Their relationship was barely hanging on by a thread. One thing was for sure—the British could *not* afford any other mishaps if they wanted the British East India Company to survive and flourish.

"If any more of your pirates come into our oceans, consider it an act of war," the Mughals declared to the British.

Now imagine the terror and fury that erupted through the British East India Company, treasury, Admiralty, and Royal Navy when they found out that one of their own privateers had robbed one of the largest Mughal ships just a few years later.

All the Admiralty could do was put Henry Avery's men on trial. Avery, who had infuriated the Indian Mughals, disappeared before any punishment could reach him, so all the blame was placed on his crew. This particular case threatened the Crown's international reputation. When the trial was described in the newspapers, the writers took great pains to exaggerate the crew's actions as evidence that pirates could practically ruin the world.

"This piracy began in Europe, carried on through Africa, and ended in the West Indies; so that, in a manner, all the world is concerned with this trial."[55] The crew intended, the trial claimed, to make Britain seem like a "harbor, receptacle, and a nest of pirates. Our friends will be shocked to hear that the enemies to our merchants and fellow mankind could find sanctuary in our noble and ancient place of trade."[56]

The court told the above-mentioned crew (in particular Joseph Dawson, Edward Forseith, William May, William Bishop, James Lewis, and John Sparkes), "The heinous crime you committed has appointed the law to give you a severe punishment by the most humiliating death possible. The judgement of the law is this: You and every one of you will be taken from here to the place from whence you came, and from there to the place of execution. There you, and every one of you, will be hanged by the necks until all of you are dead."[57]

The Pirate Created

William Kidd had already earned a reputation as a troublesome sailor. As sailor, his work took him around the Caribbean, where he mostly operated on ships that pursued the French (with whom the British were always fighting). Kidd was brash, stubborn, and not afraid to point out a captain's incompetence. He even led a mutiny on a French-English ship in the Caribbean. With the help of the crew, Kidd became captain, naming the ship the *Blessed William* (of course), and headed to Nevis, a small island in the Caribbean.

In Nevis, the British asked Kidd to join a small fleet to continue fighting the French, who were trying to take control of Nevis from the English. This assignment meant Kidd was now an official privateer. His pay? Loot he managed to steal from French ships—up to £2,000 sterling, which would be equivalent to roughly £240,000 or just over $295,000 in today's currency (as of 2020).[58] In 1690, his work took him back to New England, where he captured enemy privateer ships off the coast of New York and Massachusetts.

The early 1690s were a happy time for Kidd. In 1691, he settled down and married a thrice-widowed woman named Sarah Bradley Cox Oort. She was born in England around 1665 and married her first husband, William Cox, in 1685. Sadly, he drowned only four years later. Her second husband, John Oort, died just two days before Sarah applied for a marriage license to marry William Kidd in 1691.

Just as Henry Avery disappeared, Kidd was preparing for an expedition of his own. Luckily, he was not short on money—his friend Lord Bellomont (who by then was governor of New York, Massachusetts, and New Hampshire) was financing his trip. Bellomont and the East India Company ordered Kidd to sail into the East Indies and capture any French enemy ships, as well as the pirate captain Thomas Tew and his crew. Soon after, the Kidd crew set out on a ship called the *Adventure Galley* in September 1696 toward the Cape of Good Hope. Expectations were high.

However, the journey to the southern tip of Africa proved difficult from the start. When Kidd reached the island of Grande Comore in the Indian Ocean, an outbreak of cholera spread through the ship and about a third of his crew died. Not only that, the trip had punctured the ship too many times, creating far too many leaks to continue safely. Time was running out.

Kidd became nervous. So far they had failed to capture any pirates at all, let alone Thomas Tew and his crew—the main purpose of his voyage. He had nothing to show for his travels, and he was in danger of facing a huge amount of debt if he did not bring back any prizes.

Once they finally were able to set sail, they came across some ships that were prime for a raid—a Dutchman and New York privateer. Unfortunately, these attacks were poorly planned. Much to Kidd's humiliation, the crew failed to take the ships. At this point, the sailors grew furious and began to threaten a mutiny. The next time they docked into a port, several of Kidd's men left his service. Those who stayed continued to seethe.

But Kidd's real trouble came not long after they set sail in 1697. Once again, ships to plunder were scarce. The crew had not been paid for ages, and Kidd was practically paranoid. Finally, on October 30, 1697, one of his crewmen, William Moore, spotted a Dutch ship in the distance. He sprinted below deck to Kidd to tell him what he saw. The conversation went like this (most of the dialogue is directly from eyewitness accounts, with a sprinkle of added emotion on top for dramatic flair):

"Here is our chance," Moore said. "We must attack the ship."

Kidd's heart leapt. "Is it a pirate or privateering ship?" Kidd asked.

Moore hesitated. "No, but it is a ship nonetheless."

Not good enough. "Then no. Back to your post now." Kidd sat down and turned back to his papers.

Moore ground his teeth. "Captain, the men have not been paid and are days away from mutiny. We must attack the ship."

"And I said we cannot!" Kidd was becoming furious. What business did Moore have questioning his decision? "Our King William is Dutch-born. You know this. As I said, it would be an act of piracy."

"Piracy be damned!"

"Get back to your post or I will have you in chains, you lousy dog!"

"If I am a lousy dog, you have made me so!" Moore shouted. "You have brought me to ruin and many more!"

Moore lunged for Kidd, preparing to hit him. Kidd stepped back, grabbed an iron-bound bucket from the floor, and swung it, hitting Moore on the side of his head with a sickening crack. The man collapsed.

This was now truly a disaster. Kidd could claim self-defense and normally he would not be questioned. But with the crew restless and angry, he knew they would be looking for any excuse to end him.

"Admiralty law allows captains to use violence against their crew," he would have reasoned with himself. "I am not at fault." Unless, of course, the action was murder. He refused to let that be a concern and summoned the ship's surgeon.

Moore was taken to the infirmary. His head was bleeding and a black bruise had already swelled up where he had been hit. The surgeon was immediately suspicious. While the surgeon was not one of the mutinous members of the crew, he had still lost confidence in his captain.

"Captain, I do not wish to know the circumstances, but may I remind you that under Admiralty law the murder of a crew mate is not permitted?" the surgeon said, picking his words carefully.

Kidd did not confirm nor deny his actions. All he said was, "I have good friends in England and they will bring me off for that." He then left the infirmary. When the surgeon reported the following morning that Moore had died in the night, Kidd had no reaction.

But this was the breaking point. Kidd could no longer deny to himself the true danger that he was in. Orders be damned, he had to have something to show for himself, and his men had to be placated lest he face his ruin.

After Moore's death, Kidd's whole attitude changed. His caution disappeared and he ordered his crew to chase any ship that came their way.

Finally, good fortune fell upon Kidd. (Or was it perhaps his doom, coming to punish him for murder?) On January 30, 1698, two years after they began the voyage, they came upon an Indian ship called the

Quedah Merchant. Kidd ordered his men to raise their French flag to hail the ship. Once close enough to board, they attacked with gusto. Armenian merchants besieged Kidd's ship. But how could Kidd's men be afraid, knowing a ship laden with spices, silks, satins, muslins, gold, and silver was just within reach? Everyone on the *Adventure Galley* rejoiced and fought with joy, drunk on their good fortune. At last, they captured the captain. The ship was theirs!

The ecstasy was short-lived. When Kidd went to speak to the captain, he came upon a dreadful shock. The captain was neither Indian, Armenian or French. He was an Englishman named Wright. As captain, he had just been sailing under French permission under the protection of the French crown on an Armenian-built ship. What a nightmare. Though Kidd was commissioned to attack French ships, rendering this a legitimate capture, Kidd was still stunned. *He had attacked an Englishman.*

"We must return the ship to its rightful captain," Kidd said to his crew.

"We will not," one of them shouted back. "This is a French ship!"

"A French ship captained by an Englishman," Kidd said. "We cannot steal from an Englishman!"

"We have been ordered to take French ships and this is a French ship, captain be damned!"

There was nothing Kidd could do. If he wanted to prevent mutiny and remain a captain, he would have to proceed.

After some hesitation, Kidd relented. "We shall keep the ship."

The crew rejoiced and as a compromise they let some of the hostage crew leave on the *Adventure Galley*. The ship immediately set sail to England to deliver the news.

Sure enough, the Admiralty and East India Company were furious. This was a complicated matter, but one thing was for sure—Kidd had now put the English relationship with India in danger. While Armenian merchants had hired out the *Quedah Merchant* to let the French use it to carry out their trade, it was still an Indian ship by origin, laden with Indian goods. Those goods were meant to be sold abroad with the proceeds going back to the Mughal Emperor. This was just *three years* after the East India Company had promised the Mughals that they would never allow piracy to affect them again. Once again, an Englishman had robbed India. Kidd had to be dealt with immediately, lest the East India Company lose the Mughal's goodwill and trade, and with it, England's livelihood.

Thus, the Admiralty officials made a decision. Captain Kidd was, indeed, a pirate and he had to be hunted as such.

The East India Company and Admiralty gave the orders: "Pursue and seize the said Kidd and his accomplices for the notorious piracies they have committed."[59]

The Royal Navy set out for the East Indies. The official manhunt had begun.

Kidd was oblivious. It wasn't until he and his men landed at Madagascar to lie low for a while and replenish their stores that he discovered he was one of the most wanted men in England. The news reached them within days of docking their ship. They had to make a run for it. Some of his crew jumped ship and disappeared into Madagascar to avoid any connection to Kidd and piracy. Kidd could not waste any time looking for them. He had to get out of the East Indies. Fast.

The obvious choice was to head to the Caribbean, where he knew
many pirates continued to operate. He could hide out there. However,
it was an awkward time. In 1692, Port Royal had sunk in a powerful
earthquake and the Royal Navy had immediately stepped in to
establish a strict legal hold. The waters would be teeming with naval
officials. Nassau was not yet a bustling pirate city. Kidd had few
options in the Caribbean, but there was one thing he could do to try
to shake the Navy off his tail...

Once he made it into the Caribbean, he connected with an Irish pirate
named William Burke, who sold the *Adventure Galley* and its goods
on Kidd's behalf. Kidd used some of the money to buy himself a sloop
and headed up the North American coast toward New York.

New York was a natural destination for Kidd. His wife was there,
and his old friend and investor, Lord Bellomont, was the governor.
It would still be risky business, so Kidd did something that would
establish his place in history and change the way pirates were seen
forever: he hid some of his cash on Gardiner's Island just off the coast
of New York to use as a bargaining tool if needed.

As governor, Bellomont was already aware of the accusations against
Kidd. As soon as he found out, he had worked out a game plan.
Many already knew he was one of Kidd's financiers and close friends.
However, as a new governor, he could not afford any scandal. His
association with the most wanted pirate in the world could be his
ultimate downfall. Not to mention that the authorities might find a
way to accuse him of piracy simply based on his relationship with
Kidd. The only way to save his life and reputation was to betray his
friend and have him sent back to England in chains.

Engraved Portrait of Sir Robert Coote, First Earl of Bellomont, c. 1888
Wiki Commons

One thing Bellomont could work to his advantage was his location.
He was in Boston, away from New York, when the news about Kidd
reached him. This distance could give him some leeway and could
be a useful excuse if needed. From afar, Bellomont could also make
sure that Kidd would not disappear into New York. He knew that
Kidd would be desperate. Sure enough, Bellomont soon received a
frantic letter with a New York return address from Kidd, begging for
protection. Kidd included instructions for how to get in touch and
promised him the money he had hidden away in Gardiner's Island.
Bellomont wrote back, telling Kidd to come to Boston, promising
him protection and help to escape from the British authorities once
and for all.

Captain Kidd landed in Boston on July 6, 1699, where authorities seized him at once. He knew who had betrayed him. Officers threw him into Stone Prison in the center of Boston, notorious for harboring accused pirates and witches. Its three-foot-thick walls were solid stone and the windows were barred with iron. Wooden planks separated the cells and iron spikes covered the doors. The passageways were described as being "like the dark valley of the shadow of death."[60] It would be impossible to escape.

Bellomont had to cover all of his bases to extinguish any associations he had with Kidd. After doing that, he sent men to Gardiner's Island to find the money that Kidd had buried. Knowing the contents of Kidd's stolen ship, Bellomont assumed the actual cache would be full of gold, coins, and jewels of all kinds. When he saw that the prize was just a bag of money not worth more than a few hundred pounds, Bellomont seized and arrested Kidd's wife, Sarah, in a fury. In prison, Bellomont's cronies questioned her relentlessly about the location of Kidd's prize. She knew nothing of it. She stayed in prison for months while Bellomont searched her home and went through all of her correspondence. Finally, Bellomont had no choice but to let her go, since there was no evidence of any collusion. In the meantime, word had spread that her husband was in prison for piracy. After Sarah was freed, she was completely ostracized by New York society. Even her servants abandoned her to save their own reputations.

Meanwhile, Kidd languished in solitary confinement in Stone Prison for the next year. The jail was damp and cold, with very little light coming in through the iron-barred windows. One can only imagine the physical state Kidd was in by the time he was removed.

Finally, British forces transported Kidd back to England so the English Parliament could officially question him. Upon his arrival, they sent him to Newgate Prison. It was a horrible place—even worse than Stone Prison. An open sewer ran through the lower level of the prison. Prisoners were kept in chains and shackles, severely limiting their movement. There was no protection when rain caused sewage water to seep in. The place was so dirty that doctors refused to enter to treat any prisoners. Those fortunate enough to have some money bought alcohol, so drunkenness abounded, which only made conditions even more dangerous. Lice were everywhere.

By time Kidd came to trial, the legal system had shifted dramatically. In the 1500s and early 1600s, trials featured an informed jury who made decisions about a criminal's fate. However, by the time Kidd was put on trial, the court used juries mostly after guilty verdicts, which meant that his trial was pretty much for show.[61] Kidd went on the stand already presumed guilty. Though the law still required that a person be judged by their peers, the instruction the court gave the jury at Kidd's trial was extremely skewed, ensuring Kidd's death sentence. The whole purpose of the trial was to humiliate Kidd and prove the power of the English legal system. This was exactly what the Admiralty wanted.

Kidd would not go down without a fight, however. He needed the one thing that could possibly save him from certain death: his letters of marque and passes granted by England and France to show that he could rob ships as long as he thought they were Dutch. It was a weak loophole, he knew, but it was all he had.

The Trial of Captain Kidd

Captain Kidd's trial took place at the Admiralty Sessions at the Old Bailey, London's largest and most famous courthouse, known for trying all kinds of crimes, on May 8 and 9, 1701.

The members of the court appeared in session early one morning. Despite the daylight, the Old Bailey's courtroom was dark, with small windows and little natural light. Those presiding over the trial would have worn black lawyers' robes with puffed and powdered wigs to make sure their status was unquestioned. The room was filled to capacity with people desperate to get a look at this famous pirate who had so angered their king and country. After a few moments, officials led Kidd into the court. It was time for the trial to begin. The following courtroom scenes include all exact quotes from the trial, with some modifications for a twenty-first century audience, along with a bit of added emotion for drama.

"Captain William Kidd, hold up your hand," the Councilor of Arraignments ordered.

"Please, your lordships. I would like to have counsel," Kidd replied, without raising his hand. A gasp went through the audience.

The Recorder paused his writing and leaned forward. "What would you need counsel for?"

"My lord, there are some matters of the law I have related to the indictment and I would like to have some counsel on the matter."

Dr. Oxendon, the judge, scoffed. "What matter of law would you need?"

"And how does he know what matter he is charged with? I haven't told him!" the Council of Arraignments broke in.

"Mr. Kidd, you have to tell us what matter of law you need counsel for," the Recorder said, exasperated.

"They're matters of law, my lord," Kidd said. Laughter rang through the audience.

The Recorder narrowed his eyes and shook his head. "Mr. Kidd, do you even know what you're talking about in terms of matters of law?"

Kidd looked up and stared right back at the Recorder. He turned his gaze to the Councilor of Arraignments and Dr. Oxendon. He gave a half-smile and said, "I know what I mean. I want to put off my trial as long as I can. So I can get my evidence ready, you see."

The audience was practically in an uproar. No matter the century, everyone loves a good courtroom drama. The judge called for order and then leaned over and spoke to Kidd, his anger evident.

"Mr. Kidd, you must give us your plea before we can even consider granting you counsel. If you do not, then we must proceed."

"I beg your patience, my lord," Kidd cried out, beads of sweat breaking out on his forehead. The room had already become stifling. "I have passes—French passes. I just need time to get them."

"That is no matter of law," the Recorder said flippantly. "You have had plenty of notice for your trial date. You should have used that time to prepare for it."

"But, my lord—"

"How long have you had to prepare for today, Mr. Kidd?"

"My lord, if you will permit me—"

"How long?" roared the Recorder.

Kidd felt his heart sink. Without his passes he was doomed before the trial could really begin. "About two weeks," he muttered.

Dr. Oxendon sighed. He leaned back and tapped on the desk for a moment. "Can you give us any names of any people that could be of use to you in your defense?"

"I sent for them, but they would not come," Kidd said bitterly.

"And why not?"

"I referred them to my Lord Bellomont in New England."

The lawyers murmured amongst each other. This was certainly a sad fate for Kidd, knowing that he and Bellomont had once been close friends.

"Mr. Kidd," the Recorder said, with more patience this time, "I do regret that the Court sees no reason to put off your trial. You must plead."

"But—" Kidd started.

"Mr. Kidd, hold up your hand," the Councilor of Arraignments ordered.

The back and forth continued for several minutes. Kidd, seeing his chance at survival, could barely keep himself from shouting in frustration at these men who refused to listen to him.

"My lords, you must let me send for my papers. Please!" Kidd hated them and hated himself even more for being reduced to begging like a dog.

"Hold up your hand."

"Let me send for my papers!"

The trial was getting out of control. Kidd would not back down and the audience was practically out of control with their excitement over the drama that kept unfolding.

"If you do not plead, the Court will pass judgment on you!" The Recorder's voice echoed across the chamber, silencing the room. "If you were indicted for felony and do not plead, then we will consider it to be your guilty confession."

"I cannot plead until my French passes are delivered to me. My justification depends on them."

"Mr. Kidd," the Recorder said in practically a whisper. The room was dead silent as everyone listened. "If you will not plead, you must have judgement passed against you."

"I cannot plead until I have these papers. Look around, my lord, I do not even have witnesses here!" Kidd shouted, gesturing around the courtroom. "If I plead, I will be passing death onto my own self."

The lawyers all began to speak at once.

"You are the accessory to your own death, if you do not plead."

"Kidd, are you guilty or not guilty?"

"He does not understand the law. You have to read the statute back to him."

The arguments swirled around Kidd. He felt he would vomit, but he stood his ground, saying over and over that he would not continue until he had his own evidence and witnesses granted to him. Finally, the Recorder held up his hand to silence everyone. He stood up and walked over to where Kidd stood, who had tears of desperation and rage streaming down his face.

"If you say 'guilty,' then that is the end of it. But if you say 'not guilty,' we can examine your case further." The Recorder stepped back and took his seat.

The court officer approached Kidd and spoke quietly to him. After several minutes, the officer addressed the court. "He said he will plead."

The Councilor of Arraignments stood up in triumph. Kidd stood with his shoulders hunched, his head hanging down. "William Kidd, are you guilty or not guilty, by God and my country?"

After a moment, Kidd said, "Not guilty." The crowd broke into conversation all around the room.

"How will you be tried?"

"By God and my country," Kidd whispered.

"Then send you a good deliverance."

The officer grasped Kidd's chains and began to pull him toward to the door. "My Lord, I beg you to put off my trial for a few days!" Kidd shouted as he struggled against his chains. "Just three or four days until I have my papers!"

"We must prepare your trial. Now that you have pleaded to the court, we will consider your motion and your reasons," the Council of Arraignment said flippantly. The whole room, including Kidd, knew this was a lie.[62]

Finally, after this argument ended, the court could deliver its official indictment. From its wording, their position and condemnation of his actions were clear from the beginning, with or without his evidence being presented.

"The jurors of our sovereign Lord the King, do, upon their oath present
that William Kidd, late of London, Mariner, not having the fear of God
in him but rather having been moved and seduced by the Devil…did
make an assault upon one William Moore, in the peace of God…with
a certain wooden bucket bound with iron top. William Kidd then and
there held the bucket with his right hand and violently, feloniously, and
voluntarily through his malice beat and struck William Moore a little
above his right ear and gave him a mortal bruise… And so the jurors
aforesaid, upon their oath, do say that William Kidd…did kill and
murder William Moore on the high sea…within the jurisdiction of the
Admiralty of England against the peace of our said Sovereign Lord the
King, his Crown and Dignity."[63]

At last, the trial began. Fortunately, the court granted Kidd a defense
lawyer named Dr. Oldish. The lawyer used the existence of Kidd's
letters of marque as the key point of the defense. On Kidd's behalf,
Oldish implored the judge to allow a delay in the trial so the passes
could be obtained. Kidd hoped that his lawyer's request would
be granted.

"It is with a valid reason that this trial should be delayed," Oldish
declared. "He wants some of the papers for his defense. It's true that he
has been charged with several accounts of piracy, but they had French
passes when the attacks happened. If they had those letters of marque,
then the attacks were lawful."

Unfortunately, the French passes were gone. Kidd's old friend and
now betrayer, Lord Bellomont, had taken the passes from Kidd. At this
point, a witness named Mr. Lemmon shows up in the trial transcript.
The witness corroborated Kidd's story and emphasized that the English
had employed Kidd as a privateer and that he was "doing his King and
Country service." Lemmon also insisted that Bellomont had confiscated
the passes. No matter. The trial would proceed without the evidence.[64]

Kidd was on trial for both crimes of piracy and murder. The justification
for the latter? Kidd had fought with William Moore, leading to the
latter's death. Whether it was deliberate did not matter. The trial
began with his murder charge. The prosecution started the trial with
an opening statement vilifying Kidd, claiming that it was a "most
barbarous fact" because Moore did not seem to have provoked his
captain in any way.

"This William Moore was a gunner in the ship, and this William Kidd abuses him, cause him a 'lousy dog,' and upon a civil answer he takes his bucket and knocks him on the head, whereof he died the next day."

To Kidd's shock, Joseph Palmer, one of his crew, came forward to offer his observation of the event. Kidd raged inside. How was it that he could not find witnesses for himself, and yet Palmer showed up out of the blue claiming that Kidd murdered his crewmate for no reason? He went as far as to claim that Moore cried out, saying that Kidd was about to kill him, and that Kidd shouted that he was a "villain." Did he not remember Moore taunting Kidd and threatening mutiny if he did not attack a ship outside their jurisdiction?

When Kidd was finally allowed his chance to speak, he shouted right back at Palmer.

"What was the occasion that I hit Moore?" Kidd demanded.

"The words that I told you before. When you called him a villain!"

"Was there no other ship?"

Palmer paused at that. He was caught. He knew very well that the argument was about illegally attacking a Dutch ship. In fact, he had urged Moore to provoke Kidd into doing it. Palmer considered lying to the court, but he took an oath before the judge and God to swear to the truth.

"Yes," he admitted.

"What was the ship?"

"A Dutch ship."

Kidd sat back, likely in triumph. "My Lords, this ship was a league from us. My men demanded that we take her but I would not allow it. Moore accused me of blocking everyone's rightful due. He was mutinous. That's when I struck him. I could not allow a mutiny on board the ship."

"No," Palmer shouted. "You chased the Dutchman! You had us chase her all night even though they showed their colors!"

"That is not the point!" The crowd gasped. Kidd immediately tried to backtrack. "Was there no mutiny on board?"

"There was no mutiny!"

"Was there not a mutiny because I would not take that Dutchman?"

"No, none at all!"

At this the judge pounded his gavel to silence the court. The audience was too heated and the men were practically at each other's throats.

Round and round this discourse went, with Palmer recounting the story of Kidd's fight with Moore. This time, however, Kidd was not allowed to interject. Then, to make matters worse, another member of his crew, Brandinham, was called forward to testify about what happened after Moore's death.

"About two months after Moore died, we neared the coast of Malabar. Captain Kidd said to several of us, 'I don't care about the death of my gunner or for any other of my actions over the course of this voyage. I have good friends in England. They will get me [out of] this."

More members of his crew came forward, including the ship's surgeon. One after the other, they recounted their own version of the events, all of which were basically the same story. Kidd wanted to attack a ship, Moore implored him not to, and Kidd struck him the fatal blow.

Finally, it was time to deliver Kidd's sentence.

The Indictment

There was no time to rest after the shock of this verdict. Immediately, the court moved on to his next indictment: piracy. It was no use, however. No matter what outcome came of this part of the trial, Kidd was a dead man. So be it. Kidd was nevertheless more determined than ever to save his reputation.

The prosecutors recounted the events that led up to the capture of the *Quedah Merchant*. Once again, Kidd would have to plead for his French passes to prove that he had lawful cause to rob this ship. Brandinham was the star witness for this case, who said that there were no letters of marque either on Kidd's ship or on the *Quedah Merchant*. Had both ships carried French passes, the robbery would have been lawful. After Brandinham gave his testimony, Kidd got his chance to fire back questions.

"Did you not see any French passes aboard the *Quedah Merchant*?"

"You told me you had them, but I never saw them," Brandinham answered.

"Did you never declare that you saw these French passes?"

"No, I did not see them," Brandinham said firmly. "I only heard you say that you had them."[65]

The rest of the trial was a disaster. Witness after witness came forward to say the same thing. They all seemed to have heard Kidd say that the ships both carried these passes, but no one ever saw one. The court even brought in some of the Armenian sailors, who said that they had no such passes to rob anyone. They were simply merchants. The case was done for.

After the final piece of evidence in Kidd's trial was presented, Justice Turton turned to the jury and delivered the following speech:

"Gentlemen, the business you are to look into is the piratical taking of these ships. The witnesses have positively and directly proven not only the taking of the ships, but the seizure of the ships and the sales of their goods. There has been no evidence to suggest that the witnesses have lied to the court. They are the ones most likely to know what happened because they were there during the whole voyage. If you give any credit to these witnesses, then you know that the person on the stand is guilty of the piracy he is charged with. I will leave you to your consideration."[66]

It should not be a surprise that the jury almost immediately found Kidd guilty of his crimes. After all, the evidence was stacked against him, and the British authorities had their own motives. They had to keep the Indian Mughals happy to keep their trade going. While the British were still hunting Kidd, the head of the East India Company had sent letters to the General of Bombay. One such letter from 1698 read, "Kidd and his accomplices will be brought to very quick and public punishments. We hope this promise will remove any reproach that lies upon our nation."[67]

This time, when the jury was excused to make their verdict, they were only gone for a half an hour. Kidd was found guilty on five counts of piracy.

"Captain William Kidd, you will be transported to Execution Dock where you will hang and go back from whence you came. What say you?" asked the judge.

After a pause, Kidd replied bitterly, "I have nothing to say, for I have been sworn against by perjured and wicked people."

"So be it," said the judge.

His hanging was set for May 23, 1701. Kidd was taken back to his cell to wait for the noose.

The Hanging of Captain Kidd

The following is a dramatization adapted from the Ordinary of Newgate's original account.

It should have been no surprise that Captain William Kidd showed up to his execution rip-roaringly drunk. The audience expected nothing less. After all, he had been found guilty as a pirate and pirates were known to drink to excess.

As the cart came into view on Wapping High Street, the audience began to laugh and jeer in delight. The guards grabbed Kidd by the arms and dragged him off the cart, only to immediately stumble to the ground. This resulted in fresh laughter from the crowd.

"Get up, you filthy lout," shouted one of the guards as he jerked Kidd to his feet.

Kidd swore and spat at him in response, which elicited a gasp from the closest onlookers. Without mercy, the guards shoved him onto the scaffold. Even in his inebriated state, Kidd could make out the noose in front of him, the water lapping onto the scaffold, and the hundreds of jeering onlookers before him.

"No!" He struggled and flailed his arms blindly as the executioner grabbed him from behind and jerked the noose around his neck. The rough hemp of the rope scratched and bit into his skin. The world spun and Kidd vomited—a bitter slop of dark rum and bile from an empty stomach—and felt his bladder release as he saw his death before him. Those closest to the scaffold jumped back to avoid the splash of sick.

"I'm not the pirate you seek!" Kidd tried to choke out. The tight rope around his neck combined with his drunken slurring rendered his words unintelligible. That did not matter. Any struggle from a condemned prisoner brought joy to the crowd. After all, he had violated the rules of God and society. He owed it to them to meet the punishment fitted to his crime.

With a loud crack, he felt the platform beneath his feet disappear. His stomach leaped into his throat as a floating sensation reached his head. He felt his heart striking in his chest.

He choked on his shriek as the rope pulled taut and the noose jerked his neck with a supernatural force. Pain like fire shot into his neck, his throat, his head. He could not take in any air. His legs began to kick uncontrollably as his body struggled to stay alive.

There was a loud snap and he suddenly felt the sickening falling sensation again, only this time he crashed against the ground. The rope fell loose around him, frayed where it had snapped. He lay there stunned, barely registering the horrified gasps of the crowd.

"Am I in hell?" he thought to himself. *"Am I cursed to repeat my doomed end for all of eternity?"*

After a moment, he felt someone yank him to his feet. His burning lungs fought for air and, with each breath, his mind began to clear. He coughed and tried to swallow, but his throat was too swollen. But suddenly, he was more alert than he had ever been in his life.

Kidd did not struggle as he was pulled back onto the scaffold. The guards tied his hands behind the pole so he could not escape as they looped a fresh rope. He looked out over the crowd. Men, women, and children in various states of cleanliness and finery looked back at him. Silence had fallen over them as they witnessed this stunning turn of events.

"Is this a sign from God?" Kidd asked himself.

As if the Ordinary of Newgate, the spiritual advisor of those condemned to death, had heard Kidd's thoughts, he addressed the crowd.

"My good people, this is a sign from God. Our prisoner has refused to confess to his crimes and has shown no remorse. He even submitted to his wicked habits and arrived before us in a drunken state as only befits a pirate. God, in his righteousness, has thus condemned this man to death…twice." His voice rose forcefully on the final word. He paused for effect before turning to Kidd. "You have one more opportunity. Do you repent?"

Kidd paused before responding in a choked rasp, "I have nothing to say except that I have been perjured by wicked people."

Only the Ordinary and those closest to the scaffold could hear his gasping response. They whispered it through the crowd and murmurings grew into new shouts. The Ordinary held up his hand and the crowd fell silent.

"So be it," he said. "You are now sentenced to return from whence you came. May God have mercy on your soul."

Kidd said nothing and stared defiantly over the crowd, not meeting anyone's eyes. He swallowed and set his jaw refusing to show any fear or emotion. The law sought to take his life unjustly, he felt, and he would give no satisfaction in return. His heart pounded as a new rope was secured around his neck once more. As he started to take a deep breath, the platform once more disappeared from under his feet.

A shooting pain was followed by a loud crack. The sounds around him faded as the world went black.

Captain Kidd hanging in chains.

The Hanging of Captain Kidd, The Pirates Own Book by Charles Ellms, 1837
Wiki Commons

After Kidd's death, the British were able to prove to their Indian trading partners that they had eradicated the notorious pirate who had dared to humiliate all parties. Unfortunately, the ship and goods could never be returned, which was a sore consequence. Neither party was thrilled at this outcome, but at least Kidd had been stopped. It did not entirely make up for Henry Avery's crimes and insults, but the British stayed true to their word. Trade was allowed to continue between the Indian Mughals and the East India Company.

As for Kidd's wife Sarah, little is known. Records show that she married a man named Christopher Rouseby just a few months after Kidd was hanged, and they lived quietly in New York after that. After Rouseby died, she used her money from this and her previous marriages to open a tavern. The business was successful, and she operated it until she died in 1744, leaving all of her money to her children.

Tunes of the Tides

The whole saga behind Kidd's trial was so full of drama and betrayal that word quickly traveled throughout the streets about how the notorious pirate had been abandoned by his friends and colleagues and sentenced to death. His trial became such a spectacle that the Admiralty Court shut the Old Bailey's doors and stopped allowing people in. So how could people who had missed the trial find out what happened? And how could people who had missed the execution learn the background of Captain Kidd? The answer was to run to the local print shops, where items were produced swiftly and cheaply. Even though Kidd's death was so public, people were aching for more. On May 24, the transcript of his trial was published verbatim at the low price of 1 pence. On May 25, the trial had sold out at every shop. On May 26, a second printing was released.

Newspapers and pamphlets were great at spreading news and glorified rumors, but there was one language that transcended these more than any other: the ballad. Ballads, or tales told in song form, celebrated events such as battles, feuds, murders, executions, and tragedies. They were often funny, political, romantic, and/or lewd.

Ballads reflected the lives and attitudes of ordinary people. With the advent of the printing press, dingy rooms in the backs of print shops churned out ballads by the thousands.[68]

Ballads used popular tunes so people could remember them easily. Popular ballads, for instance, spread rumors across Britain and the colonies about swashbuckling pirates. These ballads were about real pirates and their exploits, informing people about their lives. Ballads did not just tell stories from an outsider's perspective. The subjects of crime ballads told their stories in the first person. These ballads featured the speaker already caught and prepped for execution, confessing youthful disobedience while describing his career.[69] The music coupled with such exciting subjects made ballads one of the most popular ways to spread the history of the misdeeds and violence of pirates.

Sing a Song for Kidd

Kidd might have been dead, but his legacy was not. Far from it. Many people knew who he was by the time news of the chase hit the newspapers, but everyone knew about him after his death. Presses printed his trial, along with the Ordinary's account, verbatim and sold it out within a day. Ballads, poems, and hunts for his rumored buried treasure began in earnest and continue to this day. Without Kidd, pirates would not have become the popular figures that they are today. In fact, his death is what really set off a widespread fascination with pirates.

The first publications of Kidd's trial and last dying speech brought him to people's attention and made him a legend. For those who could not or did not come across these works, there were songs to be sung. Sailors and pub goers sang ballads about Kidd far and wide to describe his struggle in detail. The ballads turned Kidd into a sympathetic character, which says a lot about how people viewed pirates at this point.

One of the popular ballads to emerge was the "Elegy of Captain Kidd." It elegy begins:

> When any Great and Famous Man does Die,
> The World expects to have an ELEGY
> Produc'd, to his Immortal Memory:
> The End of which, we know, is to declare
> What those Great Deeds and Noble Actions were
> Which did Complete his Noble Character.

The song then goes into colorful detail about Kidd's savagery and bravery. Kidd is not exactly painted as a man of upright standing, but he is certainly depicted as a bold and brash sailor who is not afraid of anything.

> Kidd was a Man of such undaunted Spirit,
> He'd face Hell-Gates, and all the Devils in it,
> Were't possible to STEAL: A Golden Prize
> Did so bewitch his Heart, and charms his Eyes!
> When on the Seas proud Waves he boldly rid,
> All stroke to fly the Great and Mighty KIDD
> So terrible was. He, where e'er he came
> To ROB, or PLUNDER, that his very Name
> Wou'd cause a Trembling Fear and Dread in those
> Who were his Friends, as well as his foes...

It is impossible for me to read these lyrics or sing the song without feeling some sort of cheer. *Yes, Kidd was a man who could face the Devil himself to receive the might to steal one of the greatest ships of all time!* Unfortunately, his success was also his downfall. He fell victim to his own ego. Like Icarus, he flew too close to the sun.

> These Actions raised his Face, and made him Great;
> Still climbing high'r, he fell by his own Weight:
> GOOD FORTUNE left him, and his Pow'r failed him,
> The DEVIL (ready for him), Goal'd and Hang'd him,
> To no one's Sorrow, rather by Joy display;
> Who weeps to see a conquer'd BEAST OF PREY.

Because Kidd's life ended in disgrace, the elegy closes with a warning. Most such elegies closed in this style for dramatic effect. Kidd's life was full of drama, so naturally there was much to be wrought from his story. His life translated well into an epic tale with a final graphic moral, not too different from the last dying speeches that most criminals were forced to perform:

> Reader, Near this Tomb don't stand,
> Without some Essence in thy Hand;
> For here KIDD'S stinking Corps does lie,
> The Scent of Which may thee infect;
> He Base did Live, and Base did Die,
> Therefore his Tomb and Corps reject.
> Put by he in WHITNEY'S Grave did lie,
> That all might Piss on him, as they pass'd by:
> One rais'd his Face, by Robbing on SHORE,
> The Other on the SEA. —Both now no more.[70]

Years later, in the late 1700s, another ballad about Kidd became popular. This one was sung in first-person perspective, as if Kidd finally had the chance to give his testimony or, at the very least, restore his reputation. The ballad starts out like a traditional speech in that it warns the audience against the temptations of piracy.

> You Captains brave and bold, hear our cries
> You Captains brave and bold, though you seem uncontroul'd
> Don't for the sake of gold lose your souls.

The ballad then shifts to Kidd's perspective, who admits his wrongdoings from the get-go. He first focuses on the shame he brought upon his family.

> My parents taught me well, when I sail'd
> …My parents taught me well, to shun the gates of hell
> But 'gainst them I did rebel, when I sail'd…
> I curs'd my father dear, when I sail'd
> I curs'd my father dear, and her that did me bear…

The ballad approaches a close with Kidd admitting that he is getting what he deserves. He accepts his fate and the fact that his death will be a public event, which will leave him without dignity.

> To Newgate now I'm cast, with a sad and heavy heart
> To receive my just desert, I must die.
> …To Execution Dock I must go
> To Execution Dock, will many thousand flock
> But I must bear the shock, and must die.

Finally, he closes his song with the anticipated moral lesson, but not without dropping some tantalizing hints about his treasure.

...Come all you young and old, see me die
Come all you young and old, you're welcome to my gold,
For by't I've lost my soul, and must die.
...Take warning now by me, for I must die,
Take warning now by me, and shun bad company
Lest you come to hell with me, for I must die...[71]

The repetitive lines and simple rhymes allow the lyrics to fit with any tune. This way, anyone could enjoy the tale. Over time, the facts of history were lost, but his memory lived on in a song that undoubtedly brought people joy, especially when the song could be coupled with long-standing legends of Kidd's buried treasure.

X Marks No Spot

Lord Bellomont's 1699 letter initiated the rumors about Kidd's treasure. After Bellomont lured Kidd to New York under the false promise of safety, he learned that Kidd "has left a great Moorish ship that he took in India...in a creek on the coast of Hispaniola, with goods to the value of £30,000: that he had brought a small ship...that had several bales of East India goods, three score pound weight of gold in dust and ingots, about a hundred weight in silver, and several other things that he believed would sell for about £10,000."[72]

This is the only official written piece of evidence that mentions any real collection of wealth hidden by Kidd. Word about it spread almost immediately. Some of Kidd's accomplices knew that these rumors were everywhere and tried to use the gossip to their advantage. For instance, a letter from Philadelphia reported, "We have four men in prison taken up as pirates who are supposedly Kidd's men...we have various reports about their riches and some talk of much money hidden between here and the Capes."[73] Another letter, written to the

Lords Justices in England by the East India Company, stated that
Kidd had sailed into the American colonies with "a great treasure
of gold, silver, jewels, and the merchandise being the produce of his
piracies."[74] So the rumors about Kidd, for a time, seemed to be almost
certainly true.

Then, a year after Bellomont's letter, in 1700, he completely retracted
his former statement about Kidd's amassed wealth. He claimed that
Kidd refused to tell anyone about what he stole: "Captain Kidd sent
the jailer to me two weeks ago to relay a message saying that if I let
him go to where he hid the *Quedah Merchant*, St Thomas Island, and
Curacao, he would aim to bring back fifty or three score thousand
pounds, which would be lost forever without his rescue...I told the
jailor to ask Kidd where the treasure was hidden, but he said that
Kidd would not tell anyone where it was located."[75]

It appears that Kidd dropped some hints as to where he hid his stolen
goods, but to this day, not a single person has found any real evidence
that it existed.

These tidbits put Lord Bellomont under fire, which is probably why
he did everything he could to distance himself from Kidd. Bellomont
was initially very detailed about his communication with Kidd, but
when he realized he was in danger of becoming a suspected pirate,
he denied all association with him. He had to save his reputation if
he wanted to remain governor. This did not stop the newspapers,
however. The press found a tiny piece of information and milked
it for all it was worth to sell more copies. In September 1699, the
London Post Boy published an article that claimed "Kidd sent a
present of jewels to the Countess of Bellomont, to the value of some
thousands of pounds" and that Bellomont's wife initially refused the
treasure, but the governor had ordered her to accept it.[76] Not only
did Bellomont have to protect himself, he had to make sure his wife's
name stayed clean as well.

Rumors about Kidd's treasure continued to swirl around England and the American colonies. Soon enough, Kidd became automatically associated with buried treasure, despite the fact that actual physical evidence of his riches still did not materialize! Not only that, but the supposed value kept changing, which made the matter even more confusing. The governor of Pennsylvania, William Penn, said, "I never yet fingered one piece of his silver."[77] Kidd's lost cargo of the *Quedah Merchant* was valued at £70,000[78] and even though "it could not be traced, and was never heard of again," the notion of his lost goods sparked the romance of his history.[79] The story behind Kidd's treasure gets even more confusing. Judge Samuel Sewall, an acquaintance of Lord Bellomont, wrote in his diary that he had written down Kidd's total inventory after the pirate's arrest in Boston, which included "an iron chest of gold, pearls, and 40 bails of East-India Goods..."[80]

Official sources from the *Calendar of State Papers* estimated that Kidd's lost treasure was worth £300,000 at the time.[81] The *London Post*, on the other hand, reported that Kidd's ship and cargo were worth £20,000.[82] The Massachusetts Historical Society, published Sewall's diary, in which Sewall put the value of Kidd's gold at £1,000.[83] Some later treasure-hunters claimed to be looking for gold, silver, jewels, and other goods in the Massachusetts Sound that would be worth up to £6,500. According to the Massachusetts Historical Society, Kidd told Bellomont he had hidden a cache of treasure worth anywhere between £50,000 and £60,000[84] between the islands of St. Thomas and Curacao, which no one would ever find.[85] And indeed, to this day, no one has ever found it.

So did Kidd have treasure or did he not? And if so, how much? Based on all of this contradictory evidence, how can we ever really know? Regardless, Kidd's fame has lasted longer than most pirates', because the press and other popular publications have immortalized the stories about his treasure.[86]

The rumors about Kidd's buried treasure continued to circulate long after his death. In the 1820s, stories were published that claimed Kidd had had a secret hideout in Kiddenhooghten, New York, having buried fifty boxes of gold.[87] Other alleged inventory lists of Kidd's treasure surfaced, which contained items such as gold dust, gold bars, coined gold and silver, and precious stones. One person even went so far as to claim that he had a strip of gold cloth passed down to him from his father, who had received it from an elderly neighbor who claimed that Kidd had given it to her when he landed in the islands of the Malay Archipelago.[88]

By the mid-1800s, the stories began to go even further. New claims emerged that people had actually found his treasure. Though the stories proved to be false or outright fabricated, it did not matter. Kidd's treasure must exist, people reasoned. Some reports stated that his gold and silver washed up on the shores of New York's Hudson River and that more great treasures were expected.[89] Other reports came out that said people found sealed bottles containing letters and maps written and drawn by Kidd.[90] Naturally, no evidence really existed.

Whether or not any of these stories were true, they told readers just how much wealth a pirate could collect on his own. As pirates, they could become independently wealthy and free of any social obligation. Captain Kidd appeared to be the epitome of that. After all, he started out as a privateer, married an extremely wealthy woman, and supposedly came into vast amounts of treasure—even though he died before he could take advantage of it.

The rumors continued. Some people were so desperate to find Kidd's treasure that they tried to con people into expeditions. The most famous of these concerned the Kidd-Palmer Charts. These were a series of Kidd's alleged maps that pinpointed the location of his treasure in the South China Sea. Hubert Palmer, an English antiques collector, claimed to have found these maps inside a chest he'd purchased that had been on Kidd's ship. As the discoverer, Palmer found it fitting to name the map after himself. When the British Museum verified these maps were legitimate, a frenzy of speculation around the legend of Captain Kidd started up once more.[91]

The excitement died in 1951. That year, someone filed a fraud report with Scotland Yard against a man who had advertised an expedition to travel to the South China Sea to find Kidd's buried treasure using the Kidd-Palmer Charts. The man in charge of the expedition, James Brownlie, advertised the adventure in the *Daily Mail* and required personal investments from those interested in joining the mission.[92] The two men who sued Brownlie for fraud had both invested over £1,500 in the expedition, only to see the trip postponed due to an erroneous claim of "bad weather" and "necessary repairs."[93] A likely story. Brownlie claimed that he would fund the expedition himself, haters be damned. Then, for some unknown reason, he canceled the adventure.[94]

May 7, 2015, marks the most recent news regarding Kidd as of this writing. Reports broke all around the world that someone had finally found Kidd's treasure off the coast of Madagascar in the form of silver ingots aboard a sunken ship. Initially, this seemed possible because Kidd had spent time in Madagascar and had allegedly hidden his prizes in different places.[95] However, just a little over a month later, the United Nations stated that the "treasure" had no relation to Captain Kidd at all. In fact, it was not even treasure. The ingots turned out not to be silver at all, but 95 percent lead and 5 percent rubble. An official investigation of the sunken ship eventually found that it was not the one captained by Kidd. Even more comical, the ruins of the sunken ship turned out to be a broken part of the Sainte-Marie port from hundreds of years ago.[96]

Although Kidd died centuries ago, rumors of his treasure continue to exist to this day.

Captain Kidd: The Man, the Myth, the Legend

Over time, people became more and more enamored with the idea of Kidd rather than the reality. Some even began to question his guilt. In 1874, the London magazine *Belgravia* published an article titled "A Cruise with Kidd" that suggested he had received a most unjust punishment. "He did some queer things, no doubt, but he was hanged for doing them, whilst so many who did infinitely worse than he died in their beds in the odour of sanctity, and, according to all the rules of fair play, ought to be now suffering a good deal more than he."

The article continued with a great effort to exonerate him, ideally to convince those with the authority to grant him a posthumous pardon. The author argued that Kidd was a skilled sailor before he turned pirate "who had done the state some service, having fought the king's enemies on the occasion of sea-fights in the West Indies, and borne himself well therein." Not only was he a skilled privateer, Kidd had also had commissions from the king to rob enemy ships. The article's author ultimately argued that the King had framed Kidd because he felt that Kidd had unfairly taken too many spoils for himself in too violent a manner.

"He was done worse than many of his contemporaries, who were pardoned [for their crimes] and employed in the King's service… As this is the age of reviving the verdicts of the past and rehabilitating the characters of reputed ruffians, let us not omit to do even-handed justice to the memory and reputation of Kidd."

Unfortunately, this article was not taken seriously by any authorities.[97] That should come as no surprise, since the author claimed to have gotten his information from a séance.

Questions about his guilt persisted, however. Interest and sympathy toward his plight continued well into the twentieth century. In 1936, a group of historians and researchers petitioned to have Kidd posthumously pardoned. According to records from the Home Office, "an interested group of persons in the United States with a request that they may be furnished with information regarding the procedure which should be observed in presenting a petition to the Crown, praying for a posthumous pardon for the notorious Captain Kidd" had approached the British Library of Information in New York. This "interested party" had allegedly discovered "certain evidence in South America" that proved Kidd should never have been tried and executed.[98] Once again, authorities thwarted the sympathizers and threw out their petition.

More than two hundred years later, his legacy still heavily influences modern pirate stories. Without him, it is possible that history and popular culture would not have immortalized all the other pirates we know and love today.

CHAPTER 3

SUPPRESSING PIRATES
AND BITTERSWEET
HEARTBREAK

C aptain Kidd became an iconic figure even before his death. He was one of the first pirates ever to make waves in the newspapers on both sides of the Atlantic Ocean. The publication of his trial and dying speech totally transformed his image and changed his narrative.[99] The popular reports published Kidd's declarations that he felt justified in all of his actions. But being tried for piracy, found guilty, and hanged for it changed his reputation for centuries to come. The never-ending rumors about his lost buried treasure perpetuate Kidd's modern notoriety.

Our pirate-loving popular culture is a uniquely modern phenomenon. As we know, pirates helped colonists by bringing in valuable goods that were unobtainable otherwise. This constant flow of commerce allowed wealth to flow into the North American colonies and plantation islands. If it were not for British interference, the perception of piracy might have remained more positive.

With the oceans swarming with pirates and colonies out of control, someone had to take charge. When Britain started to colonize the Caribbean and North America, the High Court of Admiralty's role started to grow. When piracy exploded uncontrollably at the turn of the eighteenth century, the Admiralty had only one specific job: to get rid of pirates.

The goal to eradicate piracy was, of course, a bit convoluted. With the French and Spanish also setting up camp in the Americas, how could they determine what were British waters? In that case, we refer back to what we learned in Chapter One. Henry VIII had thought through the complications of international waters and preemptively passed the *Offenses of the Sea Act*, just in case he decided to start expanding the British world.[100] Now Britain could claim virtually *any* part of the ocean its own.

A Legal Pissing Contest

The British American colonies' good relationships with pirates drove many of the complaints sent to the colonies' government officials. The transcript of a regular meeting at the Council of Maryland on November 29, 1701, gave a summary of some of these issues. The notes describe how the British North American colonies of Maryland, Pennsylvania, and New Jersey were helping pirates and were happy to let them live anywhere they wanted for the colonies' benefit: "A reliable source tells that pirates have taken advantage of Pennsylvania's government for several years and contributed much to enriching those places…New Jersey has also been a receptacle for pirates with their goods and has been encouraging smugglers and pirates to sell their goods there."[101]

Minutes like these were full of the frustrations of Admiralty officials. The source of these frustrations? Most governors either turned a blind eye to pirates or were outright happy to help them. The Admiralty had had enough. Fortune favored them when a pesky law was passed, the Navigation Acts of 1651, which banned all trade outside of British rule. Britain already struggled to assert its dominance over America against the French and Spanish, and its own people were making the process nearly impossible. Though the colonies were unhappy, Britain tried to rationalize the Navigation Acts by saying that the Acts were meant to increase English trade and keep their colonial relationships strong against their European rivals.

Jamaica was also dissatisfied with the proposal. "England does not supply us with enough goods that we couldn't have gotten from our neighbors, the French and the Dutch, who would sell us their products for cheap," said Sir William Beeston, Jamaica's lieutenant-governor.[102]

The colonists gave Britain the proverbial middle finger and turned their backs on the law, continuing to support pirate commerce. The British bit their thumbs right back. In yet another attempt to stop the colonists from trading with their bitter rivals, the British passed another law called the Barbados Act. The Act barred anyone from bringing foreign sugar, rum, and molasses into their ports. However, this law turned out to be useless. North American captains could simply claim that any supply of sugar, rum, or molasses came from Jamaica or Barbados (British colonies) as long as the supply had been picked up at those ports.[103]

The reality was that the Navigation Acts crippled local economies.[104] Pretty much every single New England settlement was a port town or city completely dependent on maritime work and trade, which Britain now severely limited. The southern colonies produced other material goods, such as tobacco and rice, that were valuable trade commodities. The strict rules put in place by the Navigation Acts ushered in the beginning of a black-market system run by pirates and other smugglers. Though these smugglers were breaking the law, local courts generally did not want to arrest pirates because so many people empathized with them.[105]

Some colonies just flat-out didn't care about enforcing Britain's trade laws. The governor of Rhode Island, for instance, did not even bother pretending to obey the Navigation Acts. In fact, he openly allowed and encouraged illegal trade. The Council of Trade and Plantations declared that Rhode Island was a "receptacle full of pirates."[106] The people of New Jersey, Pennsylvania, Maryland, and Virginia welcomed pirates with open arms. Philadelphia in particular became a great place to lie low. City residents were known to offer pirates fresh supplies if they stayed offshore or hid in town. In return, the pirates supplied them with plundered goods and riches.[107]

Meanwhile, the Carolinas became known as another "pirate hideaway" and the "second Jamaica."[108] During the mid-seventeenth-century wars against Spain, pirates would refresh their supplies in South Carolina ports. They paid in cash and developed friendly commercial relationships, which made the merchants want the pirates to keep coming back. This relationship would remain until the infamous pirate Blackbeard blockaded the port in 1718.[109]

The officials attempting to uphold the Navigation Acts begged England for more resources for protection, lamenting that the colonies were falling into complete anarchy.[110] Others cried about the dangers that pirates presented, including hurting merchant ships: "These men will cause utter destruction and ruin of his Majesty's plantation trade on the Continent," the Council of Virginia proclaimed.[111]

Their cries fell on deaf ears. The local Admiralty Courts were on their own to face the impossible task of controlling the colonists. There was only one solution: to tighten the noose.

The Noose Tightens

The colonies had always been allowed certain freedoms, such as governing themselves and creating their own laws separate from those of England.[112] Since they were so far away from their ruler, colonial governments adjusted or even expanded their colonial charters as they saw fit. King Charles I did try to keep a tight hold on the New England colonies, but he was too far away to prevent local independence.[113] After a long period of ruling themselves, it's no wonder that the British attempting to enforce their own laws abroad would strain the relationship between the colonies and motherland.[114]

When piracy grew, the Admiralty Court established its own courts in the American colonies to capture and try pirates as fast as possible. This served as an excuse to stretch the Court's power to every British American colony.[115] The pirate's circumstances did not matter—if the Admiralty were to accuse someone of piracy, they would have to enjoy making their new home in a disgusting jail cell.[116]

The motherland demanded that colonists execute all pirates in exactly the way the Admiralty ordered—or else the court would consider the colonists pirates as well. This infuriated the colonists. They, naturally, rebelled. Many secretly helped pirates or outright defied the Admiralty's orders. No way would the British tell them what to do! Even Caribbean-based leaders colluded with pirates, further upsetting the English authorities. In the Bahamas, Colonel Nicholas Trott frequently worked with the infamous pirate Henry Avery and his crew in 1695. A governor in the Bahamas once even committed piracy himself.[117]

Needless to say, there were strong reactions against executing pirates. Governor Lord Hamilton of Jamaica wrote to the Council of Trade and Plantations in England to describe how a mob in Port Royal rescued a pirate from the gallows. The pirate had robbed a Spanish ship, ensuring his death sentence. This unnamed pirate was dragged onto the scaffold, and the crowd began to protest. The pirate refused to give a speech, so the Admiralty official hit him from behind, causing an uproar. The audience surged forward onto the gallows and attacked the Admiralty officials and executioner. During the hubbub, someone managed to cut the rope and the pirate was led to safety. The shock of these two events led Hamilton to issue a proclamation that promised a reward and pardon to any person or pirate who came forward with information about them. No one said a word.[118]

"Begging Your Pardon, Sir..."

If the Admiralty could not catch all pirates, they could ensnare them. Enter the *Act for the Effectual Suppression of Piracy* (mentioned in Chapter 1), which promised pirates a full pardon if they turned themselves in. *Wink.* The catch? The pirates also had to name their accomplices and betray their brethren.[119] As a reward, they would go free with a clean record and keep all of their goods and money.[120] However, the Admiralty could not act on just the pirates' word. They had to have proof. Once the pirates confessed and named their accomplices, they were thrown into a jail cell until the Admiralty could find their colleagues. If the alleged pirates were not found, their accusers were either executed or, if they were lucky, forced into British naval servitude. If their word proved true, the Admiralty set the pirates free with their pardon.

Granting pardons did two things. First, pardons sent a message that emphasized the extent of royal authority, which must be obeyed at all costs. Second, pardons showed that the king or queen could be kind, merciful, and just enough to grant pleas.[121] Pardons kept the number of hangings in check as well, so that the court only hung an "appropriate" number of pirates. Too many hangings made the monarch look cruel and therefore fearsome. Those types of monarchs were at risk of unrest or worse—revolution. But too few executions signaled a weak monarchy...which could also result in a violent uprising of the people. The number of hangings had to appear strict but fair, frightening people just enough to induce them to obey the law.[122]

Believe it not, British officials were eager to pardon pirates. If officials did that, they'd essentially be freeing these pirates from prison and moving them into the workforce. This would be the perfect opportunity to add experienced and knowledgeable sailors to the Admiralty's employ.[123] All the pirates would need to do was find some sort of proof of innocence, or, at the least (in some very rare cases), swear that they would never act as a pirate again.

Some pirates were successful at gaining clemency without proof. Sometimes good evidence of their character or other factors worked in their favor. One of the pirates under command of Henry Avery, Robert Seely, received a full pardon due to his "youthful ignorance." "The tenderness of his youth allowed him to be carried away by the lure of Henry Avery."[124]

Officials also pardoned two members of Kidd's former crew: Robert Brandingham and Joseph Palmer. Robert and Joseph were fortunate enough to get character witnesses to swear on their behalf and, as we know, they also decided to testify against their former captain. Obviously, it was really the latter reason that they received pardons. It might have been a grave betrayal to Kidd, but most of his crew were fed up with him to the point where they did not care if he lived or died.[125]

If a pirate happened to have friends or relatives brave enough to step in on his behalf to give evidence of prior good behavior, such as previous steady employment, good family relationships, sober and honest living, and a general good establishment in his home community, the judge and jury could use the information to grant mercy.[126]

A full pardon conferred more prizes than walking away free. The pirate would receive money based on the rank of the pirates he turned in. The commanding officer would get him £100 and anyone else with an inferior rank would bring him £20 each,[127] a very considerable sum of money that could support him for years![128]

This was not good enough, however. The Admiralty had to relax their criteria a bit to get more pirates to turn themselves in. By providing legitimate proof of their innocence, the Admiralty said, the pardoned pirates could walk free without any risk of transportation. Transportation was a mighty threat to pirates. The Admiralty sometimes forced guilty pirates onto ships headed for either the Caribbean or the North American continent, where their fate of hard labor awaited them.[129] If their proof did not pan out, they could get transportation rather than jail time. The only exception, naturally, was Captain Kidd. The Admiralty considered him too notorious to pardon—no matter what evidence could have been brought forth. The Admiralty had to make Kidd into an example.[130]

But the Admiralty was a fickle beast. Though they did pardon the majority of pirates, the Admiralty still forced a huge number of them into transportation or service in the Royal Navy. It was a lucrative business to transport pirates. On rare occasions, officials forced pirates to work alongside indentured servants and enslaved people. Transporting pirates, however, was the best way to expand the Royal Navy. After all, they were experienced sailors and fighters. The best part was that they could also tell officials where pirate hideouts were located.

A Motley Crew

Despite all of these efforts, the *Act for the Effectual Suppression of Piracy* turned out to be a total failure. All three of them! If anything, piracy increased. The failure of the decree, however, was not for lack of trying. Messages about the *Effectual Suppression of Piracy* were sent all up and down the North American coast and throughout the Caribbean. Presses printed copies of it in newspapers and pamphlets sent far and wide. Officials even sent copies as far north as

Newfoundland, Canada, to no avail. As a last-ditch attempt, British officials even tried to fudge their maritime borders in an attempt to capture pirates that were technically outside of their authority and colonial boundaries.[131] Nothing worked. Nothing could stop piracy in the Atlantic.

At the root of the Act's failure was this—most pirates were loath to turn each other in. There was an unwritten pact between all pirates that they must be loyal to each other. Betraying each other was tantamount to treason and guaranteed a whole fleet of enemies. Unless, of course, you were Edward Teach, a.k.a. Blackbeard.

Blackbeard vs. Bonnet

Blackbeard was one of the most famous pirates during the Golden Age of Piracy, despite having been a pirate for only two years. His real name was Edward Teach, and he was born in Bristol, England, in 1680. Edward Teach started out as a privateer and then became a pirate under the tutelage of Hornigold. When Hornigold noticed Teach's charisma and intelligence, he took him under his wing and made him his protégé. After Hornigold retired, Teach became captain and started his own reputation as a fearsome pirate. Teach's alias, Blackbeard, came from his looks. He had a very shocking style (by eighteenth-century standards) with a long black beard (of course) and unruly hair. Funnily enough, he wasn't actually a very successful or deadly pirate. He didn't become that wealthy and he didn't kill that many people. Again, he only operated for two years: 1716 to 1718.

Captain Teach commonly call'd Black Beard, Joseph Nicholls, 1736
Courtesy of the John Carter Brown Library

After Hornigold's death, Blackbeard sailed to Nassau to build up a crew. There, Blackbeard met his new partner, Stede Bonnet. After meeting, they enthusiastically decided to join forces and sail together. However, that joy was short-lived. Blackbeard soon regretted the decision to join Bonnet. To put it simply, Bonnet was not a fellow enemy of all mankind.

A successful and wealthy planter from Jamaica, Bonnet basically woke up one day and decided to abandon his wife and children to sail under the Jolly Roger. We may never know the actual reason why, but *The General History of the Pyrates* suggests that his wife was a "nag" and that he wanted to escape her. Naturally, Bonnet bought his own ship and declared himself a pirate captain. The title was useless, however, since no one could respect a self-proclaimed captain who had not actually earned his title. An inexperienced sailor, he suffered a leg injury during his first battle alongside Blackbeard and was lame for the rest of his life. Afterwards, Bonnet became too cautious and downright cowardly for Blackbeard to tolerate as a captain. Plus, they were becoming too recognizable. The ship that Bonnet had purchased was large and easy to recognize. That and Blackbeard's infamous hair style made him too good a target. It was time for a fresh start.

Engraving of Stede Bonnet, A General History of the Pyrates, 1724
Wiki Commons

Blackbeard hatched a plan to get rid of Bonnet once and for all. He
gathered forty of his most trusted crew members to fill them in.
That night, Blackbeard and his team enacted their plan. They got the
whole crew drunk while they sailed into the Beaufort Inlet on the
coast of North Carolina. Under the cover of nightfall and drunken
chaos, Blackbeard stole away while his men hid on shore. Blackbeard
went into nearby Bath Town to find an Admiralty office. There, he
immediately confessed his crimes and asked for a pardon. He named
all of the crew on the ship, including Bonnet.

Bonnet and his crew awoke to find themselves betrayed. Realizing
what Blackbeard had done, they frantically tried to get back to sea, but
their ship was too deep into the shoals. They were marooned. Bonnet,
the coward, abandoned his crew. He took off in the night to find work
as a pirate elsewhere.

The remaining pirates Blackbeard had named decided to raid
the city's stores and went on a bender. Two days later, everyone
was passed out on the *Queen Anne's Revenge* after a bacchanalia
of drinking. When they awoke, not only did they have the worst
hangovers of their lives, they found themselves surrounded by the
Admiralty. Officials promptly arrested them all while Blackbeard and
his forty selected crew sailed away.

Blackbeard made Bath Town, North Carolina, his home over the next
several months. He even settled down, got married, and made a living
smuggling in goods. Sure, the residents were wary of him and some
outright disliked him, but everyone benefitted from his ventures,
so they left him alone. Before long, Blackbeard became bored and
restless, and this settled lifestyle lost its appeal. Less than a year after
betraying Bonnet, Blackbeard was back on the ocean to plunder.

Unfortunately, Blackbeard's foray back onto the sea would be short-
lived. In November of 1718, North Carolina's coast guard (headed
by Lieutenant Charles Maynard, off the coast of Ocracoke Island)

attacked Blackbeard's ship. Blackbeard and Maynard had an epic face-off in which Maynard stabbed Blackbeard in the leg.

"Well done, lad!" Blackbeard shouted. But before Blackbeard could fight back, Maynard sliced Blackbeard's head cleanly off his neck with his sword. To prove Blackbeard's death, Lieutenant Maynard attached the head to a ship called *Jane* and sailed it up and down the New England coast.[132]

Black Beard's Head on the end of the Bowsprit.

Black Beard's Head on the end of a Bowsprit
Courtesy of the Royal Maritime Museum, Greenwich, UK

In the meantime, Stede Bonnet continued his short-lived, haphazard career. Shortly after escaping the authorities, he joined forces with Charles Vane, one of the cruelest pirates ever to sail, before taking another ship of his own. This did not last long. Stede was soon captured off the coast of South Carolina. The South Carolina hangman executed Bonnet and his new crew for all to see.[133]

The Hanging of Major Stede Bonnet, 1725
Courtesy of the John Carter Brown Library

Pirate Wives

As shocking as this might have sounded to the King, pirates were mostly just normal people. They had families and communities that valued them.

That's right. Many pirates were family men, devoted to their parents, spouses, children, and siblings. Their families' livelihoods often depended on them. While the men were off pirating, the rest of the family had to fend for themselves.

This was not uncommon in the sailing world, either. Women who married sailors knew that they were in for a challenging life. Sailors were often away for several months out of the year, or even a few years at a time. Their wages were sent home to their families, but they would have to wait a very long time to see any money come in. Money was also a point of leverage for many sailors. The Royal Navy, for instance, held onto its sailors' pay for up to six months to prevent desertion.

Death at sea was also a very real risk. Sailors were always one step away from malnutrition, dehydration, injury, and illness. One wrong turn of the weather could sink a whole ship, sending everyone to the bottom of Davey Jones's Locker.

> Davey Jones's Locker? What exactly was this "locker"?
> Unfortunately, this is one of many historical mysteries. No one knows who Davey Jones was, if he even existed, or what "locker" truly meant. The first mention of the term comes from the book *The Four Years Voyages of Captain George Roberts*, generally attributed to Daniel Defoe and published in 1726. More likely than not, Defoe created this term to add a spice of mystery and drama. Over time, it became a commonly used term to simply mean a watery grave.

Other ships (yes, including pirates') attacking the sailors was also an imminent threat. Attacks basically guaranteed injuries and deaths. If a sailor were to die, the Navy's reparations were few and too small to give any comfort to a sailor's surviving relatives. If a woman under the age of thirty-five (a.k.a., still considered to be of child-bearing age) was widowed, her immediate solution was marriage. But what if a woman could not or would not remarry?

While their husbands were away, or if they were killed, the women of maritime families would have to take over the business or find work. They typically lived on the waterfront along narrow streets lined with taverns, boarding houses, tenements, shops, and private homes. Women were often shop owners along these streets, running taverns and boarding houses. Pirates preferred to frequent these places because of their maternal feel, which was very welcome for sailors far away from home.

Though some women were able to become business owners, most women and their children were doomed to poverty if their husband or father died. If the family was in debt, they would not receive the sailor's wages. If their deceased relative was a pirate (and not a member of the Navy), all they could do was hope and pray that other family members or friends would be brave enough to step in and help. Pirates' family members would often come forward to be character witnesses in attempts to have them pardoned for their crimes.

The death of one pirate, or several, could be the life and death of a community's survival. Havens in Tortuga, Port Royal, and Nassau left legacies that continued to thrive even after the Royal Navy took the over cities piece by piece. If married pirates were put on trial and condemned for their crimes, their wives would sometimes attempt to petition for their release claiming that their husband's death would put them into destitution. The women set up petitions and promised that their husbands would repent for their crimes if they were freed.

One of them was written in 1701 and signed by forty-eight women pleading with Queen Anne. It reads as follows: "Your petitioners most humbly pray your Majesty for your gracious and merciful consideration to grant pardons. Your Majesty's gracious intentions would be welcomed by these wives and families and other relations. They would reap in the satisfaction of Your Majesty's mercy and allow them to lead a better course of life in their own country. We promise that all merchants and the Nation will be freed from disturbance of their trade…"[134]

Queen Anne would not heed their pleas. All of the men were executed, leaving the women and their families in poverty.

Pirates were very aware of the consequences their deaths could have on their families. Captain William Lawrence, who was sentenced to die for his crimes, wrote a letter to his mother before his execution to offer words of comfort and to assure her that he was prepared to die. He knew that the impact of his death would extend beyond his mother's grief. He was widowed with two children, both of whom lived with his mother while he was away at sea. The children would grieve as well, and suffer from social ostracism. In his letter, he emphasized his wish for his children to live "honest" lives. He handed his children's care entirely over to his mother and begged her to be "father and mother, as well as grandmother, over my dear and tender infants, in whom I hope that God may grant such honest principles and morals in their hearts."[135]

The shame the pirates' families experienced was paradoxical. While many people supported pirates, no one wanted to be associated with them, lest they become known as a pirate's accomplice. This association meant society often shunned the families of those pirates forced to the scaffold. The immediate family would do everything they could to shield their other relatives from the scandal, probably in hopes that the extended family would help in turn. One pirate named

Walter Kennedy used his dying words to speak out for his wife. While at the scaffold, he admitted to his crimes and sought forgiveness. He finished his speech by begging the powers that be to spare his wife any humiliation.

"She is a pious woman," he implored. "She always hated my vices."[136]

The pirate John Massey, who was executed alongside Kennedy on July 26, 1723, also took his wife into consideration before his death. He begged for a closed casket after he was removed from the noose. He did not want his wife or any of his other relatives to see his body. He also requested to be buried as close to his mother as possible.[137]

Captain Joseph Halsey, a relatively young pirate captain at only twenty-three years old, was found guilty of murder and piracy on the high seas. He was from Boston, but the Admiralty had him transported back to London to be hanged at Execution Dock on March 14, 1759. He was supposed to give a speech atoning for his crimes at his execution, but instead he wrote a letter to his mother. In it, he insisted to her that he was innocent. He blamed enemies who deliberately offered false accusations. He wrote that he hoped his siblings would live better lives than his. The letter ended with tender words of comfort.

"I am very sorry mother, to think I should be called so soon out of this world by an untimely end, for I had always hoped to be able to help you. I would have done very well had it not been for those rogues. It has cost me all my wages, my venture, and my life. Don't be sad. It cannot be helped. I'll send you home my shirts, buckles, and hats. Remember me, mother."[138]

Not even a pirate could deny their family. Comfort was all he could offer at this point. Not only was the downfall of her son tragic enough, it would take upwards of six months for Halsey's mother to even find out that he had died.

Seventeenth- and eighteenth-century folks loved pirates not only because of the wealth they brought, but also because of their humanity. Pirates' neighbors loved and respected then. Governors, of course, enjoyed the riches they brought in. With the execution of pirates, families lost their fathers, brothers, and sons. The rise in pirates' overall popularity steadily increased social dissatisfaction with their public executions. You might now be wondering…Was killing pirates even worth it?

CHAPTER 4

WE HAVE ALWAYS
LOVED PIRATES

A Literary Phenomenon

In 1724, a two-volume collection of pirate biographies called *The General History of the Pyrates* was published by a man named Captain Charles Johnson. The book became an immediate sensation. Some of its selling points were the fascinating biographies of Anne Bonny, Mary Read, Blackbeard, and, of course, Captain Kidd. Readers were hooked. The collection of biographies proved so popular that book shops ordered it over and over into the 1800s, with updates in each new edition. *The General History of the Pyrates* inspired virtually every piece of pirate folklore that we know and love today. Today, you can find a copy at your local bookstore or read it online.

Newspapers printed and posted ads for the book on both sides of the Atlantic. American readers were particularly keen on Captain Charles Johnson's stories. *The American Weekly Journal* advertised the book with this blurb: "*The General History of the Pyrates*, from their first rise and settlement in the Island of Providence [Nassau, Bahamas] to the present time. With the remarkable actions and adventures of two female pirates, Mary Read and Anne Bonny. To which is added a short abstract of the statute and civil law in relation to piracy. By Capt. Charles Johnson."[139]

A GENERAL
HISTORY
OF THE
PYRATES,
FROM

Their firſt RISE and SETTLEMENT in the Iſland of
Providence, to the preſent Time.

With the remarkable Actions and Adventures of the two Female Pyrates

MARY READ and ANNE BONNY;

Contain'd in the following Chapters,

To which is added,

A ſhort ABSTRACT of the Statute and Civil
Law, in Relation to Pyracy.

The ſecond EDITION, with conſiderable ADDITIONS

By Captain CHARLES JOHNSON.

LONDON:
Printed for, and ſold by *T. Warner*, at the *Black-Boy* in *Pater-
Noſter-Row*, 1724.

A General History of the Pyrates, 1724
Wiki Commons

The popularity of *The General History of the Pyrates* encouraged
printing shops to advertise gilded editions of the book, which
included "twenty beautiful cuts [images], being the representation of
each pirate."[140] The addition of illustrations only added to the book's
popularity because now people could really see it all—not just the
publicly executed pirates, but *all* of the most famous pirates of the
age. The book became an invaluable resource. In one instance, legal
officers even used the book to find evidence that proved a pirate
catcher deserved his unpaid reward. Rumor has it that the officer and
crew responsible for the capture of Bartholomew Roberts in 1722 did
not know that the British government technically owed the capturers

over £1,900 as a reward.[141] If the captain had not happened to read
the book one afternoon, he would not have seen the reprinted copy
of the *King's Proclamation for the Effectual Suppression of Piracy*,
included in *The General History of the Pyrates*, which guaranteed such
a reward.[142]

Fueled by the success of *A General History of the Pyrates*, publishers
wanted to make more money from similar books. Why not cash in?
Just as the *Harry Potter* series spawned countless young adult epic
fantasy series, Johnson's bestselling book encouraged the publishing
of more and more collected volumes about criminals throughout the
eighteenth century. Two of the most popular were *The Complete State
Trials and Proceedings* (1776) and Charles Leslie's *A New History of
Jamaica* (1740).[143] The former was an eight-volume set of trials from
the reign of Edward VI (1547) to the contemporary time (1730, the
reign of George II). Since pirate trials had been bestsellers just a few
years before, these volumes were the ultimate cash-grab.

It might seem surprising that a history book about Jamaica would
prove so popular. But it wasn't simply a dry textbook. Readers could
look forward to descriptions of the geography and population of the
island, the first voyages to the Caribbean, and chapters about pirates
such as Blackbeard.[144] Though the book was published over a decade
after the peak of piracy, the popularity of pirates was anything but
gone. The population was eager to read more about these larger-
than-life sailors. These figures were already transforming into
literary heroes.

The printing industry could barely keep up with demand. British
and American official documents were copied and published as fast
as possible to be shipped across the ocean. American readers were
desperate to stay current with English bestsellers. As long as the
publications included details about the exoticism of the colonies,

crimes, and pirates, they were pretty much guaranteed to make a huge amount of money.[145]

But what about readers who could not afford whole books?

Enter pamphlet, stage right.

Not to be confused with newspapers, pamphlets were short booklets, typically between one and twelve sheets of paper, folded four ways.[146] Pamphlets were cheap, and it only took a few hours to print dozens of copies, which peddlers distributed on the streets. Pamphlets were, well, *juicier*. This is where people could find other sources of news, propaganda, and sensational superstitious stories, like those of witchcraft, executions, ghosts, and hallucinations.[147] In the pamphlets, writers depicted crimes and punishments with graphic, brutal details. Bloodshed, shrieks of pain, gore—the horrific details would provoke terror and awe in readers.[148] People read the pamphlets aloud on street corners, taverns, public houses, salons—you name it. Often you could find someone standing on a box to look over their eager crowd and reading the pamphlet as if they were on stage.

While newspapers had to stick to rules like word counts and deadlines, the pamphlet didn't. The pamphlet offered far more creativity as a medium. Pamphleteers penned mariners' stories to their heart's content. They devoted their art to the lives of notorious delinquents. These writers had the freedom to embellish facts as much as they wanted, turn the news into stories, and present facts as entertainment to readers. They also found good money in writing trial transcriptions, thanks to their anonymous liberty to stretch the truth as much as they liked.

Apart from newspapers and pamphlets, trial transcriptions were some of the best ways for people to learn about pirates. At first, trial reports were highly moralized third-person narratives, or more objective observations of what was said in court. As these publications became more popular, the descriptions became much more vivid and outrageous. City booksellers enjoyed publishing transcriptions because they sold just as much as newspapers and pamphlets, but the shops were able to hike up their prices knowing that people would clamor for the trial transcriptions' outlandish style.

Although transcriptions of pirates' trials were taken as entertainment, they did have a legitimate purpose. Booksellers often sold the transcriptions in large collections to inform readers about the state of crime and justice in England. Sometimes these collections contained cases that went back for several hundred years.[149] The trials of the pirates Captain Kidd, John Quelch, Thomas Green, Captain Ogle, and John Gow were all published between 1701 and 1725, and they sold for between one and three pence.[150] Judges and lawyers were able to use published trials to settle contradictions and controversies. The government also found many uses for them. For instance, victims of theft could use the transcriptions to regain their stolen property in civil suits. Most importantly, however, the British government used published trials to show the honor of British justice, which foreign statesmen and merchants could depend upon for security.[151]

Pirates also benefitted when their actions made it into print. In order to successfully rob ships, they had to scare the hell out of their victims. After an attack, they had to make sure that they could maintain their reputations. Newspapers and pamphlets were the perfect way for them to do that. The *American Weekly Mercury* published an article about a gruesome pirate attack that included descriptions from the pirates themselves: "The pirates gave us an account of their violent actions, including the slaughter of their crews, burning of ships, and a particularly proud act in which they cut off one of the Master's ears and slit his nose."[152]

Pirates were very aware of the threat they presented to everyone and they happily took advantage of this. Some pirates even mocked the Crown and the Admiralty authorities up to the moment of their death. In one case, a pirate referred to only as "Brett" outright gloried in his upcoming execution rather than show fear. "When he got into a cart at Newgate he shook hands with many of his friends, seemed quite composed, and had a wide smile on his face. When he sat down in the cart, he took off his hat and threw it to his friends."[153]

We know that contemporary society viewed pirates as promotors of lawlessness.[154] Their devil-may-care attitudes allowed pirates to rise above their social stations, become rich, and help communities. Plus, they sought adventure on the high seas, sailing to exotic lands and engaging in swashbuckling fights that could only be meant for heroes. We *still* view pirates this way. Though there were not that many pirates around during the Golden Age of Piracy, they still managed to threaten the world's greatest empire at the time, while also helping the future United States.

Pirates were such celebrities during their heyday that they were considered spectacular phenomena. They had a strange magnetic quality that made them attractive to all.[155] Pirates knew this. They marketed themselves as flashy villains, akin to Blackbeard's smoking beard and fancy outfits, and as entertainment while they reportedly strolled through markets in groups, giving out gifts or trinkets to passersby. They were sometimes referred to as "musical" pirates because they sang popular sea shanties as they walked through the streets.[156]

Perhaps it was pirates' unbounded unpredictability that made them so attractive. They were strong in that they were not afraid to sail against the most powerful nations in the world, but they were vulnerable because their lives were short and their capture meant certain death. They were innocent in that they felt justified in their actions and happened to have the necessary skills to be successful…at least until they were captured. These unlikely heroes just needed a way to protect themselves to survive.

Keep to the Code

Pirates had to have a very orderly manner of operation to be successful, safe, and keep their crews happy. In fact, all merchants and sailors had laws of behavior to maintain order and decorum on a ship. Punishments for breaking these rules could be severe. So there had to be a standardized form. In order for the pirate ship to operate successfully, pirates adhered to a set of rules that became known as the Pirates' Code.

Yes, this is, in fact, a real piece of pirate history—not just a legend that inspired books and movies (like the *Pirates of the Caribbean* series). There are very few surviving pieces of the actual documents, but Alexander Exquemelin, author of *The History of the Buccaneers of America*, claimed that the pirate Henry Morgan (the namesake of Captain Morgan rum) had a code of conduct and honor for his men to abide by. A common struggle for survival bound pirates together. Knowing the world was out to get them, the pirates made a world for themselves in which people could be dealt with justly.

But what were these codes, and who created them? And how were they communicated?

The codes (also known as "articles") explained the following:

- How to distribute loot

- How to choose superiors (including the captain)

- The consequences for behaviors such as gambling, fighting, and getting drunk

- Compensation for injuries, entertainment

- Other factors specific to a particular pirates' code

Many pirate ships required their crew to swear an oath to the Articles and even to sign them, if they were written down. If they refused, the other pirates would maroon the traitors on a deserted island. As for how they communicated these rules, that question is harder to answer. Most pirates, unfortunately, did not leave any written records. While Alexander Exquemelin published a partial set of codes in his book *The Buccaneers of America* (1678) that were attributed to Henry Morgan, Captain Charles Johnson recorded two sets of pirate codes from Bartholomew Roberts and John Phillips in *A General History of the Pyrates*. But Edward Low's set of codes is one of the most famous because it actually appeared in North American newspapers. If we take a look at Low's codes, we'll see that there are definitely some similarities across his and those of other pirates.

Captain Bartholomew Roberts, also known as Black Bart, was a Welsh pirate who successfully robbed about 470 ships during his three-year career from 1719 to 1722. Yes, *470* ships. Historians consider him the most successful pirate who ever lived. He would be a billionaire by today's standards.

Captain Bartholomew Roberts, Joseph Nicholls, 1936
Courtesy of the John Carter Brown Library

How did he become so successful? Well, he developed the following
behavior code:

I.   EVERY MAN HAS A VOTE IN AFFAIRS OF THE MOMENT;
      HAS EQUAL TITLE TO THE FRESH PROVISIONS, OR STRONG
      LIQUORS, AT ANY TIME SEIZED, AND MAY USE THEM AT
      PLEASURE, UNLESS A SCARCITY MAKE IT NECESSARY, FOR THE
      GOOD OF ALL, TO VOTE A RETRENCHMENT.

All goods on the ship were split evenly, including alcohol (which was great). It makes sense that they would restrict this law of abundance if supplies ran low.

> **II.** Every man to be called fairly in turn, by list, on board of prizes, because, (over and above their proper share), they were on these occasions allowed a shift of clothes: but if they defrauded the company to the value of a dollar, in plate, jewels, or money, marooning was their punishment.

This was really common practice. Stealing supplies and shares from their prizes was not tolerated whatsoever. Internal theft guaranteed the pirate a one-way ticket to a miserable spit of sand in the middle of the ocean.

> **III.** No person to game at cards or dice for money.

Gambling was always looked down upon. It was difficult and expensive enough to rob another ship, and having gamblers who would steal the booty from others would be unacceptable. Plus, outrageous debt caused fighting amongst the crew. Gamblers be warned.

> **IV.** The lights and candles to be put out at eight o'clock at night: If any of the crew, after that hour, still remained inclined for drinking, they were to do it on an open deck.

Roberts commanded nearly three hundred pirates. A strict schedule was necessary for things to stay in top working order, hence the curfew. Certainly the men below deck were grateful for strictly-enforced quiet hours so they could function the next day.

> **V.** To keep their piece, pistols, and cutlass clean, and fit for service.

A dirty weapon was a useless weapon. A useless weapon made one a useless fighter. A useless fighter was a danger to the whole ship. Pirates could not afford to be lazy.

> **VI.** No boy or woman to be allowed amongst them. If any man were found seducing any of the latter sex, and carried her to the sea, disguised, he was to suffer death.

Sex was complicated, but when hasn't it been? Hang tight; we'll discuss this more soon.

> **VII.** To desert the ship, or their quarters in battle, was punished with death or marooning.

Betrayal of the crew was another guaranteed ticket to being stranded in an oceanic hell.

> **VIII.** No striking one another on board, but every man's quarrels to be ended on shore, at sword and pistol.

When there are a lot of people working in close quarters for a long time, fights are bound to break out. Unlike fighting on the spacious land, fighting on a ship would be practically impossible to break up. Those quarreling were basically detained below deck until the ship came across an island. Then the pirates were to disembark and engage in a duel until the matter was settled.

> IX. NO MAN TO TALK OF BREAKING UP THEIR WAY OF LIVING, TILL EACH HAD SHARED 1000 L [1000 DOLLARS, AS THEY WOULD SAY DURING THIS TIME]. IF IN ORDER TO DO THIS, ANY MAN SHOULD LOSE A LIMB, OR BECOME A CRIPPLE IN THEIR SERVICE, HE WAS TO HAVE 800 DOLLARS, OUT OF THE PUBLIC STOCK, AND FOR LESSER HURTS, PROPORTIONALLY.

Fair shares guaranteed fair compensation.

> X. THE CAPTAIN AND QUARTER-MASTER TO RECEIVE TWO SHARES OF A PRIZE [THE VALUE OF THE STOLEN GOODS]; THE MASTER, BOATSWAIN, AND GUNNER, ONE SHARE AND A HALF, AND OTHER OFFICERS ONE SHARE AND A QUARTER.

This was pretty standard amongst all the known codes.

> XI. THE MUSICIANS TO HAVE REST ON THE SABBATH DAY, BUT THE OTHER SIX DAYS AND NIGHTS, NONE WITHOUT SPECIAL FAVOR.[157]
>
> —CAPTAIN CHARLES JOHNSON, *A GENERAL HISTORY OF THE PYRATES*

This is interesting! This is one of the few pieces of proof that pirates had specific entertainment and leisure time. Pirates often described their life on pirate ships as "merry," probably because of the ever-present musical life on board. Pirates enjoyed singing and dancing while playing musical instruments to pass the time at sea.[158] It looks like these musicians in particular were, therefore, seen as important enough to be granted a rest day.

Roberts's ship looks like the ideal place to be, for the most part. The code ensured that no one would be cheated out of their fair share and that desertion would have dire consequences. Not only would pirate life be fair and orderly, Roberts also allowed entertainment in the form of music and moderate drinking, although preferred his crew to stick to tea to stay sharp. And to make sure they would have plenty of alcohol to sell later.

Captain John Phillips was an English pirate who operated between 1721 and 1724 and captained a small ship called *Revenge*. Unlike Roberts, Phillips did not operate a large fleet, nor was he hugely successful (at least in comparison). He only commanded one schooner, with eleven men under his command. Because of the tiny crew, he had to work much harder to ensure that everything was in working order and that they would obey him. As a result, his pirate code mainly concerned behavior and fair regulations:

> I.   EVERY MAN SHALL OBEY CIVIL COMMAND; THE CAPTAIN SHALL HAVE ONE FULL SHARE AND A HALF IN ALL PRIZES; THE MASTER, CARPENTER, BOATSWAIN, AND GUNNER SHALL HAVE ONE SHARE AND A QUARTER.

Again, this was standard. The similarities between this and Roberts's tenth article are clear.

> II.   IF ANY MAN SHALL OFFER TO RUN AWAY, OR KEEP ANY SECRET
>   FROM THE COMPANY, HE SHALL BE MAROONED WITH ONE
>   BOTTLE OF POWDER, ONE BOTTLE OF WATER, AND SMALL
>   ARM AND SHOT.

You might remember from the first *Pirates of the Caribbean* film that Captain Jack Sparrow was marooned on a desert island with a pistol that only contained one bullet. After weeks of going mad with heat, hunger, and thirst, that gun would begin to look very friendly. Since Phillips was the only pirate to have this specific rule, he may have been the inspiration behind this plot point.

> III.   IF ANY MAN SHALL STEAL ANYTHING IN THE COMPANY, OR
>   GAME TO THE VALUE OF A PIECE OF EIGHT[159], HE SHALL BE
>   MAROONED OR SHOT.

If a crew member were to steal something from the ship, it was often to gamble it off. As we know, pirate captains reviled gambling. Let's face it—yes, if a pirate stole from his own crewmates, he deserved the worst. Pirates considered themselves brothers. Stealing from each other was no less than betrayal.

> IV.   IF AT ANY TIME WE SHOULD MEET ANOTHER MAROONER
>   (THAT IS, PIRATE), THAT MAN SHALL SIGN HIS ARTICLES
>   WITHOUT THE CONSENT OF OUR COMPANY, SHALL SUFFER
>   SUCH PUNISHMENT AS THE CAPTAIN AND COMPANY
>   THINK FIT.

If the crew were to find a marooned pirate and the pirate were to
sneak up on board and try to sign the inviolable Articles, the crew
would have to punish the marooned pirate severely. A pirate was
generally marooned for fighting or threatening to kill a member of
his crew. If he snuck onto a ship and tried to sign the Articles, which
would make it nearly impossible to expel him because it was basically
a contract, the entire ship could be at risk from a volatile person.

> **V.** THAT MAN THAT SHALL STRIKE ANOTHER WHILST THESE
> ARTICLES ARE IN FORCE, SHALL RECEIVE MOSES'S LAW (THAT
> IS, 40 STRIPES LACKING ONE) ON THE BARE BACK.

Violence begets violence. If a pirate hit a fellow crew member, he
would receive thirty-nine lashes as punishment. Fighting could not
be tolerated because it could create social instability, which could put
their whole operation at risk.

> **VI.** THAT MAN THAT SHALL SNAP HIS ARMS [WEAPONS], SMOKE
> HIS TOBACCO IN THE HOLD WITHOUT A CAP TO HIS PIPE, OR
> CARRY A CANDLE WITHOUT A LANTERN, SHALL SUFFER THE
> SAME PUNISHMENT AS IN THE FORMER ARTICLE.

This rule was extremely important. Snapping arms meant pulling the
trigger or firing a pistol. Gunpowder was stored below deck; shooting
a pistol could cause sparks. The only person allowed to deal with fire
or anything else flammable was the cook. Otherwise, bringing down
lit tobacco or candles was a recipe for disaster. All of these factors
could ignite the gunpowder and cause an explosion.

VII. THAT MAN THAT SHALL NOT KEEP HIS ARMS CLEAN, FIT FOR
ENGAGEMENT, OR NEGLECT HIS BUSINESS, SHALL BE CUT OFF
FROM HIS SHARE, AND SUFFER SUCH OTHER PUNISHMENT AS
THE CAPTAIN AND COMPANY SEE FIT.

Pirates needed all hands on deck when they were about to engage in
a fight. If someone was lazy with the upkeep of his guns and swords,
such as letting them get dirty or rusty, he could risk the entire crew.
Since this would be seen as not doing his share of the work, he
naturally would not get his fair share of the loot.

VIII. IF ANY MAN SHALL LOSE A JOINT IN TIME OF AN
ENGAGEMENT, HE SHALL HAVE 400 PIECES OF EIGHT, IF A
LIMB, 800.

In today's money, that means pirates would have gotten either
$60,000 or up to $120,000. What excellent compensation!

IX. IF AT ANY TIME WE MEET WITH A PRUDENT WOMAN [ANY
WOMAN WHO WAS NOT A SEX WORKER], THAT MAN THAT
OFFERS TO MEDDLE WITH HER, WITHOUT HER CONSENT,
SHALL SUFFER PRESENT DEATH.

—CAPTAIN CHARLES JOHNSON, *A GENERAL HISTORY OF
THE PYRATES*

This could basically be the subject for a whole other book. In a
nutshell, rape has always been a high crime with a death sentence.
Unfortunately, the woman had to be proven a victim rather than a
seductress. Social conventions and constrained roles made it nearly
impossible for a woman to prove herself anything other than a

temptress. Though rape was difficult to prove during this time, pirates were very strict on punishing it severely.[160]

Edward Low's code was probably the most famous pirate code of its time. Not only did it appear in the *General History of the Pyrates*, it was also printed in the *Boston News-Letter*.

As we learned earlier, Edward Low was an English pirate who, like Captain John Phillips, operated between 1721 and 1724. Low was one of the most infamous pirates of the time because, unlike most other pirates, he was violent and vicious. A true sadist and likely a psychopath, he was known to enjoy torturing his victims before murdering them. According to the *General History of the Pyrates*, Low had also enjoyed gambling and stealing from people since his childhood days in Westminster, England. Over time his petty theft graduated to breaking and entering until his older brother convinced him to go to sea with him, perhaps in an attempt to curb his behavior.

Once Low became a pirate, he immediately became known for being particularly brutal, especially to his victims. When he and his men took a Portuguese ship, Low and his crew were said to have "cut and mangle" their victims in a "barbarous manner." They tied the men up and cut their skin to ribbons. Then they hoisted the men by the strips of their skin, set them back down, cut them some more, and repeat the vicious cycle. During this particular process, Low sustained an injury that required stitches, but his ship's surgeon did a poor job, so Low ripped out the stitches and re-stitched himself. The man was relentless, and he terrified all of the American colonies.

Edward Low Shoots a Man, 1725
Courtesy of the John Carter Brown Library

What does a brutal leader do to maintain control? He sets up a draconian set of orders with just enough give to keep the peace. (Note: Some of his codes were the same as Philips's, so I've left those out here.)

II.   HE THAT SHALL BE FOUND GUILTY OF TAKING UP ANY
       UNLAWFUL WEAPON ON BOARD THE PRIVATEER OR ANY
       OTHER PRIZE BY US TAKEN, SO AS TO STRIKE OR ABUSE ONE
       ANOTHER IN ANY REGARD, SHALL SUFFER WHAT PUNISHMENT
       THE CAPTAIN AND THE MAJORITY OF THE COMPANY SEE FIT.

A collectively decided punishment is a running regulation with Low.
As a result, punishments were undoubtedly harsher than normal. In
life, when someone does you wrong and really makes you angry and
then gets punished, don't you secretly wish they'd gotten a harsher
punishment, no matter what it was? Now was their chance to dole out
the punishment of their vindictive dreams.

> **III.** HE THAT SHALL BE FOUND GUILTY OF COWARDICE IN THE
> TIME OF ENGAGEMENTS SHALL SUFFER WHAT PUNISHMENT
> THE CAPTAIN AND THE MAJORITY OF THE COMPANY SHALL
> THINK FIT.

Cowardice is subjective, so this could be an extremely brutal and
unfair assessment from the Captain and crew. Running away from
battle would definitely put the whole crew in danger, but what exactly
does Low mean here by cowardice? We will never know.

> **IV.** IF ANY GOLD, JEWELS, SILVER, ETC. BE FOUND ON BOARD
> OF ANY PRIZE OR PRIZES TO THE VALUE OF A PIECE OF
> EIGHT AND THE FINDER DO NOT DELIVER IT TO THE
> QUARTERMASTER IN THE SPACE OF 24 HOURS HE SHALL
> SUFFER WHAT PUNISHMENT THE CAPTAIN AND THE MAJORITY
> OF THE COMPANY SHALL THINK FIT.

This is an important rule. Not reporting the prizes was tantamount
to stealing from the whole company. I, for one, do not want to
imagine what sort of punishment the rest of the crew would dream up
for stealing.

> **V.**   HE THAT IS FOUND GUILTY OF GAMING OR DEFRAUDING
>   ONE ANOTHER TO THE VALUE OF A ROYAL OF PLATE [MONEY
>   WORTH THE VALUE OF THE GAMBLED GOODS] SHALL SUFFER
>   WHAT PUNISHMENT THE CAPTAIN AND THE MAJORITY OF THE
>   COMPANY SHALL THINK FIT.

Similar to Phillips, gambling was a huge risk on a ship. (Of course, this did not stop Low from gambling, but he was never known to be an honorable captain.) In this case, however, it provided ample opportunity to basically destroy a debtor in their midst.

> **VII.**   GOOD QUARTERS TO BE GIVEN WHEN CRAVED.

Giving quarters means granting mercy, so this seems to be a little out of character of Low. In fact, it almost seems…nice? Generally, if a captured sailor was granted mercy in or after battle, he would be less inclined to resist being forced into piracy, so this was likely a mere benefit for Low.

> **VIII.**   HE THAT SEES A SAIL FIRST SHALL HAVE THE BEST PISTOL OR
>   SMALL ARM ABOARD OF HER.

Basically, it's winner takes all, in a manner of speaking. The person who spotted the danger was gifted the absolute best weapon, because, clearly, they would be the most deserving of surviving the battle!

IX. HE THAT SHALL BE GUILTY OF DRUNKENNESS IN TIME OF ENGAGEMENT SHALL SUFFER WHAT PUNISHMENT THE CAPTAIN AND THE MAJORITY OF THE COMPANY SHALL THINK FIT.

—*THE BOSTON NEWS-LETTER*

Low was known for being the harshest captain when it came to drinking rules. He was absolutely militant about sobriety on the ship. Any hint of drunkenness led to marooning because inebriation could put everyone at risk.

On the one hand, these rules made pirate ships seem strict and orderly, and made sure everything ran as smoothly as possible. On the other hand, the *Boston News-Letter* made sure to inform local readers of these laws, but to what purpose? If these rules applied to an ordinary merchant ship or the Royal Navy, Bostonians and other Massachusetts colonists who relied on the maritime industry would have been relieved to know that the ships were kept in such rigid working order. However, the notion that pirate ships operated in such a meticulous fashion would have undoubtedly been seen as intimidating, if not threatening. In this case, the *Boston News-Letter* printed these codes not just to inform the reader, but to warn them. The people had to know just what kind of foe they were dealing with.

Whether Captain Kidd had his own set of Articles is unknown. If he did, he himself would have likely been in violation of several of them on his ship. His promises of quick wealth did not initially deliver, so this could have been seen as "defrauding one another." His initial hesitance to rob a ship outside of the letter of marque might have been called cowardice. Those examples are up to interpretation. However, he was certainly guilty of taking an unlawful weapon (a bucket) and striking a crewmate with it so hard that the man died. If he were not captain and if the ship were not in precarious circumstances as it fled from the Royal Navy, he almost certainly

would have been ousted as captain and marooned with a single shot…
if the crew felt merciful.

Pirates and Relationships

Pirates and the Ladies

Relationships were a complicated matter with pirates. Generally, it
was preferred that they not bring women on ships with them, to avoid
any complications or fights. With the lack of women on board, pirates
had to make up for lost time once they were on shore. The waterfront
at any given port city was crowded with taverns, many of which were
run by women. In London, these women would be known as the
"Wapping Landladies" ("Wapping" as in the neighborhood in east
London where pirates were executed) and earned their living off the
numerous ports along the Thames. Taverns were generally family-
owned, but it was the landlady and her daughter who were in charge
and set the tone for the establishment. Licenses for alehouses were
generally under the husband's name, unless he died. Then the widow
would inherit the tavern and become the official business owner.[161]

Pirates would come into taverns and shower these women with their
earnings, buy them drinks, and pay for their company. Some well-
known attractive women, particularly Flemish women who were
known for their beauty, were hired as tavern sex workers to increase
business. Many of these women enjoyed the company of pirates. One
woman said,

"I know very many sailors—six, eight, ten, oh! More than that.
They are my husbands. I am not married, of course not, but
they think me their wife while they are on shore."[162]

—David Cordingly, *Seafaring Women*

The high turnover of sailors in London ports attracted not just local sex workers but those from continental Europe as well. There was no shortage of work in these areas.

One of the most famous sex workers was a woman named Damaris Page. She was born in Stepney (a small hamlet of London) in 1620 and became a sex worker as a teenager. After about fifteen years she was able to move on from sex work to running her own brothels for ordinary seamen on the Ratcliffe Highway and naval officers on Rosemary Lane. She married several times, was accused of murder for helping a woman have a brutal abortion using a two-pronged fork, and escaped her subsequent death sentence because of her own pregnancy.

Most sex workers, unfortunately, were not able to establish themselves as business owners like Damaris. Most were forced into the business because of poverty. Others preferred this line of work to spending up to sixteen hours a day in a laundry. The vast majority of them chose to work in dockside areas because of the numerous sailors (including pirates) who sailed in and out of port all year long. They never ran out of work.[163]

Anne Bonny and Mary Read

Women were known to have romantic and sexual relationships with each other in this era as well. Female pirate sexuality has always been a source of fascination for pirate historians, but none have held more interest than Anne Bonny and Mary Read. These two women sailed under Captain Jack Rackham between August and November 1720.

Though their career lasted only two short months, their lives became some of the most intriguing stories ever to come out of this time period. The two of them lived in different gender roles at different times and became involved in a romantic relationship.[164] These women subverted social rules and shocked the Atlantic world. At the same time, they also demonstrated just how a woman could make an adventurous life for herself during a time in which her options were marriage or domestic servitude…if she was lucky.

Anne was an illegitimate child born in Cork, Ireland, to a servant mother and an attorney father. Mary, from London, was born in the same circumstances. They were both raised as boys primarily to help reduce the scandal of being born out of wedlock.

When Anne's mother died in childbirth, Anne's father raised Anne as a boy, knowing it would be better for her to be an illegitimate son than an illegitimate daughter. He and his true wife separated after Anne was born, and he secretly moved with Anne to London as he set up a practice. Once Anne's father's estranged in-laws found out about her existence, he took her to the Carolinas so they could start a new life. Mary's mother, in contrast, passed Mary off as a boy in an attempt to receive an allowance from Mary's father's family.

Both women were forced to live as their biological sex by the time they hit thirteen years old. To Mary, this would have been quite the shock, because she had not known that she was female. Her mother simply never told her! As was the custom for girls of this age, they were both hired as maids.

Anne did not last very long in this position. She was fired for fighting with boys, one of whom she stabbed after he made fun of her red hair. Mary also did not take to the servant life, nor to presenting as female, so she donned male clothes and headed across the English Channel to serve in the British Army as a man.

When Anne was sixteen, she infuriated her father by marrying James Bonny, a common sailor. Having grown up on the Irish and Carolina coasts, she would have had frequent contact with seamen. Sailing also offered a new life that could free her from the bondage of female servitude. Once she was married, she and James joined a pirate ship and sailed south toward the Caribbean. In 1718, they reached Nassau.

Mary, under the name Mark Read, began her service in the British Army in modern-day Belgium. She quickly became known as one of the fiercest fighters with the greatest stamina. While serving, she fell in love with a fellow soldier. She revealed herself to him and they married in secret. Tragically, he died soon after, and Mary had to mourn in secret. Her devastation affected her service until she was discharged for her unexplained depression and poor performance. She refused to head back to England where she would be forced to work as a domestic, so she kept her male identity and joined a ship's crew headed for the Caribbean.

In the meantime, life was not going quite as planned for Anne in Nassau. James seemed tired of the sailing life and declared that he wanted to give up piracy and settle down. This was absolutely abhorrent to Anne, who had spent the last several years in the unique position of being a female pirate alongside her husband. More importantly, she had managed to break away from social constraints and yearned to continue adventuring on the sea. If they settled down on land, she would have to take up a traditional woman's role, and this would not do for her. She began hanging out in taverns and sleeping with sailors and pirates who passed through the city. James, in the meantime, had struck up a friendship with the governor of Nassau, Woodes Rogers, and agreed to take a job as a pirate hunter. This infuriated Anne, as it went against everything they had ever

stood for. They had been pirates themselves! Now her husband
wanted to throw away their life and betray their people?

Anne separated from her husband and struck up a relationship with
a pirate captain named Jack Rackham, who had come to Nassau to
find some new crew members. Rackham initially worked under the
fearsome Charles Vane as a lieutenant, until he and the rest of the
crew voted Vane out of his captaincy. (Vane, of course, managed
to continue his pirate career elsewhere.) Rackham was sworn in as
captain and had success capturing small ships in and around the
Caribbean. In 1719, Rackham sailed into Nassau and made it his
home base, where he met Anne Bonny two years later. The two
fell in love and wanted to marry, but James refused a divorce. On
August 22, 1720, Anne and Jack stole away on his ship and declared
themselves married.

Jack Rackham, A General History of the Pyrates, 1724
Wiki Commons

Anne soon noticed a new young sailor named Mark who had joined their ship. He was smart, strong, and a great fighter. Anne loved her husband, but she was attracted to this other man too. She decided to seduce him by cornering Mark in a storeroom, only, to her shock, to have Mark reveal himself to her. Mark Read was actually Mary Read. Gender did not matter to either of them, and they began a secret relationship. When Rackham realized this, he was so jealous that he demanded they *both* declare themselves married to him.

Mary decided to stop hiding her sex and began to openly fight as a woman. Both women's sex and appearance shocked their victims into submission. The images below paint quite the picture. They wore their hair long and flowing and often kept their shirts open to display their breasts.

Anne Bonny, *A General History of the Pyrates*, 1724
Courtesy of the John Carter Brown Library

Mary Read, A General History of the Pyrates, 1724
Courtesy of the John Carter Brown Library

Anne and Mary quickly gained a reputation as fighters. They swore
more than the men on the ship and also fought more fiercely than
any member of the crew. Unfortunately, their career was short-
lived. In October of 1720, known pirate hunter Captain Jonathan
Barnet stalked them into a shallow Jamaican bay where he attacked
Rackham's ship. Rackham and all of his crew, except the women, were

too drunk to fight, so they went below deck, leaving Anne and Mary
to fight on their own. They were captured, but their bravery and skill
had impressed Barnet.

Anne would never forgive Rackham's cowardice and lack of
leadership. According to *A General History of the Pyrates*, on the day
he was to hang for his crimes, he asked to speak to Anne. She was led
to his cell, where he begged for words of comfort from his wife. She
looked at him coldly and said, "I'm sorry to see you like this, but if
you had fought like a man you need not hang like a dog."

She walked away and never saw him again.

Anne and Mary each ended up escaping the noose in her own way.
They were both pregnant during the fight, which was discovered at
their trial. This granted them a stay of execution until their children
were born. Mary, unfortunately, died in childbirth. Anne somehow
left prison. It is generally accepted by historians that her father paid
her ransom and she went back to North Carolina where she had her
child, remarried, and lived until 1782.[165]

People all over flocked to read their story. After all, this was a time
in which it was rare for women to work outside the home, let alone
become pirates. Is it possible that they were the only women to work
as pirates? Absolutely not. Other women went to sea for various
reasons, but the most common one was to escape social constraints.
Many women took to the sea disguised as men and fought in sea
battles. In fact, captains' logs and newspaper articles show us that
at least twenty women served in the Royal Navy between 1650
and 1815.[166] But the real number is likely much higher. If women
disguised themselves as men, their true identities would not be
recorded. Pirates hardly left any of their own records, so there is
no definite information there. We also have to acknowledge the
possibility that writings simply—intentionally or not—left out
the women.

Gay Pirates

What else about sex on the ship? Pirates' sexuality is a such source
of fascination that it has become the punchline of some modern-
day jokes. In popular culture, we sometimes hear the term "gay
pirates" with the implied meaning of someone who is on the ultimate
fringes of society. However, homosexuality among sailors, including
pirates, was not uncommon. Two of the pirate codes mention the
consequences of bringing women and boys onto the ship for sexual
pleasure. If one takes a second glance at the two codes regarding
relationships, one will notice that they specifically say that pirates
cannot bring anyone on board. They do not say anything about
relationships with those already on the ship.

As long as there have been people with sex drives, there have
been people engaged in heterosexual relationships, homosexual
relationships, polyamorous relationships—every kind you
can imagine.

When male Europeans began colonizing the Caribbean during the
seventeenth century, there was a huge shortage of women. Intense
sexual frustration would build up quickly, especially amongst
sailors who were in tight quarters around each other for months on
end. Privacy was nonexistent, so sexual acts such as masturbation
would have been hard to hide. Tight quarters, the anxiety of life
at sea, the dangers that came with it, and closeness would create
the perfect recipe to develop sexual relationships. It was common
knowledge that gay relationships, or at least gay sex, was practiced by
numerous sailors.

Homosexuality was technically illegal, but as long as marriages
produced children, people usually turned a blind eye. However, the
fact that so many men were having sex with each other horrified
the governors. In 1645, the French governor of Tortuga (Haiti),

Jean La Vasseur, thought that the reason men were having sexual relationships was because of the lack of women throughout the islands. To solve this problem, he imported 1,650 female sex workers to the island to give men a sexual outlet.[167] Did it work? It's a mystery, but it certainly is interesting to imagine what type of orgies sprang out of this scenario!

These interactions were not always just about sex, however. Many pirates also formed romantic relationships with each other. There are documented cases of seventeenth-century pirates who practiced *matelotage*, meaning that they became legally bound to each other. The term comes from the French word *matelot*, which simply means "sailor." It became associated with seventeenth-century Caribbean pirates because they became known for having bonds with each other that were almost like marriage. Two pirates on the same ship could become institutionally linked to each other.[168] It's possible that pirates engaged in *matelotage* for legal and financial reasons. For all intents and purposes, if a pirate died, his partner would receive his share of pay, not unlike a widow receiving her late husband's pension. And, of course, it could be because the pair were genuinely in love.

One of Captain Kidd's crewmates, Robert Culliford, may have been one of these men in a loving relationship with a fellow pirate. Before Kidd set out for the East Indies, he and Culliford served on the same ship in the 1680s. Kidd became captain of the ship after it was attacked, but Culliford staged a mutiny. Naturally, the two parted on terrible terms. That did not stop them from running into each other over the next decade, particularly when Kidd was on the run and stopped briefly in Madagascar. Many members of Kidd's crew had abandoned him and joined up with Culliford to avoid being associated with the most wanted pirate in the world.

Afterward, Culliford sailed with a man named John Swann. The two of them became very close when they were imprisoned together from

1692 to 1696 and, over time, they developed a romantic relationship.
They were not very open about it, but they lived together on St.
Mary Island just off the coast of Madagascar.[169] However, they parted
ways in 1698, when Culliford reconciled with Kidd and decided
to continue pirating in the Indian Ocean and Swann decided to
stay in Madagascar. Not long after, however, when they heard that
pirates could be pardoned if they turned themselves in, they both,
independently, decided to take the pardon. They ended up receiving
the pardon together in Madagascar, but they did not reunite, as
Swann decided to head to Barbados. The two never saw each other
again.[170] Sadly, Culliford was one of several pirates who were executed
for being associated with Kidd.

Captain Kidd showed people that anyone could upend their social
status and remake themselves at sea. Anne Bonny and Mary Read
showed women that they could take control of their lives and brave
adventures better than any man. Culliford and Swann showed an
inkling of hope for legalization of gay marriage in the twenty-first
century. Pirates were sources of inspiration and examples of what
people can do to uplift themselves into glory…and what one can do
to fall out of it.

CHAPTER 5

KILLING PIRATES:
A FUN DAY OUT!

I magine waking up one day feeling particularly excited because of an event you are going to attend. This event is free for everyone and by no means exclusive, but that makes it no less exciting. Everyone you know is going to be there. There will be food, drinks, jokes, and impatient shouting. Today, you are all there to see a performance. You have seen this performance many times before, but each time it is a little bit different. You leap out of bed to get ready for the day.

You dress quickly and gulp down a bit of breakfast, which is most likely yesterday's leftovers poured into a pot, mixed with water, oats, and grains and heated up into a hearty dish called pottage. You and your family each take a full bowl and a mug of ale. You have to eat quickly and get going if you would like to get a good view.

The sky begins to turn a light gray and you all know it's time to go. This event usually starts mid-morning, and it will be easily over an hour's walk to the east end of the city.

The day is proving to be another typical gray, damp day. It rained in the night, so puddles dot the cobblestones, making them treacherously slippery. The main road is muddy and smells rank—a disgusting mix of dirt, mold, piss, dung, and who knows what else. You breathe it in. Ah, London.

Despite the early morning, the city is already bustling. People are heading into the city to open shops, make their daily purchases, and head to various appointments. Others are only starting to make the trek home after working at the docks all night, drinking, or being a person of pleasure.

You decide to walk along the Thames. It is still crowded, but you will get to your destination sooner, as it is right on the bank of the river. The walk takes you down past St. Paul's Cathedral and London Bridge. You pass through the city as you continue east. The Tower of London looms over this end of the city, dark and ominous against the clouds.

Finally you reach your destination: Wapping, the sailing neighborhood. The area is crowded, dark, and dirty. The buildings are all somewhat decrepit, and some of their wooden walls are visibly rotting. And yet, there is a buzz of energy around the place. Sailors head to the docks. Tavern wenches open the windows and doors as meals are prepared. There are jovial shouts as people greet each other.

Up ahead, you see a large crowd already formed on a dock. A shiver goes down your spine as you see the noose swing in the breeze.

Today a pirate is going to die.

And what a day for it! Nothing is better than attending an execution! People from all over the city gather, vendors walk about selling food and ale, and entertainment is guaranteed. The poor wretch will be forced to make a speech atoning for his crimes, which everyone knows is pure performance, but that makes it even more exciting. It is like watching one of those vulgar plays that everyone secretly enjoys. The drama grows throughout the event, often culminating in the screams of the criminal's family or friend. Sometimes the man at the noose begins to scream or cry for his mother. It is heart-wrenching, but you almost feel as if you are watching it from outside yourself.

You have heard many times that pirates are the worst criminals who ever existed. Not even the deepest circle of hell will take them, so people say. Notices posted around the city declare that pirates are destroying His Majesty's nation. However, there is no angry energy at Execution Dock. The people are excited for the hanging, yes, but they are there for their own curiosity rather than to see the King's justice. Pirates, in a way, are just like most of the people who have gathered at the dock. They are young, and their origins are usually working-class. And yet, these misunderstood figures are known to send heaps of money home to their parents and/or loved ones. They can get rich quickly. So even though the Crown is trying to make everyone hate pirates, you all cannot help but be thrilled by them.

You find your spot in the crowd. You spot some friends and you wave to each other in excitement. It is too crowded to actually head over to them but you will catch up with them to debrief later, likely over a pint. Food vendors shove their way through the crowd, trying to sell meat pies. Ale is spilling on the ground. It is hard to breathe among all the people here, but that does not matter.

After several minutes, the sun starts to peek out from behind the clouds. As if by a divine sign, something sparkles in the distance. A cheer goes up, deafening. The sun has caught the silver oar, the symbol of the Admiralty. The pirate is on his way!

The shouts get louder and louder as the cart draws near. At the head of the procession is the Admiralty official followed by the Ordinary of Newgate, the spiritual advisor for condemned criminals, and then the pirate himself with his hands tied behind his back. The officials pulls the pirate out of the cart amid the shouts of the crowd. The Admiralty official has to push people aside to get the pirate onto the dock. A final cheer goes through the crowd when a noose is placed around the man's neck.

The Ordinary then starts to make his speech. No one pays attention as he drones on about sin, criminal acts, just punishments, and how this pirate has offended God and can only hope for mercy. After what feels like ages, the Ordinary shuts up and grabs the pirate's hand and pulls him forward. The pirate stumbles a bit. His face is white. Sweat pours down his face. Or are they tears? He is filthy from his time languishing in Newgate. Those closest to the scaffold can smell the grime on him.

The crowd falls silent. It becomes so quiet that the city appears to have stopped altogether. After a few moments, the pirate starts to speak. In a shaky voice, he recounts his life and actions and how he became a pirate. He asks forgiveness for the robbery and murder he committed at sea. Now comes the part where he warns others against turning pirate, lest they meet the same fate.

However, this time something else happens. The pirate suddenly turns toward the Admiralty official and says, "If you and your superiors gave us better treatment on your ships, we would not have to turn pirate. If you showed kindness and mercy and fairness, we would not have to become those you hunt." Then he spits on the ground.

The crowd goes wild. Pirates are known to sometimes go off-script, and this is one of the best events you have ever seen. A pirate whose last words were to scold the Admiralty—the very organization that pushed him into that way of life!

The pirate says no more as a canvas sack is placed over his head. The noose is tightened and the scaffold floor releases. The rope is too short to kill him instantly. There is a sickening thump as his body jerks against the pulling of the rope. His arms and legs being to jerk, kick, and flail all about. Sometimes this last minutes. Other times it can last over an hour. This is the worst part. The ritual itself is over and now you must watch the reality of the situation. Some in the crowd gasp. They can hear the pirate choking out pleas for help in a choked, garbled voice. It turns your stomach. A few people near him run forward and grab his legs. Together they pull as fast and hard as they can. There is a collective gasp throughout the crowd as a loud crack echoes around them. After a moment, the pirate goes limp.

After a moment, a murmur goes through the crowd, and people start to drift away. The pirate will hang until the day after tomorrow to serve as a warning. The ritual is over. The Crown has shoved its

message into the people's faces: Become a pirate and you will hang
without dignity. No one is powerful enough to defy the King.

But once people leave the dock, they go about their day and look
forward to the next event.

"And You Shall Return from Whence You Came."

As we know, if you wanted to witness a hanging, the best place to
be was London. Public executions of traitors and all manner of
common criminals had been frequent fun days in the city since the
1200s. The hangings took place near what is now known as Marble
Arch on the western border of Hyde Park. The location was known
as Tyburn, which featured a large tree with long branches that
towered over the others, the perfect behemoth to aid in the deaths
of thousands. This became known as the "Tyburn Tree." The place
became so synonymous with death that permanent gallows were
erected in 1571.[171]

Pirates, on the other hand, got special treatment. Execution Dock did not only hold notoriety for witnesses. Pirates were very aware of it as the location of their death. Their executions drew crowds by the thousands. The people who gathered were hungry to witness the infamous rebels who, until that point, they knew of only through word of mouth.[172] The infamous home of the pirates' death was located in Wapping in London's East End, on the banks of the Thames. The neighborhood had existed since the mid-1300s, when a wall was built along the Thames to prevent flooding. A wharf was created to add more security, and then people began establishing homes and businesses. The area tended to attract seafaring men and tradesmen.[173] During the 1400s, more wharfs were built, along with warehouses and other docks where small boats could be secured. By 1516, the area had grown to the point where royal ships began to dock and replenish their supplies.

By the turn of the eighteenth century, Wapping was an official port neighborhood. There was a lot of work available along with many businesses, but the area was considered less civilized than other areas in London because so many sailors drifted in and out of the port. The area also attracted immigrants from the Low Countries in Europe and, of course, pirates.[174]

Port neighborhoods like Wapping were considered more dangerous parts of town, where drink flowed freely and people cruised the streets looking for fun, pleasure, or work.[175] Criminal activity steadily increased as the area became more crowded. Public houses, or pubs for short, were often robbed, and patrons were known to get attacked or start fights.[176]

The transient sailing population kept sex work in high demand. Many were sex workers by trade while others by circumstance. Since men came and went, unplanned pregnancies were frequent.

The increasing number of seafaring men made Wapping the most logical place to execute criminals for crimes committed on the sea. Pirates were hanged at Execution Dock as early as the reign of Henry VI (1422–1461). The first recording of a pirate's execution is from his reign, which described a pair of pirates who were hanged there for the murder of three adults and a child in a Flemish ship. After they were killed, "they hanged until the tide had washed over them three times."[177] This became the standard tradition for all executed pirates, except for Kidd. His body was tarred and strung up in an iron case, also known as a gibbet, for over twenty years.

If you go to London today, you will find a pub called the Prospect of Whitby (est. 1520), which sits on the bank of the Thames in Wapping. Behind it on the riverbank stands a replica of Execution Dock. Although its architect and creation date are unknown, the scaffold reminds us that this London location was notorious as a receptacle and execution site for pirates from as early as the fifteenth century until the site's last public execution in 1830. In fact, the location bears such infamy that another pub just down the road, the Town of Ramsgate, also claims to sit on the original location Execution Dock.[178]

"You Will Hang from the Neck Until Dead."

Public executions were meant to be demonstrations of power or punishment by death. Hangings were death-torture, or "the art of maintaining life by pain, but subdividing it into a thousand deaths."[179] Pirates were unlucky enough to be tied to shorter nooses. This meant that when the floor dropped out from under them, their neck would not break. Instead, they would be wracked with excruciating pain as the shockwave radiated down their spine. The noose would

tighten against their throat, quickly cutting off the air supply. Intense
pressure would immediately build up in the throat and face as the
person turned bright red. It would feel as if their head was being
squeezed until it was fit to burst. As their brain starved for air, the
body would start to jerk uncontrollably in a vain attempt to keep
shocking itself back to life. This became known as the Marshal's
Dance. The crowd would watch the pirate flail about desperately
as excrement streamed down his legs onto the ground below. The
process could take up to an agonizing forty-five minutes. Sometimes
witnesses would be so overcome with horror that they would pull on
the man's legs to break his neck and end his misery.[180]

These events were marketed as entertainment. Thousands of people
would travel for miles to attend a hanging. They were such popular
events that they were carried out like ceremony. The prisoner was
led to the place of execution in a cart. Their hands were tied in front
of them to make them appear tame and penitent. Once the person
arrived, they would be forced to put on an exciting performance
known as the "last dying speech." At this point, the crowd would go
wild. The poor soul would confess their crimes and ask forgiveness
over the shouts and jeers of the crowd. The people in charge of the
event would join in by screaming out the confessed crimes to make
sure no one missed a word. This would elicit louder cries, to the point
of a frenzy. By the time the noose went around the person's neck, no
one would be able to hear any distinct words.

These executions were performed at low tide to symbolize the place of
the pirate's crimes. Criminal executions often took place at the scene
of the crime. If they were unable to return to that place, an execution
would happen in a symbolic location. For example, Tyburn was used
for land-based crimes. Execution Dock on the bank of the Thames,
on the other hand, was the perfect location to execute accused pirates
because it symbolized the sea. The Admiralty Court was in charge of

all crimes and misdemeanors that were committed on any body of water up to the low-tide mark.[181]

For time and efficiency, sometimes large groups of people were executed together, and this was a real treat for spectators. In 1710, a group of fifty-two pirates were arrested at once and twenty-four of them were hanged together at Execution Dock, which made for a huge occasion. This day was so momentous that the Ordinary of Newgate mentioned it in his records for over eight years.[182] This was the largest group execution, but there were several others. For instance, twenty-four French pirates were hanged together in 1700, which would have been an exciting event for London society. Many vendors would walk through the crowd trying to sell their goods, taking advantage of emotions running high. Some would be drunk with bloodlust, while the pirates' loved ones would grieve openly. England and France had long been both enemies and frenemies, so it would have been gratifying (with a touch of schadenfreude) to watch the French pirates all hang together.[183]

Pirates in the British American colonies were also often executed in groups. Nearly 10 percent of all public executions were of pirates.[184] The main difference was that the actual execution ceremony did not have a consistent ritual. While the silver oar of the Admiralty still led a procession in Boston and New York, in the Caribbean, pirates were taken to their place of execution without it.[185]

Pirates Beyond Their Death

Pirates' public executions were not over once the pirate was dead. The memory of the action lived much longer for those who witnessed such an event. Judge Samuel Sewall, the justice who oversaw the trial and execution of the pirate John Quelch and his crew in Boston, wrote in his diary: "When I came to see how the river was covered with people, I was amazed. There were 100 boats or some 150 boats and canoes, so said Cousin Moody of York. Mr. Cotton Mather came with Capt. Quelch and six others for their execution from the prison to Scarlet's Wharf. There they were taken into a boat and taken to the place of execution about halfway between Hanson's Point and Broughton's Warehouse...When the scaffold was hoisted to its proper height, the seven pirates were taken upon it. Mr. Mather prayed for them while standing in the boat. Ropes were all fastened to the gallows. When the scaffold was set to sink, there was such a screech of women that my wife heard it sitting in our entry next to our orchard, and was much surprised at it. Our house was a mile from the place."[186]

Execution Dock was memorable enough to be depicted in late-eighteenth-century paintings of the Thames. A 1782 painting called *A Prospective View of the River Thames*, by an unknown artist, depicted the view of the King's Arm at Blackwall, Shooter's Hill in Woolwich. The painting shows the Blackwall Yard on the left, Woolwich on the right of center on the south bank of the river, and Shooter's Hill on the far right side of the piece. There is a small ship in the river, and right below its stern, the gibbeted body of a pirate can be seen as a warning to sailors.[187]

A *Perspective View of the* River Thames *&c taken from the kings Arms at* BLACKWALL.
1 Shooters Hill.   2 Woolwich.   3 The East India Dock Yard.

A Prospective View of the River Thames, 1782
Courtesy of the Royal Maritime Museum, Greenwich, UK

The hanging pirate is a lonely figure, barely noticeable upon first view. The artist illustrated the Thames's maritime history through the placement of the small Indiaman ship, the docks and the sailors on the south bank of the river, and other ships sailing down further. The inclusion of the nondescript gibbeted figure tells us that the bloody history of the Thames has never been expunged from history. The fact that gibbeted people were a common sight along the shores of the river is always in the background—both literally and metaphorically.

All the deaths in Wapping dubbed the area "the fatal place" in all the London newspapers. Every article that discussed Execution Dock made sure to have its location included on the off-chance readers might forget. Here are a couple of examples. After Philip Roche's execution, the reading audience was reminded that "Philip Roche, the pirate, convicted at the Admiralty Court, was executed at Execution-Dock in Wapping." Again, when a group of nine pirates were hung together, the report said, "Nine malefactors, convicted of piracy and murder at the recent Admiralty trials, were executed at Execution Dock in Wapping." Even as late as 1784, the *General Evening Post* described how a group of pirates' sentences would be "performed at the place where pirates hang in Wapping, called Execution Dock."[188]

Execution Dock was so famous that people knew about it in the American colonies. In 1732, a pirate named John Ellis was captured and convicted of piracy and met his death there at Execution Dock, in Wapping. Both the *Boston Gazette* and the *American Weekly Mercury* published the same letter from March 11, 1732, that said, "Yesterday the dead warrant came down to Newgate, ordering the execution of John Ellis, the pirate, at Execution Dock on Monday next."[189] Articles about Execution Dock hangings continued to be printed in the American colonies for the rest of century. In 1772, for instance, a man named John Shoals was tried and convicted at the Old Bailey, London's major criminal court, for piracy off the coast of Africa in 1722. Naturally, he hanged in Wapping.[190]

The Celebrity of Execution Dock

Execution Dock saw its last pirate hang in 1830, thirty years before the public execution ritual ended in Britain altogether. New attitudes toward crime in the nineteenth century called for a reform of punishment. The wave split those who were for public executions and those who were against them. These arguments surrounded a school of thought known as "civilized morality," an idea that suggested that the death penalty was inconsistent with the values of a humane civilization.[191] Growing criticisms began changing the attitudes surrounding the ritual. Critics felt that the sight of violence corrupted people. Indeed, these events were often unruly, or even broke out into riots, with conflict between spectators who sympathized with those on the scaffold and those who did not. Some of the critics complained that the hangings lacked dignity because they were badly staged and did not actually carry the serious, frightening message intended to deter audiences from turning into pirates.[192] Public executions stopped acting as warnings. They turned into theater that proved order was precarious and it was the audience who held true power.[193] They were meant to be somber events to teach the audience moral lessons and warn them against committing future crimes. Instead, the opposite happened: executions became spectacles of entertainment.

Interest in Execution Dock grew again in the late nineteenth century, when a British periodical called *The Speaker* published an article about the location. The article gave a history of the High Court of Admiralty and included the details of how the procession of a pirate's execution played out, which, naturally, mentioned the Admiralty's famous silver oar that sparkled in the sun. The article spoke in the second person, as if the reader were the pirate being executed.

"You departed this life with no little ceremony. You set off from Newgate at about ten in the morning. You sat on the elevated stage in the cart, the executioners behind you, the Marshal of the Admiralty in his carriage in front...However, even the law had not finished with you. Even dead, your body was forfeit for the King, and might still serve as a warning to others. After being done to death by the gallows at Execution Dock, you and your fellows were hung in chains on gibbets placed at intervals down the river, the 'chains' being a sort of iron cage turning on a swivel so that you might swing freely with the wind. Occasionally, you were dipped in a coating of tar, to prolong the spectacle so edifying to nautical men as they fared up and down the river... Men still living have seen those gruesome sights, or at least heard them described by eyewitnesses."[194]

Public executions were the most effective way for contemporary people to see pirates in the flesh. Most factual knowledge of them came from witnesses of these events, whose words immortalized pirates into collective memory. Accounts of pirates, their executions, and people's observations were written down and published for wide consumption. If some could not attend the executions, then their knowledge depended solely on printed reports or gossip, such as newspapers or independently printed tales. The legacies of these pirates' popular ends carried their memories through the rest of the eighteenth century and to today.

CHAPTER 6

FIGHT THE
ESTABLISHMENT

T he shock at, and secret delight in, Kidd's drunk and surly behavior was only to be expected from much of the audience in eighteenth-century England. It was around this time that a new idea about collective "politeness" began to spread through the populace. This idea of politeness went beyond saying "please" and "thank you"; it extended to improving moral and social mores to the point of completely reforming them.

An intensely polite society was especially appealing to those who had risen through the ranks of society by trading overseas and selling slaves. Their newfound wealth urged them to echo the upper class's ways of speaking, manners, dress, choice of hobbies, and knowledge about the world. The most important part of this new lifestyle was understanding that any personal conduct would be judged by others.[195] Thinking constantly about others' judgment especially applied to men, because these polite notions were meant to extend to British leaders and lawmakers.[196]

Of course, a newfound zeal for politeness meant that pirates, who had once had good standing with many societies around the Atlantic, came to be judged and examined as if through a microscope. Because pirates robbed ships without any regard to what country the vessels belonged to, they came to be seen as enemies to the individual, society, and nation. Many laws against piracy in North America, Britain, and the Caribbean were direct reflections of the growing habits of politeness. One of the most offensive behaviors was public drunkenness—like Kidd's performance at the scaffold.[197]

Despite (or perhaps because of) these emerging codes of conduct, the relationships between people, their leaders, and the law became very heated. Like today, anti-establishment attitudes existed during the seventeenth and eighteenth centuries. The people distrusted their government. This distrust made them believe that pirates were simply brave rebels fighting against a corrupt system. *Pirates* were the ones fighting for the cause. Naturally, people supported that. One could argue that the people's relationship to the law was like that of a child and their parent. The laws that told people what to do could evoke powerful feelings from childhood, such as the complex feelings of love and hatred, ambivalence, and defiance that would be forced into submission.[198]

One of the ways the state tried to force people into submission was by taking advantage of polite society. The image of pirates had to shift from romantic, Robin Hood-esque figures into wicked criminals. And what better way to spread the immoral consequences of piracy than the printing press, making any printed material newly available to the masses? Or for the people to witness the pirates at their public executions? These events included religious advisors, such as the Ordinary of Newgate in London, and Reverend Cotton Mather in New England, both of whom published sermons warning against the ills of piracy. The pirates' speeches at the scaffold were also transcribed and published verbatim. The government urged publishers to print copy after copy of these documents, with a huge emphasis on how pirates insulted God and society and how these doomed sailors wept, attempting to atone for their sins, and got down on their knees to pray for forgiveness by God and Man.[199] The goal: to use religious sentiment to turn people against pirates.

The rise of polite society should have turned people off pirates completely, but human nature stepped in. One could assume that the Ordinary of Newgate's reflections and Cotton Mather's sermons sold because people agreed with their arguments about pirates being evil. However, what these advisors did not anticipate was that they created a fascinating narrative. Pirates were people who rebelled against the establishment. They took orders from no one. People may not have been able to climb the social ladder during this time, but they still managed to transcend it by taking their fate into their own hands. Their plundered goods went back to the community! Like Robin

Hood of yore, they stole from the rich and gave to the poor. Or, in this case, they gave it to their homes or colonies, all of which were deprived of excellent things, such as French wine or Indian spices and silks, that people could not buy otherwise. And in return, people and governors supported pirates by buying their booty, financing their adventures, and giving them a place to stay or hide (depending on the situation). Think about it—authority figures targeting those who rejected society's straitjacket completely? People were *transfixed*. Freedom from constraints has always been a natural desire. Sales of publications about pirates skyrocketed, proving that people like Captain Kidd—who the government saw only as a betrayer of his nation who refused to adhere to the expected public execution ritual—only fascinated people more and more.

Ridding people of this fascination would prove a difficult task. Pirates were seen as agents of social change through their rejection of their country and popular norms. With new class systems emerging, creating friction between the long-standing system of social immobility, pirates were viewed with awe and even, in some cases, hope.

Society might have become obsessed with being "polite," and the state might have capitalized on it to turn the public against pirates, but the state's exploitation proved to have the opposite effect. Instead, those who did not have previous relationships with pirates began to root for the *pirates* (not the state!). What marginalized person could not get behind someone who rebelled against authority? These social changes intended for the "good of the people" only helped increase people's fascination with pirates.

Puritanism was a major religious component of life in Massachusetts, one of the most powerful American colonies. Religious fervor, then, severely influenced the way people viewed behavior and morality. In the increasingly Puritan Massachusetts society, pirates' crimes were viewed as sin and the courts there functioned more as churches preaching to the sinners rather than as rulers of the law.[200]

On the other hand, the southern colonies—especially South Carolina—had more in common with the West Indies in terms of their view of pirates. Like the Caribbean plantation islands, South Carolina had a similar culture and economy. Lives in both locations depended on slaves and the agricultural goods they sold and traded, unlike their northern religious neighbors whose economies relied on the fishing and logging industries.[201] The South had little time to make religious ideals a priority. Physical objects—tobacco, indigo, cotton, rice—were more useful things to worship. Naturally, since their lifestyle matched that of the Caribbean, the South was often viewed as riotous and immoral. Not only that, but the South, due to its climate and harder way of life, also had higher mortality rates and a greater shortage of women. Population in South Carolina lagged behind that of the other southern colonies.[202] Since the South did not make religion a priority and was more focused on making money and getting goods, the pirates were more inclined to head there. They knew they would be safe from those who wanted to capture and kill them.

As we've discussed, the West Indies had a long history as a pirate haven because the pirates were seen as the heroes who brought wealth and prosperity to the plantation islands. However, as the Royal Navy stepped in and began to hunt pirates more than ever before, many pirates had no choice but to head northward. Colonies such as South Carolina and Pennsylvania were ideal places, since both of their economies were based in the coastal cities. Earlier in the book, we discussed how the Navigation Act made it nearly impossible for colonies to engage in legal trade with countries other than Britain. Pirates, naturally, became the Robin Hoods who brought the colonies excellent treasures.

Pirates vs. the Establishment

The emergence of a polite society was not specific to England. The printing industry and gossip allowed this idea to travel across the Atlantic Ocean to the American colonies. Colonial America attempted to emulate England as much as possible. Both sides of the ocean had increased literacy rates and an abundance of taverns, coffee houses, salons, meeting houses, and council chambers for people to discuss their views of society and how to stop criminal behavior.[203] Polite society was much slower to arrive in the Caribbean due to a lack of printing presses until about 1715 so, in the meantime, various laws were established in attempts to enforce a "civilized" society.[204] Emphasizing pirates' immoral actions redefined the public's view of criminals.

One of the ways people could adhere to the tenets of "politeness" was by following social expectations and specific rituals. The executions were given a specific theatrical ritual structure that the audience came to expect. The custom was necessary to show submission to the government's authority and end-of-life moral regret and reform. The formalities around pirates' public executions did not only exist in England; they were followed throughout the British Atlantic colonies. "Polite society" was spreading.

But how on earth could public hangings be considered "polite?" Is there anything ruder than…killing someone? An important thing to understand is that this idea of politeness was not just an *individual's* action. It is not just you saying please and thank you and dressing appropriately. The idea is that there have to be fair *consequences* for those who do not adhere to politeness. If you show up drunk in public and make an absolute asshat of yourself, then you have to pay the consequences in order to teach others a lesson. Throw you into the stocks in the center of town for all to see! This punishment tells other people, "This is what you get for making a fool of yourself and, by extension, your community. Do. Not. Do. It."

Pirates were total social rejects. Swearing, drinking, and sleeping around is one thing. But betraying your king and country, robbing your people, and—worst of all—killing your countrymen? There is nothing worse than that, and there must be retribution to destroy you and warn others against becoming you.

Therefore, hangings were not just for the guilty party. These sentences were also intended for the spectators. The Ordinary's published accounts were deliberately written for a general audience. Admiralty officials knew that these would be widely attended events. Everything had to go smoothly. The scaffold had to be in good repair, erected, and ready for the ceremony. The area had to be clean and presentable to make it desirable for people of all classes. Sheriffs and marshals were assigned as guards in order to "keep the King's peace" and to make sure the pirate's cart arrived safely.[205]

The executions were practically a ceremony with three specific stages. The pirate was led onto the scaffold where the religious advisor introduced the doomed person and gave a summary of their crimes. This was followed by what was known as a pirate's "last dying speech." This speech forced the pirate to admit to their crimes, atone for their crimes, and to warn everybody against the temptation to follow the wicked path to piracy.

Pirates did not make any attempt to hide their contempt for the government and their accusers. Newspaper reports described them as being "obdurate" and hardened in their sin.[206] Many stayed steadfast and defiant until the day of their death by refusing to participate in the execution ritual. Some were known to insult their superiors in their last dying speeches. Some refused to give a speech at all, as in the case of Captain Kidd. One pirate named Captain John Downes was described as so stubborn that he refused to show "the appearance of a mortified man." Two hours before his execution he boasted about how much wealth he'd stolen during his piratical career.[207] Another pirate even threatened to come back from the dead as a ghost to haunt his prosecutor for the rest of the man's life.[208]

While Kidd refused to submit to the ritual, his fellow sailor who was executed with him, Darby Mullins, followed this ritual to a tee.[209] Mullins "heartily begged Pardon of God and the World" for his crimes of piracy. He admitted that he was a sinner for swearing, cursing, and blaspheming the Sabbath. (Whether or not his social crimes actually included blasphemy was irrelevant.) This speech followed a dramatic performance by the Ordinary of Newgate, who loudly proclaimed with awe that, Mullins being uneducated and illiterate, it was natural to assume that he did not care about the Bible and its teachings, so it was practically a miracle that he desired salvation at all.[210]

Illustrations of these hangings began to be circulated throughout all of the major British and British Atlantic cities. The woodcut below shows an unnamed pirate (meant to represent all pirates) about to be hanged at Execution Dock in London.

The Hanging of a Pirate at Execution Dock, 17th Century
Courtesy of the Royal Maritime Museum, Greenwich, UK

The crowd of onlookers surrounds the pirate while the Admiralty Official sits on his horse, holding the silver oar on the left. Just to the left of the oar, the pirate stands next to the Ordinary, while a man below the scaffold checks the trapdoor to make sure it is working properly. The most interesting thing about this image, however, is the detailed audience engagement. The close proximity of the crowd suggests that the witnesses are intended to be active participants in the pirate's demise, signifying the insult the pirate has inflicted on his nation and countrymen.

Newspapers included numerous details to show the public just how subversive pirates could be at their executions. In Charleston, South Carolina, the pirates John Rose Archer and William White were executed together. According to the paper *The Boston News-Letter*, the pirates' flag was placed at the end of their gallows for all to see. The flag had two images: one side had a "…dart in the heart, with drops of blood proceeding from it; on the other side an hourglass. The sight is [frightening]."[211] The not-so-subtle symbol of death was designed to terrify their victims into surrendering at sea. The flag dripping with blood was meant to horrify the audience. Instead, the details just added to the excitement and drama of the event. Then (most likely coerced into the ritual), the two pirates gave their traditional speeches in which they warned the audience against the sins of swearing, blaspheming, disobedience to one's parents, and drunkenness. One of them even went so far as to tell the audience to choose death over piracy.[212]

"Why Is All the Rum Gone?"

Pubs were popular establishments for people to come together over pints of beer to discuss the news and politics of the day. Pubs, of course, were *also* places for secret treasonous meetings and, naturally, fights. They became known as establishments where people could go to unleash their bad side until they lacked any sort of self-control.[213]

Despite the prevalence of pub culture, drinking and outward signs of drunkenness have unsurprisingly been looked down upon in North America since the eighteenth century. In the South, lawmakers were so disgusted by sailors' drinking habits that they passed laws heavily restricting their alcohol use.[214] (I'd venture to say that drinking to excess until stumbling and swearing has always been judged openly.) Alcohol was pretty much *the* symbol of bad behavior and poor reputation, especially during this period. However, despite England's long-standing pub culture, rules and politics about drinking habits have been a subject of debate since the 1600s.[215]

We like to think of pirates as devil-may-care men who like to party, just like the beloved modern character Jack Sparrow. However, newspaper articles insinuated that pirates' drinking habits were the cause of their doom. One evening in 1718, a group of pirates stole a ship filled to the brim with all kinds of bottled wine and liquor off of the coast of Massachusetts. A find like this would make them very rich men. Knowing that they could still make hordes of money, they decided to take advantage of their loot and began drinking in celebration. They whooped with laughter and toasted their good fortune. The actual captain of the ship saw an opportunity and encouraged his crew to keep partying. Once all the pirates had passed out, the captain retook control of his ship and crashed it onto the rocky coast of Massachusetts. The pirates were so drunk that the crash did not even make them stir. When they final woke up, they found themselves surrounded by Admiralty officials who promptly, upon the captain betraying them, shackled and arrested the whole group.[216]

Not even the Caribbean was immune to bias against drinking. For years Jamaica, for example, had been known as the "Sodom of the Sea." Religious society thought the population was idle, debauched, lecherous, and constantly publicly drunk.[217] The Caribbean should have been a key source of wealth for Great Britain, but with so many people living lawlessly, it was impossible to know what quantities of sugar and other goods were being produced. Plus, this reputation prevented upper-crust society from wanting to move there, which meant the population could not be expanded enough to develop rich sugar cane plantations built on the backs of enslaved people.

In an attempt to "clean up" Jamaica's act (or, more specifically, Port Royal's act), the Council of Trade and Plantations began to write laws that attempted to regulate the behavior of Jamaica's inhabitants. As early as 1664, laws were passed to stop "tipling [drinking to excess], cursing, and swearing."[218]

Naturally, this did not sit well with Port Royal's citizens. Always the rebels, pirates scorned these laws and social pressures. They openly and proudly drank for entertainment. In fact, the pirate Blackbeard is rumored to have encouraged drinking on his ship to keep morale high. Port Royal alone was home to nineteen taverns.[219] The people continued to ignore the laws and, if anything, their drinking got *worse*. To make the problem even larger, more and more prostitutes arrived on the island, namely from France and England, adding to the people's "lecherous" behavior.[220] One of the quays in Port Royal became known as "Drunkard's Key" not only because of all the drinking, but because of the many pirates and privateers who frequented the area after unpacking their plundered goods.[221] Fresh supplies of wine, ales, and liquor filled local taverns to the brim with drink and customers.

The "out-of-control" behavior in Jamaica would prove short-lived. In 1692 a massive earthquake struck the island and practically leveled the capital city, Kingston. Most of nearby Port Royal, a spit of land that jutted out from the coast of Kingston, sank into the sea. The British saw their opportunity.

Amid this chaos, the Royal Navy swooped in, banished all pirates from the area, and set up offices to enforce strict regulations. First, alehouses and taverns were banned from selling alcohol without permits. The permits had to be renewed annually, which further hurt these establishments financially. This was to prevent any and all "disorders committed in his said House or any Thing there done contrary to the laws of England or this Island." Second, public profanity or blasphemy meant to "dishonor Almighty God" was punishable by law with a fine of twenty pounds."[222] Anyone found guilty of public drunkenness, swearing, or blaspheming was banned from finding future employment to prevent future "embarrassment" and scandals.[223]

God's Judgement

North American colonies might have been very strict about their religious beliefs, but sailors' religious habits faded away once they were at sea. Their apathy toward religion might have been a result of the tough and dangerous work at sea. There simply was no time or desire to bother with religion while away from church and home. An independent society of a ship full of mostly religiously dissatisfied men basically guaranteed that blasphemous and foul language ran aplenty.[224] Sailors also had other hardships to endure without the comforts of home and a religious routine. Food was often lacking in essential nutrients or spoiled. Water could become brackish or too low. Working conditions were extremely dangerous and accidents ran aplenty. Storms could strike at any time, which could irrevocably damage ships. Rules on merchant and naval ships were strict and the punishments severe. Take all of these factors and add them to the fact that taverns and brothels set themselves up right at the docks, and you'll find the perfect equation for what would be considered "sinful" behavior. Life at sea was dangerous and lonely. It is not surprising that the sailors would spend their earnings on drink and prostitutes to forget their troubles and find warm companionship (often on ships and with men as well).[225]

Sailors might have also gotten into traditionally sinful habits because their work included long periods of idleness. Long hours during the fighting off-seasons led to boredom, feelings of uselessness, and restlessness. Land-based workers, who did not have that experience, did not sympathize with sailors. They felt that sailors were lazy, which led to their drinking and "whoring." The idea was that, if sailors were given more honest work, especially in the plantation colonies, the number of pirates would decrease. It was impossible for piracy to completely disappear, but their numbers could stay low if those captured were sentenced to hard labor rather than death.[226]

This objective opinion drifted toward pirates. Some felt that pirates were competent sailors (quite the understatement), but simply lacked the amount of steady employment necessary to keep them honest. After all, if sailors were given more honest work, especially in the plantation colonies of the South, the number of pirates would decrease. Right? Those who had no use for pirates, such as New England sailing communities, felt that, if pirates could find a way to make themselves useful to society, they could reenter the grace of God. *The Boston News-Letter* encouraged this opinion and urged its

readers to "instruct, admonish, preach and pray for them" because
pirates "were without salvation" as they currently were .[227] In Puritan
New England, the common view was that God had written a moral
code into the hearts of everyone. This should save people from
sinful behavior, but a naturally-inclined sinful nature made a person
incapable of obedience to the church.[228] Though they assumed that
sailors *did* have God's moral code in their hearts, pirates were just
irredeemable. They were the worst sinners, who kept themselves in
the company of the devil. They rejected the social and moral codes of
civilized society.

Some of these ideas were also present in England and encouraged
judgmental views against the American colonies—especially
the southern colonies. In 1724, an Englishman named Hugh
Jones traveled through the American colonies and published his
observations of the people in Virginia. His intention was to describe
the colonists' lifestyle and how they could fix their "pirate problem."
Jones described Virginia as a place where foul and immoral behavior
was technically discouraged, but the lack of an ecclesiastical court
made it impossible to enforce any social laws.[229] With this, he felt,
how could there *not* be pirates?

Pirates' public executions were not just a way for people to get a closer
look at pirates for the first time. Religious leaders used condemned
pirates to help keep religious fervor high—and to make money. In
England, the Ordinary of Newgate offered religious counsel to the
prisoners who suffered in the dank, filthy cells of the prison. Then
the Ordinary would write all of his observations and conversations
with the pirate, embellishing at will. The Ordinary would write these
more for monetary and entertainment value than anything else. Then

the manuscript was off to the printers to become the next cheap bestseller, eaten up by readers.

In the American colonies, particularly Puritan New England, it was not just the priests and reverends who delivered religious judgement. This attitude spread to the local communities as well. Puritans, who had arrived in America to escape persecution in Europe and to practice freely, projected their values onto the pirates. As a result, American colonists were focused more on the pirates' irreligiousness than the people in England. Although the concentration of strict religious rules settled in New England, there were Puritans in every colony, so their influence bled south.[230]

The eighteenth-century printing industry was hungry to publish writings focused on crimes and other scandals, knowing their appeal. Trial transcripts and observations of pirates' behaviors and crimes were thus the perfect sort of inventory. Even though many of these publications were highly embellished, they provided some of the most detailed biographical information about pirates that we could ever possibly encounter today.[231]

CHAPTER 7

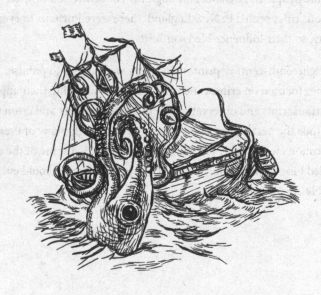

FAKE NEWS AND
ALTERNATIVE FACTS

T here was a distinct difference between the way the
American Colonies and Britain reported about pirates.
True to their reserved nature, English newspapers mostly
relied on simple details and unembellished facts. They rarely used
colorful descriptions or sensational language unless it was an
extraordinary tale to tell. On the other hand, it should be no surprise
that American newspapers used as much description, sensationalism,
and purple prose as possible to report the news while making punchy
social commentaries.

Despite the fact that many pirates had good relationships with
colonists, not all pirates were good people. There were those who
were happy to attack and pillage ships for the fun of it. Some also
took pleasure in beating or even maiming their victims. These were
the pirates who were featured in newspaper reports. Cruelty would
hopefully turn the pirates into villains in the people's eyes as another
way to deter anyone from that way of life, or at least from idealizing
those seamen.

While generic reports of piracy in English newspapers were pretty
much straightforward and to the point, the newspapers had ample
space for firsthand accounts. In 1721, the *British Gazetteer* published
a story about a crew of four hundred pirates attaching a ship called
Cassandra. At just over 1,100 words, the article contained every little
detail: the layout of the ship, who operated it, the goods it carried, and
exactly how the pirates carried out their attack.

According to the article, pirates attacked the Cassandra on the
morning of August 8, 1720. They were described as merciless men
who had "their black and bloody Flags being all the time display'd."
In a horrific act of savagery, several of the pirates cornered three of
the *Cassandra*'s crew and cut the poor men in pieces. The pirates
then took over the ship and kept everyone hostage for forty-eight
days until they arrived off the coast of what was then Bombay. Two

English ships approached, thinking it was a vessel finally arriving with overdue goods. When they realized the ship was under the control of pirates, the two English ships attacked and disposed of all four hundred pirates.[232]

These details, along with the description of the pirates' flag, were intended to tell readers about the pirates' rejection of their nationality and the brutal attacking and dismemberment of their own countrymen. Newspaper entries likes this one also helped solidify the association between the Jolly Roger and pirates.

Knowing the success of horror, not every newspaper would dare to hide the true and gory details of some pirates' dreadful actions. People have always been drawn to brutal events and news, as people today slow down on the highways to observe a major car wreck. They cannot look away. Newspapers knew the appeal of rubbernecking and used it to augment their sales.

Three weeks before Lowther's attack on the *Cassandra*, another article was also printed in the *London Journal*. This article contained the most horrifying act of violence a pirate could ever commit: forced cannibalism. The article warned people about several pirate ships operating in the West Indies, one of which included a gang who managed to attack and plunder a fleet of four ships out of New England. This gang of pirates attacked the captain, cut off his ears, and forced the poor man to eat them.[233] A year later, Lowther made his rounds in the newspapers again, only this time everybody got to read the gory details. This time the *London Journal* chose not to spare their readers. The article claimed that Lowther and his crew "… murdered 45 Spaniards in cold blood [and] cut off the Captain's lips, broiled them in front of him, forced the Captain to eat them, and then killed him along with his whole crew of 32 sailors."

The article concluded with a statement that Lowther shot himself in the head after they docked on the "Island Blanko." He was found with his brains splattered about him and his pistol at his side, looking up into oblivion.[234]

Public fascination with gruesome spectacle proved a lucrative product. Cannibalism and bodily mutilation became common tropes in London's newspaper reports about pirates. This was not a new tactic. Cannibalistic rhetoric about enemies and criminals has been in use since the Middle Ages to horrify and intrigue people.[235] An eighteenth-century account of it in a newspaper would have been shocking to read. Cannibalism was seen as the ultimate savage act. Newspapers articles did not actually mention the word "cannibal," but the graphic imagery that the article invoked "othered" the pirates. These characters were completely dehumanized to show that pirates were not normal human beings. They were completely separate from the human population.

In 1729, a pirate named John Upton was hanged for his crimes after spending five years terrorizing merchant ships.[236] His most hideous crime occurred on November 14, 1725, when he attacked a ship called the Perry Galley, captained by a man named Story King. Although King was the victim of a brutal attack, he survived to recount his tale. On that November day, Upton and his fellow pirates stormed King's ship with their cutlasses swinging to collect booty. King, being captain, was "strung up by the neck until he fainted." To revive him, the pirates stabbed the man in his buttocks. King claimed that Upton and some of his comrades stabbed and brutalized him up to twenty times. In their final act of torture, Upton cut off King's ear, boiled it, and then "thrust a pistol into his mouth and threatened to blow his brains out" if King refused to eat it.[237]

Letters of the Caribbean

What about news in the Caribbean? After all, when we think of
pirates, the first places that come to mind are from this tropical
area, and named in the popular Pirates of the Caribbean series:
Tortuga, Jamaica, and Nassau. Surely the colonists there were just as
informed of the happenings of pirates as their North American and
English comrades?

Even though American colonists had to initially rely on news out of
London, there soon came another source that contained juicier
details: letters sent out from the Caribbean via ship, or, to be more
specific, from Jamaica and Barbados. The colonists welcomed these
letters not only for their gory accounts, but also because they provided
more up-to-date information about pirates'
whereabouts. Now the North American colonies
had another direct link to their plantation island
neighbors. In addition to sharing smuggled
items and good relationships with pirates, they
could trade news and gossip without England's
interference.[238]

American newspapers often lifted news stories directly from the
Barbados Gazette. For instance, in 1739, the *Weekly Rehearsal*
published the "Account of the Murder of Capt. Christopher Brooks,
Commander of the Ship *Haswell*, of London." This was "extracted"
verbatim and told a detailed and gruesome story about Brooks'
murder, as told by his surviving first and second mates. When pirates
stormed his ship, they threw members of Brooks' crew overboard
until they were able to declare the ship a pirate ship, which they
renamed the *Jolly Rover*. Once the ship had surrendered to the pirates,
they delivered the Pirates' Code and thus the *Jolly Rover* became an
official pirate vessel. It is not hard to imagine that, although the idea
of a ship being taken was a frightening threat, people still found it

deliciously intriguing to read about how a group of rogue sailors could take over another ship and transform it into their own maritime kingdom. Pirates in general were pretty successful at doing this. During that year alone, at least four or five ships had been captured and turned pirate. The captured crew were, unfortunately, all subjected to brutal punishments at the hands of the pirates. Five of the pirates were put on the rack until every joint completely dislocated. Three of those pirates who survived the wracking were "strangled" to death. The pirate captain was given the worst punishment. He had his right hand cut off and was impaled on a spiked wheel, which rotated into and out of the water until the helpless man either drowned or bled to death.[239]

Caribbean newspapers were not exclusively loyal to their North American neighbors. They had an obligation to also trade news with England, since they were plantation colonies and did not have their own charters. Letters and oral reports made their way to London, where they were published in local papers. One paper claimed to receive daily letters for the "frightful accounts of the piracies, murders, and robberies done in the West Indies." The news would often travel from one of the islands to Boston and then to London.

One particular piece of news to make this journey was about the infamously violent pirate, Edward Low. Low murdered a merchant captain named Nathan Skiff during a fight between their ships. In an unusual act of kindness after Low captured Skiff's ship, he offered Skiff's crew places on his ship as pirates. Low's kindness was short-lived. The crew refused to switch allegiances, and many of them were shot to death as a result. Low was eventually captured, but he would not go down without a fight, or the last word.

"I will not be hanged at Execution Dock," he shouted at his captors. "I will shoot myself first!"[240]

So, how did the English settlers throughout the West Indies get information about laws against pirates, and about the pirates themselves? Like the North American colonists, Jamaican planters and colonists had to know what measures were being taken against piracy, for their own safety. While many North American cities enjoyed an amicable trade with pirates, Jamaica and other islands were more at risk of damage, because it was *their* goods that would get stolen. After the Royal Navy took heavier control of the Caribbean in the late 1690s, colonists and governors needed to work with pirates to smuggle in goods blocked by the pesky Navigation Acts. Government officials distributed Council of War meeting notes throughout the plantation islands to show Caribbean merchants exactly what was being done to protect them. Naturally, one of the most efficient ways to do this was by publishing them as newspapers.[241]

Jamaica was actually the second American colony to publish a weekly paper, the first being Boston. The papers in the Caribbean were four pages long, printed in a specific order: the first and second pages held proclamations and legal news, advertisements, and world news. The third page contained local news. The fourth page consisted entirely of advertisements.[242] The paper, called the *Jamaica Weekly Courant*, ran from 1718 to 1754. However, if a reader wanted to pore over these papers to find all the Caribbean gossip, they might be disappointed. The majority of the papers that were published before 1750 are either lost or only exist on old microfilm.

It is these Caribbean papers that brought us the only factual account of one of the most popular pieces of lore about pirates: an article about a group of pirates forcing their hostage to walk the plank. "A vessel from the West Indies brings us information that pirates have been off the coast for some time. The pirates have captured several vessels and forced the officers to walk overboard on a plank."[243]

Jamaica also provided many letters to both North America and London. Since its capital, Kingston, was home to one of the most prolific execution sites in the Caribbean, there was much news to report. It was also a great place to circulate other pirate news and gossip, given that many were so positively and negatively affected by piracy. The colonists were thirsty for news. For these colonists, it was fortunate that Jamaica was able to reproduce news from North America. A popular story that traveled around the island was a report about a large group execution of pirates. (A story even more popular because of its direct connection to Jamaica.) A Jamaican captain, Chandler, captured a pirate ship off the coast of New England. Fifty-eight of those pirates were brought to trial, forty-two were found guilty, and forty-one of them were hanged in Boston, all at once. Seven of the convicted pirates were pardoned because some felt that they were young enough to reform. They were sent back to Europe to "prevent their returning to the same bad course of life."[244]

The chase, capture, trial, and execution of Captain William Kidd tells us just how prevalent the early modern printing industry was. Just as today, newspapers and other forms of media were meant to inform, but more importantly, entertain their readers. Newspapers had a duty to tell their readers about the horrors of piracy to keep the governments happy. However, readers read between the lines and extracted the true stories: pirates were exciting. They were cool. They were sexy. Their actions could be gruesome, but when one is far removed from the actual crime, it becomes a source of entertainment rather than news. Pirates began to transform into beloved villains.

The governments would not stop here, however. If the news itself was not convincing the readers that pirates were horrible people, they would have to appeal to common sense and morals.

CHAPTER 8

LIVES FOR PROFIT

P ublications about pirates became extremely profitable during the eighteenth century. A lot of this is thanks to religious and moral authorities. In North America, the famous Reverend Cotton Mather made it his life's mission to, in his view, rehabilitate pirates. He delivered impassioned, sanctimonious sermons intended to practically shame pirates into seeking salvation. Like the Ordinary of Newgate, Mather wrote and published his sermons. He painted pirates as horrific, godless heathens. Naturally, the sermons were bestsellers throughout colonial America. His speeches also offered moral instruction to all of his observers and readers. Speeches and publications by the Ordinary of Newgate and Cotton Mather turned pirates' executions into spectacles, which in turn served only to *increase* people's fascination with the supposedly godless pirates.

In London, the Ordinary of Newgate's purpose in life was keeping his reputation as a confessor and moral guardian for those doomed to die. His observations about Captain Kidd are a perfect example of his role. He wrote that he repeatedly tried to get Kidd to admit his guilt and absolve his sins. However, Kidd remained obstinate. Kidd, according to the Ordinary, refused to admit any guilt and stated that he did not need or care to find God as he languished in prison. After the Ordinary published his account, people flocked to the printers to buy a copy. Any story—fact or fiction—was popular among readers, as long as it contained a juicy tale. Captain Kidd *certainly* provided that sort of entertainment.

America, however, was not fortunate enough to get the Ordinary's Observation Accounts. However, this did not mean that American colonists were ignorant of Kidd—otherwise he never would have become infamous. In fact, British newspapers only had information to print about Kidd because of the American newsprint industry (except for the London-based Ordinary's account, of course). The *Post Boy*, a popular London-based newspaper that had a particular interest in

Kidd, had to cite letters and articles from America bearing news that
was already several months old.[245] Despite that hurdle, Londoners
made an effort to stay informed, and were well-versed in Kidd's raids
by the time he arrived.

Pirates were not just the means to get the Ordinary's message out;
they made the Ordinary rich. The Ordinary would only sell his
observations to publishers if he were allowed to include a transcript of
the pirate's last dying speech. Now, not only could the Ordinary take
credit for his own writing, he also claimed ownership of the pirate's
own last words. With a final flourish of hyperbolic gory details, the
Ordinary would send off his manuscript to money-hungry printers,
and copies were sold at three or six pence. Much to the printers'
delight, these publications sold by the thousands. The Ordinary only
received a modest percentage of sales, but as luck would have it, the
printing industry was still quite shaky. And the printing industry's
unstable nature was the Ordinary's gain. Licenses expired fast. They
were expensive to renew. Printers often were out of work, which
meant new printers were able to rush in and take up management
so they could put their names on the front page. In fact, the industry
was so precarious that between 1720 and 1775, the names of at least
twenty-five printers appeared on the title pages of Ordinary Account
publications and reprints. A changeover of printers would happen
every other year. This meant that the Ordinary was privy to a new
advance or generous cut from the initial profits with each changeover.
He could get up to £200 a year from his writing alone, which would
be about £21,000 or $27,000 today.[246] These accounts were extremely
popular and lucrative. Ultimately, over four hundred editions were
published during the eighteenth century, which included 2,500
biographies of executed criminals.[247]

In the 1760s, many of the observations of the various Ordinaries
observations were collected into an anthology. One of the more
famous entries was about a particularly violent Irish pirate named

Philip Roche. He was condemned to death for stealing a French ship and "cruelly and barbarously attacking and murdering the captain of a French Vessel, Pierre Tartoue."

Roche was born to a wealthy family who provided him with the best education possible. He was bred to become a captain, but instead he quickly turned to piracy so he could become as rich as he wanted in the fastest way possible. When he and his men captured Tartoue's ship, they showed no mercy whatsoever. Roche and his fellow pirates "beat the brains out" of Tartoue's men and threw them overboard.

According to Roche's testimony, Captain Pierre Tartoue cried and begged for mercy. "Please," Tartoue pleaded, "did I not let you onto my ship with civility and kindness? Aren't we both Christians and children in the eyes of Jesus?" In response, Roche threw Tartoue overboard, where he drowned in the cold, black water.

"I heard Tartoue the others in the water calling upon God," Roche said at his trial. "I listened to their shouts until the waves overcame their voices."

Roche and his crew were captured soon after, perhaps in a stroke of divine punishment.

According to the Ordinary's accounts, Roche testified with such a calm matter-of-fact tone that the Ordinary was beyond horrified. "This malefactor, who shows us human nature in the most depraved manner possible is only about thirty years of age. How could a man so young have learned so much cruelty?"

Roche showed no fear or repentance about his crimes or his sentence of death. He told the Ordinary that he had been promised a pardon under the *Act of the Effectual Suppression of Piracy* as long as he named his fellow pirates. This way, his execution date would be pushed back as long as he provided enough evidence to win his pardon. The Ordinary found it even more disgusting that Roche had no qualms about betraying his crew. Even if he was a pirate, he was still a human being, but there appeared to be no soul behind his eyes. However, something must have come over Roche. At the last minute, he refused to name any members of his crew. This infuriated the Admiralty and they gave him an execution date of August 22, 1723.[248]

As his execution date came closer, the Ordinary was surprised to find that Roche became more and more subdued in his manner. "He appeared very serious and attentive. He has asked me to keep him company and read him scripture."

However, on the date of his execution, Roche's anger returned.

"I was raised as a devout Catholic. I counted on the Church of Rome to save me from my crimes," he said. "But instead I am betrayed."

This perceived betrayal broke him. Roche was so demoralized that he could not speak at all at the scaffold and refused to give the customary speech.

"He was too faint and confused," wrote the Ordinary. "He was too much in consternation."[249]

A story such as Roche's was an enticing inclusion in the published Ordinary accounts. Pirates' notoriety and subsequent popularity made them a selling point for newspapers. The Ordinary of Newgate knew exactly what he was doing here. A little over twenty years earlier, Kidd's trial had been a literary sensation that sold out immediately. Since then, newspapers had been rife with articles about pirates. Why not take the opportunity to capitalize on the condemned pirate's life? In fact, they're still profitable! You can buy your own copies online.

Pity or Mercy?

Not every piece of writing tried to make pirates look as villainous as possible. There were moments when the author clearly sympathized with the poor pirate's plight and implored his audience to feel sorry for the man as well. In the same anthology of pirate confessions that contained the tale of Philip Roche, a pirate named Walter Kennedy became somewhat famous for his actions, thanks to one Ordinary's compassionate writing.

The accounts of Walter Kennedy gave more insight into the lives of pirates than nearly any other account at the time. Kennedy painted his brethren as organized, meticulous, and skilled sailors. Captains were elected based on their intelligence and cunning, men who were kind to their crew and banned fighting. He did not defend his life as a pirate nor those of others, however. Kennedy mournfully admitted that his life as a pirate was wicked and unhappy because he and his crew spent most of their time trying to flee from capture rather than collect riches.

On the day of his execution, Kennedy wept as he said he was ready to die and hoped he could be in God's graces. Although he was married, he did not have children, which he said was his greatest relief so that he would not leave any more orphans to languish in the workhouses. As he approached the scaffold, he began to shake and his weeping turned into gasping sobs of terror. He began to cough and choke.

"Please," he said to the Ordinary as he looked out at the sea of faces before him, "May I please have some water?"

After a moment the Ordinary patted his shoulder and called for a jug. He poured Kennedy a mug of water, which he took gratefully. After a long drink with shaking hands, he managed to take a deep breath and compose himself so he could give his speech and confess to his guilt.

"Do not judge my wife for my actions," he implored the audience. His voice rose to a shout. "She is a good and pious woman and full of virtue! She left me as soon as she learned I was a pirate."[250] Before he could say another word, the rope around his neck tightened and the ground disappeared below his feet.

The same anthology featured a double execution of two pirates who did not sail together, but were convicted at a double trial on July 5, 1722: Captain John Massey and the aforementioned Philip Roche. This case was particularly difficult because the Ordinary had to counsel two men at once who were very different in personality. Massey not only regretted his life of piracy, but was also extremely devout and repentant. Roche, as we have learned, remained defiant until his bitter end. Being a pirate captain, Massey had the unfortunate sentence of an immediate hanging, while Roche was granted a temporary reprieve.

Massey claimed he had had no choice but to become a pirate. He was initially employed by the Royal Africa Company as a merchant trader. Unfortunately, the majority of his crew had weak constitutions. Nearly all of them died off the coast of Africa of either dysentery, malaria, or yellow fever. Massey was lucky to find another ship almost immediately. He was shocked, he claimed in his trial, to find out that they were actually pirates.

"I had nightmares the entire time I sailed with them!" He insisted. "Every night I dreamt that I was being led to Execution Dock. I spent my whole voyage terrified that they would cut out my tongue and throw me overboard!"

His pleas were ignored. After all, if he was a pirate captain democratically elected by a crew, then he couldn't have hated being a pirate that much, let alone felt threatened in such a manner.

Either way, Massey proved a spiritual and devout man. After his pleading failed, he accepted his sentence without any more tears. The

Ordinary said that every time he visited Massey, he found him reading scripture or praying in his cell. Massey carried this attitude with him to his death. He was openly praying as he was led to the scaffold at Execution Dock and delivered a heartfelt speech, which moved many in the crowd to tears.

At the end of his speech, Massey turned toward the Ordinary. "If I may, I have one request," he said.

"And what would that be, my son?" the Ordinary asked, a bit surprised.

"Please," Massey said in a choked voice, "please bury me in a closed coffin. Don't let my beloved wife see my body. She does not know...of this."

After a moment, the Ordinary gave a nod. He started to motion to the executioner.

"Wait, if I may!" Massey choked out. This time the Ordinary said nothing, but waited. Massey continued, "Bury me next to my mother. Or at least as close to her as possible. That's all I ask."

With a final nod from the Ordinary, Massey sighed and closed his eyes as the noose was placed around his neck.

"He was decent, grave, and penitent," the Ordinary later wrote in his report. "Courage attended him to his last moment."

The Preacher Cometh

Pirates' trials, such as Massey's, sometimes pointed out the direct effect that their deaths would have on their immediate families. This offered an opportunity for the Ordinary to continue building his platform of moral judgements. Pirates' executions were said to have left "too many widows, orphans, and families ruined."[251] Wives and close family members naturally had the closest relationships to pirates. Therefore, they often came under suspicion as accomplices to their husband's or family member's actions. A condemned pirate knew what his arrest could do to his wife's and children's reputation. He would hope that "no reflections would be made on his innocent family."[252]

A perfect example is what happened to Captain Kidd's wife, Sarah Bradley Cox Oort Kidd. Sarah was born in New York and became extremely wealthy after being widowed three times before marrying Kidd. After her husband's arrest, she herself was thrown into jail on suspicion of trying to hide his loot, or at least its whereabouts. She denied this, and after several weeks Lord Bellomont, having no evidence, had no choice but to release her. Though Sarah managed to regain her property, her life remained tainted. For several years to come, she and her servants would be under constant suspicion of having played a role in Kidd's piracy.[253]

The Ordinary saw an opportunity here to spread his agenda of morality. After Lawrence died at the scaffold, the Ordinary published his account, which included a copy of the private letter. Was the letter transcribed for the publication and then sent to his mother, or did it never reach her? We will never know.

The Ordinary of Newgate's accounts were not published very much in the American colonies, but not to worry. The colonists had Cotton Mather's impassioned and furious sermons against pirates to read instead. Cotton Mather was a third-generation preacher who quickly gained an enormous following in the New England colonies. His first foray into the execution sermon came about in March 1686, when a man named James Morgan, thirty years old, was found guilty of piracy and sentenced to hang. Nearly five thousand people in Boston came to the execution because it was the first hanging to happen in the city for seven years. Mather delivered a rousing speech that generated cheers and jeers throughout the whole crowd, causing a deafening roar.

"The people were so moved by my words that they very greedily desire a publication," he wrote in his diary that night.[254]

The result was the first of his many publications, *The Call of the Gospel*, published just months later. The sermon sold so well that printers had to order a second edition, which included a nine-page transcription of his conversations with James Morgan on his death march to the scaffold.[255] This success solidified his place as Massachusetts's religious leader and moral backbone for the next forty years.

Portrait of Reverend Cotton Mather, Peter Pelham, 1727
Courtesy of the John Carter Brown Library

There were so many similarities between Cotton Mather's sermons
and the Ordinary of Newgate's accounts that it is possible that the
Ordinary's accounts might have been the inspiration for Mather's
writings. In fact, the Ordinary's accounts might have even served as
the model for publications about executions in North America.[256]
Like the Ordinary of Newgate, Cotton Mather happily capitalized on
pirates' crimes and punishments to deliver his agenda to the pulpit.
This platform provided a perfect opportunity for Mather to deliver
his message about the consequences of "sin" and the breakdown
of morals to people beyond his church, and even to the rest of the
American colonies. Mather's message: Pirates were sinners, and they
must fear the afterlife to find true redemption. This would be a sizable
task, considering that pirates disregarded most religious beliefs.

The Ordinary of Newgate and Cotton Mather shared the same
goal: to sell religious and moral guilt to the public. Their works sold
massively within their communities. People were ravenous for the
drama. For some, it confirmed their own religious ideals, and for
others it provided titillating reading and fodder for gossip. Mather
used his speeches at the pirates' gallows as a way to demonstrate his
own righteousness, power, and influence, not just to the public, but
also to lawmakers and leaders.[257]

Pirates were unfazed by these zealous moral hunts. They had long cast
off their allegiance to their home countries and had formed their own
nations and identities at sea. This self-made freedom attracted more
and more people to the point of a mass moral fascination with pirates
that spread through communities all over.

However, Cotton Mather was undeterred. He preached that pirates
brought their damnation onto themselves because they knew the
consequences of their actions were evil. He took it upon himself
to warn young people away from the temptation to turn pirate

by quoting biblical commandments and appealing to religious upbringings and habits.

He tore into pirates at the scaffold: "Your actions break your parents' hearts to know that you are so unrepentant and obstinate that none of their pleadings or commands will save you. You are killing them."[258]

It made no difference even if pirates proved repentant. Cotton Mather did not only want to condemn pirates, he wanted to strip them of their humanity. In his eyes, there was no confession or atonement that a pirate could make to reach any level of forgiveness and salvation. "Have not their last speeches proved that their souls are full of rottenness?"[259]

Although pirates could not be saved, at least the preacher could hope to prevent future generations of pirates by reinforcing Puritan lifestyles and traditions. "Children, will you not continue to live religiously? Do not take up a lifeless religion and the irreligious life!"[260]

Religious leaders used pirates as examples of the most depraved and self-indulgent beings ever to walk the earth. Pirates dared to engage in all "sinful compliances" that challenged God's authority. They were "the worst men of all accounts."[261]

A book written by Philip Ashton only fueled these characterizations. Pirates captured Ashton off the coast of Marblehead, Massachusetts, in 1722, while he was on a sailing expedition. He described his captors as unholy degenerates who lived in utter disregard of basic morals, writing, "I soon felt that death would be better than being linked with such a vile crew of miscreants, to whom it was a sport to do mischief. All they did was drink, swear monstrously, say hideous blasphemies, demonstrate an open defiance of Heaven and contempt of Hell itself except for when they were sleeping."[262]

The only time the pirates ever fell into despair for their lives and souls
was when their ship nearly sank during a violent storm. "The poor
wretches had nowhere to go for help, for they were in open defiance
of their Maker and they could have little comfort in their beliefs in
hell…They evidently feared the Almighty, whom they defied, lest
He was to come torture them before their expected time to die. And
though they were so used to cursing and swearing that they could not
stop this habit when they were at risk of dying during this storm. You
could plainly see the inward horror and anguish of their minds, which
was visible also by their behavior. I could hear them crying out in
terror, 'Oh, how I wish I were home!'"[263]

Even though Ashton clearly observed the pirates' terror at the idea
of death and what awaited them in the afterlife, he continued his
message that pirates had no place for God in their lives. Therefore,
God could not accept them.

Despite the denunciations from the religious pulpit, not all God-
fearing people felt that pirates were irredeemable. There were many
who thought that pirates could also be "cured" by making themselves
useful to society. Perhaps it was restlessness at home or idleness at
sea that pushed them into their way of life. The idea was that some
pirates' habits and attitudes could be "softened by the practice of
agriculture, where they would have a permanent home."[264]

The majority of pirates, however, shrugged off this judgement. They
did not see themselves as religious men, so religion simply did not
matter to them. Pirates saw themselves as deliberately removed from
society, especially the church. Cursing, swearing, and blaspheming
were their trademarks. Bartholomew Roberts, also known as
Black Bart, allegedly swore at a British official "like any Devil." In
response, the British official fell to the ground in shock "swearing and
cursing as fast or faster than Roberts, which made the pirates laugh
heartily."[265] Realistically, not everyone (even those in authority) could

follow religious, social, and moral codes all the time. Nevertheless, these so-called "immoral" behaviors were specifically associated with pirates, as if everyone else in society was too pure to lower themselves in such a manner. Newspapers described pirates' speeches as barbarous, foul, scandalous, and insolent.[266] The papers encouraged people to "instruct, admonish, preach, and pray for them" as they led "wicked and vicious lives."[267] The authorities' judgements were so petty and widespread that their complaints reached to the ears of King William III.[268]

CHAPTER 9

A PIRATE'S LIFE FOR US

The legacy of pirates has been stamped permanently into the lexicon of popular culture since the Golden Age of Piracy because of the history and legend that spread thanks to the printing press. The history of pirates such as Captain Kidd was immortalized into *The General History of the Pyrates*, which in turn inspired a whole slew of other publications. In fact, there were popular books written about pirates even before Captain Charles Johnson's seminal publication, which shows that pirates were already gaining popular interest among the people. The man who started this was none other than Daniel Defoe. He incorporated the pirates' voice into his stories, which made up the first novels in the English language. These include *Robinson Crusoe* (1719), *The King of Pirates* (1720), *Captain Singleton* (1720), and *Col. Jack* (1722), just to name a few. Defoe may have used stereotypes or popular social moral standards when writing about pirates, but his pirates did possess the traits of their real-life counterparts, such as creating their own nation and hierarchies.[269]

Books like Defoe's transformed actual people into cultural icons. Pirates fit the description of the "outlaw." Their actions on the high seas were intended to invoke terror, but instead gave generations of people a broad repertoire of characters, situations, and scenarios to bring to life. They were part of the irresistible allure of the criminal hero-villain.[270]

As we have learned, the most significant pirate publication is *A General History of the Pyrates*. The author intended this work to be a history of piracy and tried to stay as close as possible to real life. The author interviewed imprisoned pirates, used source material such as published trials and last dying speeches, and survivors' testimony. However, since pirates did not leave their own actual records, he had many plot holes to fill. This required some embellishment, much of which came from rumors, newspapers, and imagination. The book was so popular that a second volume was immediately produced, published in 1728.

One of the most notable features of the second volume was the inclusion of a chapter about the female pirates, Anne Bonny and Mary Read. Unfortunately, most of it is probably fiction. It is likely that the author had to make up the vast majority of their history, since the only document about them that exists is the transcript of their trial. The trial itself does not contain any information about the women's lives before they entered piracy. Their stories are similar to Daniel Defoe's *Moll Flanders* (1721) and *Roxanna* (1724), which contained "sexual intrigue, out-of-wedlock pregnancies, cross dressing, and general licentious behavior. These were all common tropes of women warriors popularized in ballads."[271] In fact, the stories are so similar that many historians believe that Daniel Defoe is the real author of *A General History of the Pyrates*. It is safe to say that the thirst for knowledge about pirates will never die.

Captain Kidd's legacy continues practically up to present-day legends and popular culture. His infamy as a wanted pirate was widely publicized throughout England and the American colonies, which allowed readers to learn more about pirates than they ever had before. His trial was a sensation that sold out within just a day. Yes, there were other pirates who became just as, if not more, famous. But Kidd was the first pirate to receive that level of attention, which, one could say, set the standard for future fame associated with pirates. More significantly, rumors of his buried treasure have inspired numerous pieces of literature, songs, films, television shows, and even video games. The permeation of pirates in everyday cultural references means that, even if one does not know Kidd by name, one certainly knows of pirate legends that concern treasure and adventure, all of which are attributed to Kidd. Even the novel *Treasure Island*, which created the popular image that people conjure up when they think of pirates, would not exist if it were not for Kidd. His story is one of the main reasons why people came to love pirates for their adventure, mystery, and intrigue.

The Golden Era Pirates

One of the first pieces of literature to feature Captain Kidd as a major plot point was written by Edgar Allen Poe. In 1843, he published a short story called "The Gold Bug," which follows a man named William Legrand, who has returned home to Sullivan's Island in South Carolina after losing his family's fortune. He brings his servant, Jupiter, who finds a gold scarab. Jupiter is a formerly enslaved person who refused to abandon Legrand even after he was freed. Poe probably intended Jupiter to serve as comic relief, but in reality his portrayal of the character is ridiculously stereotyped. Jupiter, convinced it is made of solid gold, shows it to the story's narrator and his employer. The bug bites Legrand and he suddenly becomes mad with an obsession to find hidden treasure. He leads the narrator and Jupiter to a tree and has Jupiter climb it until he finds a skull nailed to a branch. They find another skull, and this time they also find a chest filled with gold coins and jewels.

Legrand tells the narrator that Jupiter brought back a piece of parchment with the gold bug, which he attributed to Captain Kidd.

Poe helped push forward the genre of the pirate adventure story. A little under forty years later, Robert Louis Stevenson appeared on the scene with a little story called "The Sea Cook," or, as we know it and learned about earlier in this book, *Treasure Island*.

Robert Louis Stevenson was born in Scotland in 1850. Scotland had its own colorful pirate history. Glasgow, which is still a major trading port, frequently had pirates either attack merchant ships or sail in to replenish. Stevenson knew about this history and also owned *A*

General History of the Pyrates. Like many other readers, Stevenson
found this book fascinating. One rainy night, he sat down to tell his
son a bedtime story, which gradually turned into the beginning of
his famous novel. The novel depends heavily on *A General History of
the Pyrates.*

Photograph of Robert Louis Stevenson by Henry Walter, 1893
Wiki Commons

Treasure Island was initially published as a weekly serial in 1883, until
it was bound into a single-volume book. Every image we conjure
up of pirates is thanks to this novel: eye patches, peg legs, walking
the plank, X marks the spot, and treasure hunts. Before writing it,

Stevenson had done a tour of the United States and met many Civil War veterans who had eyepatches and peg legs. He reasoned that life as a pirate would be dangerous, so it was safe to assume that many pirates had similar injuries.

Map of Treasure Island, 1883
Beidecke Library, Yale University

Jim, Long John Silver and his Parrot, N.C. Wyeth, 1911
Wiki Commons

Treasure Island was an instant sensation in Britain and America among both children and adult, of both sexes. In the early 1900s, it was adapted as a stage play, and then in several films, when "talking pictures" became the norm. Then, in the 1950s, Disney made a live-action film starring a Cornish actor named Robert Newton. Cornwall, on the west coast of England, has an extensive maritime history, and sailors made up a huge part of the population during the 1700s. Newton's accent was very strong, and is still used as the typical pirate "accent" in subsequent films and television shows. Since Long John Silver was written as an experienced sailor and a pirate, Newton exaggerated his accent and thus created the most iconic type of pirate speech, including the classic "arrrrrr, matey."

Soon after Stevenson's book was released, a fellow Scot named J. M. Barrie wrote his play *Peter Pan*, bringing the hook for a hand idea into popular pirate vocabulary. *Peter Pan* stepped alongside *Treasure Island* and became immensely popular in the Britain and the United States.[272] The perception of pirates changed forever.

Kidd's story does not feature in *Peter Pan*. However, his influence could not have been far from the author's mind, as he is included in a brief mention. The villain of the story, Captain Hook, at one point lays his ship to anchor in a creek named after Kidd: "One green light squinting over Kidd's Creek, which is the near the mouth of the pirate river, marked with the brig, the Jolly Roger, lay low in the water..."[273]

Whether or not it was a conscious decision, Kidd's spirit was everywhere.

"Yo-Ho, Yo-Ho, a Pirate's Life for Me!"

There have been numerous stage and screen adaptations of *Treasure Island* and *Peter Pan*, and they continue to inspire in all sorts of media. *Treasure Island* inspired one of the most popular rides at Disneyland, Pirates of the Caribbean, spawning one of the most successful film franchises in history, starring Johnny Depp as the bumbling Jack Sparrow. Walt Disney created the ride as a concept in the 1950s, not long after the park opened. Disney had plans to expand the park with New Orleans Square and intended to create an underground wax museum walk-through about pirates plundering a place called the Blue Bayou. The project was put on hold when Disney got involved with the World's Fair in the early 1960s.

The World's Fair was an opportunity for Disney to showcase two new technologies they had created for the park: a boat-based ride for It's A Small World, and animatronics used for the Lincoln Showcase. After the fair, the Imagineering team created a new plan for a ride that would incorporate both of these technologies. They went back to the original pirate wax museum idea and decided to create a ride instead. They used the original concept art designed by Mark Davis to create the scenery. Imagineers spent two years designing and building the ride. It opened in 1967 and was an immediate smash hit.

As a frequent Disneyland Annual Pass holder, I make sure to hit Pirates of the Caribbean every time I visit the park. Naturally, I make sure to let my friends and family know that I must go on this ride for research purposes. In fact, I went to Disneyland for my birthday in January 2020 while in the middle of writing this book. Therefore, I can give you more precise details of the experience than anyone else you know. Pirates of the Caribbean starts in a bayou where you board your boat. As you set off, you watch an old man play a banjo on his porch. Then the boat rounds a corner and you are suddenly given a warning about pirates before tumbling down a waterfall into Dead Man's Cove. A warning would not have been uncommon because many eighteenth-century newspapers printed articles to warn colonists about pirate activity offshore. You must be warned as well! Then you are all thrown into the middle of an underwater graveyard of dead pirates and their treasures. This, of course, is fiction, but the image of dead pirates would not be unfamiliar since their bodies were strung up for all to see after executions. Plus, the lore of Captain Kidd's treasure stayed in public memory.

Anyway, after rounding another corner, you all find yourselves caught between battling ships. We don't know who the pirates are fighting, but the ships would have been close enough to damage each other well with both gunshots and cannons. You manage to escape, but then you are in a Caribbean town (I'll guess Port Royal, since that Jamaican city was raided in the corresponding film) that is currently under siege by pirates. Here is where you are treated to songs, dances, pillaging, and plundering. There are fires, cannons, and exploding gunpowder. Finally, the ride ends with a journey up a ramp where you witness stolen treasure before being dropped back off in the bayou.

The ride remained relatively unchanged until the 1990s, when they altered some scenes involving pirates chasing women to having the women carry food, no longer rendering them as objects. (That said, yes, there are still several male pirates chasing women as of the time of this writing.) The biggest change came in 2006 to incorporate the characters from the *Pirates of the Caribbean* film franchise. The ride's plot has also changed. This time, Captain Barbosa raids the city to capture Jack Sparrow, who is on the run. Finally, in 2018 the bride auction scene was changed to sell items to pirates, which is headed by a red-haired female pirate inspired by Anne Bonny.[274] Familiar?

Pirates Plunder Television and Film

The Silver Screen

To step back for a moment, the type of fame generated by these books continued into the twentieth century. By the 1920s, "talking pictures" had arrived and were in full swing, where pirates made their big-screen debut. The first film about pirates was *The Black Pirate*, which came out in 1926. The movie stars Douglas Fairbanks, who was already famous for starring in *The Mask of Zorro*. The plot of the film surrounds a man named the Duke of Arnoldo, who assumes the identity of a pirate known as the Black Pirate to avenge his father's death. In this film, he kills the pirate captain and takes his ship and falls in love with a beautiful princess who has been taken hostage on board. Swordfights ensue, Arnoldo has to walk the plank but manages to retake the ship, and the princess is rescued. Although this film was not well-received by critics, it paved the way for future pirate-centric films.[275]

Other famous pirate films showcased specific legends around these swashbucklers, particularly *The Princess Bride* and the *Pirates of the Caribbean* franchise. The former conveys how pirates had to maintain a certain image to succeed, while the latter goes into the infamous pirate code (among other things, of course).

Those details shine in the 1987 film, *The Princess Bride* (based on the 1973 novel by William Goldman), with the character the Dread Pirate Roberts. This pirate was inspired by the real-life infamous pirates Blackbeard and Bartholomew Roberts, who both relied on their appearance and reputation to ensure their success.

In this film, the heroine, Buttercup, falls in love with Westley (also known as Farm Boy), who must leave her to make enough money for the two of them to marry. Unfortunately, he is declared dead at sea at the hands of the infamous Dread Pirate Roberts, who is notorious for leaving no survivors. In her grief, Buttercup agrees to marry the cruel Prince Humperdink, whose only motivation is to start a war with the rival country, Guilder. He pays kidnappers to abduct Buttercup, with the intention to blame his enemy. She and her captors are soon pursued by a lone ship captained by a "Man in Black," who is referred to as such because of the black clothing and eye mask he wears to create mystery surrounding his origins and identity. He soon reveals himself to be the Dread Pirate Roberts.

After beating the three kidnappers in a battle of skill and wit, the Dread Pirate Roberts takes Buttercup for his own. Then, the twist: Roberts is actually her one true love, Westley!

It turns out that Westley was taken hostage by Roberts, who threatened to kill him "in the morning" every night over a period of time. Eventually it was revealed that Roberts did not plan to kill him. Quite the opposite, in fact. It turned out that Roberts wanted to retire with his riches. "I'm not the real Dread Pirate Roberts," he said to Westley. "My name is Ryan." It turns out that Ryan had inherited his ship from the previous Dread Pirate Roberts, just as Westley was set to do after serving as his valet for three years. The original Dread Pirate Roberts had been retired for over fifteen years and was living like a king in Patagonia. However, the most significant part of this tale was this: "The name was the important thing to inspire the necessary fear. You see, no one would surrender to the Dread Pirate Westley."[276]

This is reminiscent of Blackbeard, who changed his real (from Edward Teach) for his role and made sure that he looked the part with a smoking beard. *The Princess Bride* certainly reminds us that it is not the actual criminal we admire and fear, but the image that they send to the public.[277]

Pirates of the Caribbean: The Curse of the Black Pearl brings out another great pirate trope. In the film, a Royal Navy captain's daughter, Elizabeth Swann, is kidnapped by pirates in Port Royal, Jamaica, because they believe she has the last Aztec gold coin from one of their prizes. Once they spent the coins, they were cursed to survive in a living purgatory. To break the curse, they need the final coin. When they break into her home to kidnap her, she says, "I invoke the right of parley. According to the Code of the Brethren set down by pirates Morgan and Bartholomew, you have to take me to your captain…If an adversary demands parley, you can do them no harm until the parley is complete."

They agree and take her to their captain, Barbossa, and the film's adventure begins. Throughout, pirates are told to "keep to the code" if something goes wrong. In this case, the particular code they were referring to was to leave behind any man who fell behind. This particular example of a pirates' code comes from legend, but is likely included to simply drive the movie's plot.

The mention of the Pirates' Code is a solid piece of maritime and pirate history from the early modern period. The pirates that Elizabeth referred to were most likely Bartholomew Portugues and Henry Morgan (who were actually privateers) active in the late 1600s Caribbean.

Black Sails

In 2015, the TV show *Black Sails* debuted. In short, it attempts to retell the history of piracy in the Caribbean by blending fact and fiction. The show serves as a prequel to *Treasure Island* by telling the story of Captain Flint and the origins of Long John Silver. Many of the main characters, such as Jack Rackham, Charles Vane, and Anne Bonny, are based on their historical counterparts. The show's attention to detail is impressive, and it portrays the realistic logistics of what it is to be a pirate. The opening scene in the pilot is an attack in which pirates plunder a ship. There is screaming and sword-fighting, false teeth made to look like fangs, and make-up to appear even more frightening. Once the ship surrenders, the pirate captain, Flint, assigns his men to check out the inventory, keep the captured crew quiet, and to speak to the captain. This is a far cry from typical cinema in which pirates like to fight, steal, and kill.

The show is set during the Golden Age of Piracy, in 1715 to be precise, which is about twenty years before *Treasure Island* takes place. The first season plot arc involves the capture of the Spanish ship *Urca de Lima*, which is said to carry a vast quantity of treasure. Treasure, as we imagine it in the form of gold and jewels, did not actually exist. However, the *Urca de Lima* was a real part of a 1715

Spanish fleet that was known to carry chests of silver. It also carried vanilla, chocolate, and incense resin, which were all extremely valuable. Unfortunately, the *Urca de Lima* and the rest of the fleet sank in a storm on the way from Havana to Spain.[278]

The show also blends fact and fiction with its central characters. Anne Bonny and her husband Jack Rackham are major characters in the ensemble cast. Anne Bonny is depicted as a fiery, fierce, and independent woman, consistent with descriptions of her historical counterpart. Rackham has a posh accent and the flamboyant air of an over-educated snob (by pirates' standards), a nod to the historic Rackham's reputation for having a good education and a love of fine clothing. He was not known as Calico Jack for nothing!

Charles Vane (one of the main antagonists on the show) enters into a rivalry with Flint, very much matching his historical counterpart. Vane is portrayed as cruel and corrupt in the show. In real life, Rackham did sail with Vane for a time as his quartermaster, although that was before he met Anne Bonny. His particularly cruel associate, Ned Low, joins the show in the second season. Benjamin Hornigold, the famed "pirate king" who transformed Nassau into a fully-functioning pirate city, has a role on the show to assist Captain Flint even though he has long been retired. In real life, Vane was his target when Hornigold acted as a pirate hunter for a period of time.[279]

What is truly unique about *Black Sails* is its openness in portraying the often-ignored queer realities of pirate ships. Captain Flint, as we know him in the first season, is everything from Stevenson's book: cunning, ruthless, and a brilliant strategist. He has a secret, however, which is revealed in the second season. (Spoiler alert!) The real reason why he turned pirate was that his English nobleman lover was taken from him during his stint in the Royal Navy. One of the other main characters, Max, is a prostitute on the island and strikes up a relationship with Anne Bonny. This mirrors Anne Bonny and

Mary Read's real-life relationship. Similar to history, Anne and Jack's marriage becomes a trio as Max becomes involved with both of them. *Black Sails* stands out as a show for dramatizing the historical realities of piracy and especially for bringing piracy's oft-ignored queerness to the forefront.

Pirate Superstitions

Another pirate myth that the film franchise stayed close to was that of the Flying Dutchman and Davy Jones' Locker. In the film, the Flying Dutchman is captained by Davy Jones, who has been cursed to live forever. The Flying Dutchman is known in sailing lore as a ghost ship that is doomed to sail the seas for all eternity. The first instance of this comes from John MacDonald's *Travels in Various Parts of Europe, Asia, and Africa During a Series of Thirty Years and Upward*: "The weather was so stormy that the sailors said they saw the Flying Dutchman. The common story is that this Dutchman came to the Cape in distress of weather and wanted to get into harbor but could not get a pilot to conduct her and was lost and that ever since in very bad weather her vision appears."[280]

Flying Dutchman by Albert Pinkham Ryder, c. 1896
Wiki Commons

The phrase "Davy Jones's Locker" has been used in history and popular culture. As we learned at the beginning of the book, the origin of the phrase is unknown, but it was prevalent in sailors' superstitions with several different meanings. Davy Jones's Locker was known as the devil disguised as the spirit of the sea.[281] Others said it was the grave of sailors who died in open water. The term may have originated from the biblical story about Jonah[282] and the whale in that the "locker" (the whale) was "kept and confined." A 1628 publication of sermons mentions this reference in regard to the death of sailors. "Of any, that has been in extreme peril, we use to say he has been where Jonah was…" The general tradition, which may

have come from Norway, came to be known as, "If a sailor is killed
in a sea-skirmish, or falls overboard and is drowned, or any other
fatality occurs that keeps his remains in the 'great deep,' his surviving
crew-mates speak about him as one who has been sent to Davy
Jones' Locker."[283]

One of the first instances of the phrase being used in writing comes
from the book *Four Years Voyages of Capt. George Roberts*, by Daniel
Defoe. The book recounts how Roberts was attacked by the violent
pirate, Edward Low. When it appeared that Roberts was at risk of
being taken, one of the crew members "…told them they should not,
for he would toss them all into Davy Jones' Locker if they did."[284]

The term was also used in common newspapers well into the
nineteenth century. In 1819, a ship called the *Socorro* sailed out of
Campeche, Mexico, and attacked an English ship off the coast of
Cuba. When the second-in-command of the *Socorro* went aboard
the English ship, he declared "he would be shown where the money
was hidden or he would send the whole of the [crew to] Davy Jones'
Locker." The event turned into a fight, but in the end the *Socorro*
only made off with a barrel of beef and a barrel of pork, four bags
of break, one hundred pounds of rice, some candles, and other
practical items.[285]

The other superstition, the Flying Dutchman, was also born out of
fear. Sailors were so afraid of dying at sea that many of them would
not even learn how to swim. They did not want to get tempted by
the water. It was considered bad luck for the whole ship if a sailor fell
into the sea and drowned at the beginning of a voyage.[286] Perhaps this
is what caused the Flying Dutchman to become cursed to sail for all
eternity, or maybe Davy Jones was one who died too early in a voyage
and in his rage continued to kill sailors as his vengeance.

Illustration of Davy Jones Sitting on his Locker by John Tenniel, 1892
Wiki Commons

Other Popular Media

Video Games

In 2013, the widely popular action-adventure video game series
Assassin's Creed by Ubisoft released a new installment: *Black Flag*.
This game series takes place over several periods of history around
the world. The game has had several series play out during the

Third Crusade, Italian Renaissance, the Colonial Era (including the American Revolution), French Revolution, Ming Dynasty, Victorian Era, Sikh Empire, October Revolution in Russia, Ptolemaic Egypt, the Peloponnesian War, and the Spanish Inquisition.

This fourth volume of *Assassin's Creed* is set during the Golden Age of Piracy between 1713 and 1715. The game includes four missions in which the player has to find pieces of a fictional map that belonged to Captain Kidd, which he gave to four members of his crew for safekeeping. Once the four pieces were found, the location of Kidd's treasure would be revealed.

The director, Ashraf Ismail, made sure to position the game in the most historically accurate way possible. There would be no parrots on the shoulders, no Kraken, and no "theme park shine" like *Pirates of the Caribbean*. He intended the game to be grittier and more authentic to the dark, rough reality of the era. In previous series, fatal fights led to immediate persecution by authorities. In Volume IV, however, this trope has been tossed out because Ismail reasoned that navigating the ocean island to island "makes this sort of 'worldwide alert' illogical."[287]

The geography is stunningly accurate as well. *Assassin's Creed IV* covers all of the Caribbean in astonishing detail. The game also centers around the three main areas of pirate activity in the Caribbean: Jamaica, Cuba, and, of course, Nassau. Nassau is the main hub because pirates, such as Benjamin Hornigold, Charles Vane, Jack Rackham, and Blackbeard (all of whom are characters in the game), were mostly linked to that island.[288] The game also took great care to get the landscape correct. The artists recreated the Caribbean Sea and made sure it was "peppered with islands," to add to the game's adventure, but also to stay authentic to the challenges of sailing throughout the Caribbean.[289]

The game is most impressive in the way it stayed true to the historical context. Taking their cue from pirates who created their own societies, *Black Flag* is "all about embracing freedom and carving your own path through the world."[290] The game even took measures to make it "less violent than its predecessors." *Black Flag* had fewer fights and stabbings to emulate the reality of pirates during the Golden Age of Piracy.

The Treaty of Utrecht, in particular, frames the game. The Treaty ended the War of Spanish Succession, which caused newly unemployed privateers to continue their work as pirates. The game used the historical context, albeit with a bit of liberty in terms of the timeline. The designers chose these pirates because the sailors were all of British origin and were either directly associated with the War of Spanish Succession as privateers, or were at least caught up in the displacement, and subsequently organized bands of pirates.

Modern-Day "Shanties"

Pirates haven't just inspired video games. A new genre of music has slowly developed over time: pirate metal. A subgenre of heavy metal, dozens of bands have chosen to play under this flag, which has been described as "part musical theater and part head-banging riffage."[291] The first band to release a pirate-themed metal album was Running Wild in 1987 with their album *Under the Jolly Roger*. The lead singer and guitarist, Rolf Kasparek, had an interest in pirates and, after reading about them for a time, decided to take what he learned and put it into a musical context.[292] Since the 1980s, the genre has grown to incorporate traditional sea shanties played on distorted guitars along with full death-metal riffs. The songs are full of tales of murder and mayhem taken from pirate folklore.

One of the best-known groups is Alestorm, a Scottish band that formed in 2004 under the leadership of lead singer, Christopher Bowes. The style came to them pretty simply. While jamming together, they started singing some sea shanties heavy-metal style. The band members had a lot of fun with it and decided to keep going. They thought it might be a funny way to get noticed. Plus, "pirates are cool," said Bowes.[293] After releasing a song on Myspace, they were signed by Napalm Records, one of the largest heavy metal record labels in the world.[294] Their first album, a concept project called *Captain Morgan's Revenge*, had more of a traditional heavy metal sound, while their second release, *Black Sails at Midnight*, incorporated more string, brass, and folk arrangements to lean into traditional sea shanties.

Their lyrics lean more toward pirate fantasies, such as quests for buried treasure. One of their first hits on *Captain Morgan's Revenge*, "Over the Seas," features the following lyrics:

> "Many moons ago, in a faraway land
> We met an old man with a hook for a hand
> He showed us a map that led to treasure untold
> He said 'I'll give ye the map, if ye give me some gold.'"[295]

"We're more like Disney pirates," Bowes said, describing himself and his bandmates. "My favorite pirate is probably Johnny Depp, [who] embodies what piracy is all about for me. Getting drunk and being a badass."[296]

Like the ballads and sea shanties of the seventeenth and eighteenth centuries, songs continue to immortalize the lives and legends of Golden Age pirates.

Bleeding into the Mainstream

Books, television, film, myths, and music have had such an impact that the influence of pirates has bled further into the mainstream. People do not want to just read about, watch, or listen to pirates. They want to become them.

In the United States, Renaissance Fairs are popular weekend events that pop up in the autumn all across the country. These weekends are a time for people to cast the modern day aside, wear corsets and breeches of old, visit artisans, attend jousts, and make merry with ale and turkey legs. Not only that, nearly 130 pirate festivals have popped up all over the United States, Canada, and United Kingdom year-round.[297] One example is Long Beach, California, which hosts the Pirate Invasion every year. According to the website, this is a time when a thousand costumed pirates and three ships "will descend on the Shoreline Park for two days of all things Pirate. Sword fights, cannon and musket battles, a treasure hunt, adult and children's costume contest, an interactive kid's zone, arts and crafts vendors, live and DJ entertainment on our stages, food and grog, a living history encampment, and a live production of *Treasure Island*."

Crowds of over fifty thousand people swarm the venue over a period of two days.[298] If there are no pirate festivals nearby, most Renaissance Fairs will have a pirate-themed weekend, which features similar events and themes. One will see a multitude of Jack Sparrows.

To create even more authenticity and fun, people have become well-versed in how to speak "pirate." September 19 has become known as International Talk Like A Pirate Day. Oregon residents John Baur and Mark Summers came up with the idea while playing tennis one day in 1995. They chose September 19 because it was Mark's ex-wife's

birthday, which was easy for them to remember. The "holiday" was
merely a joke between two friends until the award-winning humor
columnist, Dave Barry, published an article about them, which
became syndicated. Thanks to the internet, the holiday became
an international interest.[299] International Talk Like A Pirate Day
launched in 2002.

Pop culture lexicon has even showed up in news stories about
contemporary pirate problems. During the early twenty-first century,
pirates out of Somalia terrorized ships around the world. News
articles made references to pop culture when describing these acts of
piracy. In 2005, *Time Magazine* reported that pirate attacks had risen
by over thirty incidences between 2004 and 2005 with ferocity "like
a scene from a Johnny Depp movie." At the time of publication, the
article predicted that worldwide pirate incidents would climb to over
three hundred.[300] A 2010 *Time Magazine* article began, "This time
last year Somali pirates dominated headlines in the US. The hijacking
of the Maersk Alabama, a tanker captained by an American, led to a
made-for-Hollywood intervention by sharp-shooting Navy SEALS
and triggered a media frenzy about the rise of piracy off the Horn
of Africa."[301]

Interestingly enough, Hollywood did, in fact, turn this into a film.
In 2013, *Captain Phillips* aired, which starred Tom Hanks in the
titular role.

Fictionalized characters such as Stevenson's Long John Silver and
Barrie's Captain Hook permeated our perception of history to the
point where someone as outrageous as Blackbeard can only be
assumed to be fiction. Stories about pirates, both fact and fiction,
became so popular that people began to learn about pirates through

tales rather than history lessons.[302] No historical "villain" or "hero" has had such a lasting impact on culture as real-life pirates. Their memory will forever live on.

CONCLUSION

THE END OF PIRACY
AND ITS LEGACY

B y the late 1720s, the Golden Age of Piracy was waning fast. In 1718 and 1723, Charleston and Newport both held two of the largest mass executions in the history of early America.[303] Colonists accepted that the age of pirates was over and that they had no choice but to bend to Britain's will.

All of the infamous (and most violent) pirate leaders were dead by 1726—Captain Kidd, Blackbeard, Jack Rackham, Charles Vane, Stede Bonnet, Bartholomew Roberts, Edward Low, and William Fly among others.[304] The Royal Navy was flourishing more than ever, and it was impossible for pirates to continue sailing and pirating freely. Nassau was no longer the pirate republic they once knew. Organized piracy no longer existed.

After 1730, traditional piracy had been all but eradicated. Wars began to break out in the 1730s and 1740s, which brought warships back into the ocean. They required able seamen who were extremely skilled sailors and brave fighters. Former pirates had a new safety net to fall into. There would be no risk of a hanging, let alone arrest. It would be almost as if their life as a pirate had never existed.

In 1739, a war between Britain and Spain called the War of Jenkins Ear broke out and took place mostly at sea, requiring skilled sailors and fighters. Britain called upon any former pirates and told them they had a chance to continue their line of work in relative safety. Former pirates who had scattered after the deaths of Blackbeard and William Fly, those inspired by them, and other former pirate captains were glad to reenter into legitimate maritime work. Even better, their pay would be comparable to their earnings as pirates. As privateers, they could keep all of the loot they captured on attacked ships.

To some, particularly merchants and some sailing communities, and perhaps even some pirates themselves, it was a relief.

To others, the end of piracy was a period of mourning. It was a time long gone that would fade into the murky waters of memory.

However, one light shone upon the legacy of pirates: Captain Charles Johnson's *A General History of the Pyrates*. Perhaps the author knew that the end was nigh and realized that he needed to preserve their legacy. Maybe with the increasing deaths of famous pirate captains, the author and his publisher saw a lucrative opportunity. Whatever the reason, the book was a success. It preserved the stories of all the above-mentioned pirates forever.

Kidd's story heightened fascination for pirates. He was the first whose manhunt was meticulously documented for nearly two years. People were obsessed with this sailor who remained elusive to capture. Not long after, reports of his buried treasure hit the news, which spurred a heightened interest in this figure. What riches were there and where could the cache be found? This became a mystery that would last for centuries.

Many pirates who followed Kidd became inspirational in their own right. Many sailors were born poor, but thanks to piracy, they were able to rise to the top of the social ladder through their quick accumulation of wealth. Here was proof that someone born poor did not need to die poor. Until this point, the idea of rising through the ranks of society was unheard of outside of folk tales. Not only that, piracy sounded *fun*. Britain and Colonial America had strict moral and ethical laws that condemned swearing, drunkenness, and all kinds of lewd behavior. Even hair and clothing styles were prisoner to social conventions! Not for pirates, however. Stolen fine fabrics allowed pirates to dress better than other sailors. Blackbeard deliberately grew his hair long to shock people. Jack Rackham wore the nicest clothes he could. Pirates were not beholden to the law or their country. They were completely free to sail all over the world without answering to anybody but themselves. They had their own cities where they were at liberty to swear and drink in public without consequences. On land, sex was abundant because they could afford any prostitute they desired, syphilis be damned. These people were subverting all the rules of society and flaunting their rebellion with glee.

Women especially could see pirates as defiant of society's strict boundaries. Anne Bonny and Mary Read were a good example. Here were women who dressed as men, swore like the worst of them, and fought harder and braver than anyone else. They were direct proof that women were capable of much more than rearing children and keeping a house in order.

Pirates were also the epitome of grand adventure. *Treasure Island*, as discussed throughout this book, mainstreamed pirates. Nearly thirty years after the book was published, it was still a newsworthy novel. In 1907, an essay was written about why the novel should be given to children. The essay praised the book for its emphasis on the hero. That is, perhaps, why it became such a phenomenon. "[T]he world loves a hero, because there is a heroic strain in all normal men and women. Every such man or woman would like to be a hero, but many are shut off from heroism in any form dramatic enough to make it real for them, even while they are leading lives which are heroic in quiet self-denial and hidden self-effacement. To such men and women the description of the heroic life is a satisfaction and an inspiration; they hunger and thirst for it in spirit just as the body hungers and thirsts, and their desire for it is as wholesome as any other desire."[305]

Though Jim Hawkins was the hero of the novel for fighting pirates, those men came to be worshipped also because they were able to stick it to the man and make something of themselves (however exploitatively it might have been).

Pirates, like death and taxes, are always a certainty. Piracy continues to flourish today. In 2019, the ocean off West Africa became the most dangerous area in the world for ships because piracy continues to flourish there. Just like pirates of old, they are known for robbery, but now even more so for hijacking and kidnapping (just like in the historical film *Captain Phillips*, mentioned in the previous chapter). In 2013, there were no fewer than 112 pirate attacks in West African waters. Nigerian gas and oil tankers have been the main target.

Just like the pirates we have learned about, these people today are motivated by political problems, shaky law enforcement, and the need for more money. Many younger people are attracted to piracy because of high unemployment rates on land. Africa's bountiful resources attract pirates who know that they will have excellent merchant prey on their horizon. Just as it was almost three hundred years ago, it is difficult to stop these pirates. That would require more armed ships and international navies, which would make ocean travel very complicated for the region.[306]

Similar to the 1700s, today's pirates bring back resources and wealth to their homes from the goods that they steal. In a way, today's views of pirates are the same as they have been since the Golden Age of Piracy. They were the Robin Hoods of their time, stealing banned goods from wealthy merchants and selling them back to colonies in want and need. They refused to bow down to social norms and law. Piratical acts were joyously illicit.[307] These people defied the war against them, and even in death, their tales continue to be told, much like the Greek epics.

Pirates will be part of our mainstream media for a long time to come. As of the writing of this book, ABC Productions has announced it purchased the rights to an article called "The Revenge of Anne and Mary" to create a new television show about these women.[308] Another film will also join the Pirates of the Caribbean franchise, only this time the story will be about a female swashbuckler.[309] These projects are set to progress pop culture piracy by giving female pirates their due.

Those who sail under the black flag will never be gone. Their allure will never die. So pour yourself a glass of rum, raise it to the sky, and give a "yo-ho!"

BIBLIOGRAPHY

Primary Sources

Manuscript Sources

British Library, London, UK

Add. MS 61620/115b-156. "Petition of Pirate Wives." 1701.

IOR/H/36, "Extract of an Eminent Indian Merchant at Suratt Viz. Agapery." *India Office Records*. April 16, 1698.

IOR/H/36, "To Their Excellencies The Lords Justices of England The Humble Petition of the Governour & Company of Merchants of London trading into the East Indies." *India Office Records*. September 21, 1699.

RP 8780, "Autograph Letter Signed to Jonathan Dickinson, discussing trade matters including an account of the remnants of Captain Kidd's crew and tales of buried treasure." Philadelphia, July 9, 1699.

Jamaica National Library, Kingston, Jamaica

MS 60, "An Act against tipling, cursing, and swearing." *Jamaica Council Minutes* 1. November 8, 1664.

MS 60, "An Act Declaring the Laws of England in force in this Island passed to the Council." *Jamaica Council Minutes* 1. November 10, 1664.

MS 60, "At a Council Held at St. Jago de la Vega," *Jamaica Council Minutes* 3. March 14, 1674.

MS 60, "The Deposition of John Yardley Master to the Ketch John's Adventure." *Jamaica Council Minutes* 3. July 5, 1676.

MS 60, "At a Council Holden at St Jago de la Vega on Thursday May 3rd 1688." *Jamaica Council Minutes* 5, 1683-1688.

The National Archives Kew, UK

CO 139/8 Colonial Office and predecessors, *Act of Assembly Passed in the Island of Jamaica from 1681-1737 Inclusive*. London, 1738.

HCA 1/112, "Menu Respecting Execution Dock." *Execution Dock Papers*. July 18, 1806.

HO 45/19503, "Pardons: Questions of free pardon to Captain Kidd (executed in 1701)," *Home Office Records*, 1936-1944.

MEPO 2/9166 "Attempt to raise money to finance expeditions to search for Captain Kidd's Treasure in in the China Seas, 1951-1953."

Warrant to insert Robert Seely in the next general pardon for the poor convicts of Newgate for piracy, without condition for transportation, in compassion for his tender years." *State Papers*, National Archives, 1699.

SP 44/350, Secretaries of State: State Papers: Entry Books, Warrants, and Passes, Vernon, Manchester, and Hedges, 1698-1704. "Warrant to Chief Justice Holt and Sir Charl. Hedges, judge of the Admiralty Court." July 4, 1700.

"Warrants to Dr. Geo. Oxenden." May 26, 1701.

Calendar of State Papers Domestic: William III

"By the King, A Proclamation." Volume 243, March 6, 1701.

Calendar of State Papers: Colonial Series, America and the West Indies

Volume 10, 1677–1680

Volume 11, 1681–1684

Volume 12, 1685–1688

Volume 13, 1689–1692

Volume 15, 1696–1697

Volume 16, 1697–1698

Volume 17, 1699

Volume 18, 1700

Volume 19, 1701

Volume 20, 1702

Volume 22, 1704–1705

Volume 23, 1706–1708

Volume 29, 1716–1717

Volume 30, 1717–1718

Volume 31, 1719–1720

Volume 33, 1722–1723

Volume 34, 1724–1725

Volume 37, 1730

Volume 38, 1731

Volume 42, 1735–1736

Newspapers and Magazines

American

Boston Gazette

Boston News-Letter

Haverhill Gazette

Morning Herald

New-York Gazette

New-York Journal

Original Weekly Journal

Pennsylvania Chronicle

Salem Gazette

Semi-Weekly Eagle

The American Weekly Mercury

The Morning Chronicle

The Speaker: The Liberal Review

Weekly Rehearsal

British

Belgravia: A London Magazine

British Journal

Daily Journal

Daily Post

Diary or Woodfall's Register

English Post Giving an Authentick Account of the Transactions of the World Foreign and Domestick

Essex Gazette

General Evening Post

Ladies' Home Journal

London Journal

London Post and General Advertiser

London Post with Intelligence Foreign and Domestick

Monthly Chronicle

National Magazine

Post Boy

Public Ledger

St. George's Chronicle and Grenada Gazette

The Idler

Times

Weekly Journal or British Gazetteer

Weekly Journal or Saturday's Post

Caribbean

Bermuda Gazette

Jamaica Weekly Courant

Published Materials

A Person of Quality. *A Full Account of the Proceedings in Relation to Capt. Kidd in Two Letters*, London, 1701.

Adams, Reverend John. *The Flowers of Modern History*. Dublin, 1789.

Anonymous. *The liues, apprehensions, arraignments, and executions, the 19 late pyrates Namely: Capt. Harris, Jennings, Loncastle, Downes, Haulsey, and their companies. As they were severely indited on St. Margarets Hill in Southwarke, on the 22 of December last, and executed Fryday the following*. London, 1609.

Ashton, Philipp. *Ashton's Memorial: Or an Authentick Account of the Strange Adventures and Signal Deliverances of Mr. Philip Ashton*. London, 1722.

Baer, Joel H. *British Piracy in the Golden Age: History and Interpretation 1660-1730*. Vols. I-IV. London: Routledge, 2007.

Barrie, JM. *Peter Pan in the Complete Works of JM Barrie*. Sussex: Delphi Classics, 2015.

Cooper, Anthony Asher Third Earl of the Shaftesbury. *Characteristics of Men, Manners, Opinions, Times*. London, 1711. Ed. Lawrence Klein. Cambridge, 1999.

Defoe, Daniel. *The Four Voyages of Capt. George Roberts*. London, 1726.

Emyln, Sollum. *A Complete Collection of State-Trials and Proceedings for High-Treason, and Other Misdemeanours; The Fourth Edition: Commencing with the Eleventh Year of the Reign of King George III*. London, 1730.

Exquemelin, Alexander. *The History of the Buccaneers of America*. London, 1771 edition.

Farmer, John Stephen. *Slang and Its Analogues Past and Present* II. 1891.

Foote, Henry Wilder. *Annals of King's Chapel from the Puritan Age of New England to the Present Day* I. Boston, 1900.

Grose, Francis. *Dictionary of the Vulgar Tongue*. London, 1788.

Leslie, Charles. *A New History of Jamaica, from the Earliest Accounts to the Taking of Porto Bello by Vice-Admiral Vernon*. London, 1740.

Johnson, Captain Charles. *A General History of the Pyrates*. Edited by Manuel Schoenhorn. Dover, 1999.

Jones, Hugh. *The Present State of Virginia, Giving a particular and short Account of the Indian, English, and Negroe Inhabitants of that Colony*. London, 1724.

MacDonald, John. Travels in Various Parts of Europe, Asia, and Africa During a Series of Thirty Years and Upward. London, 1790.

Maggs Brothers. "An Elegy of Captain Kidd who was Executed at Execution-Dock, on Friday the 23rd of this Instant May, 1701." *Proclamations against Piracy 1603-1701*. London [No Date].

Mather, Cotton. *The Diary of Cotton Mather*, 1681-1708. Boston, 1911.

Sewall, Samuel. *The Diary of Samuel Sewall, 1674-1729 II*. Boston: Massachusetts Historical Society, 1878.

Stevenson, Robert Louis. *Treasure Island*. London: Alma Classics. Reprint Edition, 2015.

Thornbury, Walter. "The Thames Tunnel, Ratcliffe Highway, and Wapping." *Old and New London: Volume 2*, London, 1878.

The Tryals of Joseph Dawson, Edward Forseith, William May, William Bishop, James Lewis, and John Sparkes for several Piracy and Robberies by them committed, in the Company of Every the Grand Pirate, near the Coasts of the East-Indies; and several other Places on the Seas. London, 1696.

The Arraignment, Tryal, and Condemnation of Captain William Kidd for Murther and Piracy, upon Six several Indictments. London, 1701.

An Extract Abridgement of all the Tryals, Not omitting and Material Passage therein, relating to High Treasons, Piracies, &c. in the reigns of the Late King William III of Glorious Memory, and of our Present Gracious Sovereign Queen Anne, London, 1703.

The Tryals of Major Stede Bonnet and Other Pirates Who were all condemn'd for Piracy. London, 1719.

A Compleat Collection of Remarkable Tryals, of the most Notorious Malefactors, at the Sessions-House in the Old-Bailey, from the Year 1706, to the last Sessions, 1720, London, 1721.

Compleat Set of St. James's Journals.

Remarks upon the Tryal of Capt. Thomas Green and his Crew (London, 1705); *A Full and Exact Account of the Tryal of Pyrates, Lately Taken by Captain Ogle, on Board the Swallow Man of War, on the Coast of Guinea,* London, 1723.

An Account of the Conduct and Proceedings of the late John Gow, alias Smith, Captain of the late Pirates, Executed for Murther and Piracy Committed on Board the George Gally, afterwards call'd the Revenge; with A Relation of all the horrid Murthers they committed in Cold Blood, London, 1725.

A Discourse of the Laws Relating to Pirates and Piracies, and the Marine Affairs of Great Britain. London, 1726.

A Complete Collection of State-Trials and Proceedings upon High-Treason, and other Crimes and Misdemeanours; from the Reign of King Richard II to the End of the Reign of King George I, London, 1730.

A Collection of the Most Remarkable Trials of Persons for High-Treason, Murder, Rapes, Heresy, Bigamy, Burglary, and other Crimes and Misdemeanours, London, 1734.

The Ordinary of Newgate's Account of the Behavior, Confession, and Dying Words of Capt. Joseph Halsey, Who was executed at Execution-Dock on Wednesday the 14th of March, 1759, For the murder of Daniel Davidson, London, 1759.

"The Confession of Walter Kennedy, who was condemn'd at the Sessions of the Admiralty for that he with other Pirates, had robb'd and plunder'd the Ship called the Loyal Rover, etc.," *A Select and Impartial Account of the Lives, Behavior, and the Dying Words of the most Remarkable Convicts from the Year 1700, to the present Time* I, London, 1760.

"The Behavior, Confession, and Dying Words of Capt. John Massey, who was Executed at Execution Dock, on Friday the 26th of July 1723, for Piracy on the High-Seas, near St. James's Island on the Coast of North Africa," *A*

Select and Impartial Account of the Lives, Behavior, and the Dying Words of the most Remarkable Convicts from the Year 1700, to the present Time I, London, 1760.

"Captain Kidd: A Noted Pirate, who Hanged at Execution Dock in England." Boston, between 1775 and 1810.

Executive Journals of the Council of Virginia, Vol. II. Richmond, 1925.

Online Sources

Grose, Francis. *1811 Dictionary of the Vulgar Tongue*, extracted from *Project Gutenberg*. https://archive.org/details/1811dictionaryof05402gut accessed April 5 2020.

Ordinary of Newgate, "Ordinary's Accounts: Biographies of Executed Criminals," *London Lives*, http://www.londonlives.org/browse. jsp?div=OA172312232312230005, accessed October 28, 2019.

"Ordinary of Newgate's Accounts," The Proceedings of the Old Bailey: London's Central Criminal Court, 1674–1913, 2018. https://www. oldbaileyonline.org/static/Ordinarys-accounts.jsp#. Accessed August 19, 2020.

Old Bailey Online, The Trial of Roger Mean, John Russell, Edward Tankard, May 1722, accessed July 2020. www.oldbaileyonline.org.

Old Bailey Online, The Trial of Robert Coyle, February 1737, accessed November 12, 2014, www.oldbaileyonline.org.

Old Bailey Online, Ordinary of Newgate's Account, February 1950, accessed July 2020. www.oldbaileyonline.org.

Old Bailey Online, The Trial of James Lowrey, February 1751, accessed November 12, 2014, www.oldbaileyonline.org.

Newgate Calendar, "Philip Roche, Executed on the 5th of August 1723, for many Murders on the High Seas and Piracy." Newgate Calendar, August 22, 1723. http://www.exclassics.com/newgate/ng168.htm, accessed October 20, 2019.

Secondary Sources

Books

Armitage, David and Braddock, Michael. *The British Atlantic World, 1500–1800*. Basingstoke: Red Globe Press, 2009.

Bacchilega, Cristina and Brown, Marie Alohalani. *The Penguin Book of Mermaids*. New York: Penguin Classics, 2019.

Bannet, Eve Taylor. *Transatlantic Stories and the History of Reading, 1720–1810*. Cambridge: Cambridge University Press, 2011.

Beattie, J.M. *Crime and the Courts in England, 1660-1800*. Oxford: Oxford University Press, 1986.

Benton, Lauren, *A Search for Sovereignty: Law and Geography in European Empires, 1400-1900*. Cambridge: Cambridge University Press, 2009.

Bolster, Jeffrey W. *Black Jacks: African American Seamen in the Age of Sail*. Cambridge: Harvard University Press, 1997.

Brewer, John. *The Pleasures of Imagination: English Culture in the Eighteenth Century*. London: Farrar, Straus, and Giroux, 1997.

Brooks, Bayus B. *Quest for Blackbeard: The True Story of Edward Thache and His World*. Lulu.com, 2020. Kindle.

Bryson, Anna. *From Courtesy to Civility: Changing Codes of Conduct in Early Modern England*. Oxford: Oxford University Press, 1998.

Burg, B.R. *Sodomy and the Pirate Tradition: English Sea Rovers in the Seventeenth-Century Caribbean*. New York: New York University Press, 1995.

Burgess Jr., Douglas. *The Politics of Piracy: Crime and Civil Disobedience in Colonial America*. Lebanon: ForeEdge, 2014.

Cave, Roderick. *Printing and the Book Trade in the West Indies*. London: Pindar Press, 1987.

Cohen, Daniel A. *Pillars of Salt, Monuments of Grace: New England Crime Literature and the Origins of American Popular Culture, 1674-1860.* Oxford: Oxford University Press, 1993.

Cordingly, David: *Seafaring Women: Adventures of Pirate Queens, Female Stowaways, and Sailors' Wives.* New York: Random House, 2001.

—— *Under the Black Flag: The Romance and Reality of Life Among the Pirates.* New York: Random House, 2006.

Cockburn, J.S. *Crime in England, 1550-1800.* Princeton: Princeton University Press, 1977.

Crawford, Michael J. *The Autobiography of a Yankee Mariner: Christopher Prince and the American Revolution.* Washington DC: Brassey's Inc., 2002.

Darby, Madge. *Waeppa's People: History of Wapping.* Colchester: Connor & Butler, 1988.

Duncan, Martha Grace. *Romantic Outlaws, Beloved Prisons: The Unconscious Meanings of Crime and Punishment.* New York: New York University Press, 1996.

Earle, Peter. *The Pirate Wars: Pirates vs. the Legitimate Navies of the World.* London: Thomas Dunne Books, 2004.

Foucault, Michael. *Discipline and Punish: The Birth of the Prison.* Translated by Alan Sheridan. New York: Vintage Books, 1995.

Games, Alison. *Migrations and Origins of the English Atlantic World.* Cambridge: Harvard University Press, 2001.

Green, Thomas Andrew. *Verdict According to Conscience: Perspectives of the New English Criminal Trial Jury, 1200-1800.* Chicago: University of Chicago Press, 1985.

Hanna, Mark. *Pirate Nests and the Rise of the British Empire, 1570-1730.* Chapel Hill: University of North Carolina Press, 2015.

Harris, Graham. *Treasure and Intrigue: The Legacy of Captain Kidd.* Toronto: Dundurn, 2002.

Herrup, Cynthia B. *The Common Peace: Participation in the Criminal Law in Seventeenth-Century England.* Cambridge: Cambridge University Press, 1987.

Hoffer, Peter. *Law and People in Colonial America*. Baltimore: Johns Hopkins University Press, 1992.

Jameson, John Franklin. Privateering and Piracy in the Colonial Period. New York: MacMillan & Co., 1925.

Kesselring, K.J. *Mercy and Authority in the Tudor State*. Cambridge: Cambridge University Press, 2003.

Konstam, Angus. *Blackbeard: America's Most Notorious Pirate*. Hoboken: Wiley, 2007.

Kritzler, Edward. *Jewish Pirates of the Caribbean: How a Generation of Swashbuckling Jews Carved Out an Empire in the New World in Their Quest for Treasure, Religious Freedom, and Revenge*. London: Anchor, 2009.

Lane, Kris E. *Pillaging the Empire: Piracy in the Americas, 1500-1750*. New York: Routledge, 1998.

Leeson, Peter T. *The Invisible Hook: Hidden Economics of Pirates*. Princeton: Princeton University Press, 2009.

Lincoln, Margarette. *British Pirates and Society, 1680-1730*. London: Routledge, 2014.

Linebaugh, Peter. *The London Hanged: Crime and Civil Society in the Eighteenth Century*. 2nd edition. London: Verso, 2003.

Linebaugh, Peter and Rediker, Marcus. *The Many-Headed Hydra: Sailors, Slaves, Commoners, and the Hidden History of the Revolutionary Atlantic*. Boston: Beacon Press, 2013.

Little, Benerson. *The Sea Rover's Practice: Pirate Tactics and Techniques, 1630-1730*. Lincoln: Potomac Books, 2007.

Nelson, William E. *The Common Law in Colonial America, Volume II: The Middle Colonies and the Carolinas, 1660-1730*. Oxford: Oxford University Press, 2013.

Nicholls, James. *The Politics of Alcohol: A History of the Drink Question in England*. Manchester: Manchester University Press, 2009.

Policante, Amadeo, *The Pirate Myth: Genealogies of an Imperial Concept*. London: Routledge, 2015.

Pryce, Merrall Llewelyn. *Consuming Passions: The Uses of Cannibalism in Late Medieval and Early Modern Europe*. New York: Routledge, 2003.

Raymond, Joad. *Pamphlets and Pamphleteering in Early Modern Britain*. Cambridge: Cambridge University Press, 2006.

Rediker, Marcus. *Villains of All Nations: Atlantic Pirates in the Golden Age*. Boston: Beacon Press, 2004.

Ritchie, Robert C. *Captain Kidd and the War Against the Pirates*. Cambridge: Harvard University Press, 1986.

Roach, Joseph. *It*. Ann Arbor: University of Michigan Press, 2007.

Salinger, Sharon V. *Taverns and Drinking in Early America*. Baltimore: Johns Hopkins University Press, 2002.

Schmid, Susanne and Schmidt-Haberkamp, eds. Drink in the Eighteenth and Nineteenth Centuries. London: Routledge, 2009.

Silverman, Kenneth. *The Life and Times of Cotton Mather*. New York: Welcome Rain Publishers, 2001.

Skirboll, Aaron. *The Thief-Taker Hangings: How Daniel Defoe, Jonathan Wild and Jack Sheppard Captivated London and Created the Celebrity Criminal*. Guilford: Lyons Press, 2020.

Stark, Suzanne. *Female Tars: Women Aboard Ship in the Age of Sail*. Annapolis: Naval Institute Press, 1996.

Vickers, Daniel. *Young Men and the Sea: Yankee Seafarers in the Age of Sail*. New Haven: Yale University Press, 2005.

Williams, Kevin. *Read All About It! A History of the British Newspaper*. London: Routledge, 2010.

Woodard, Colin. *The Republic of Pirates: Being the True and Surprising Story of the Caribbean Pirates and the Man Who Brought Them Down*. Boston: Mariner Books, 2008.

Zacks, Robert. *The Pirate Hunter: The True Story of Captain Kidd*. New York: Hatchett Books, 2003.

Selected Chapters

Craton, Michael. "Reluctant Creoles: Planters' World in the British West Indies," in *Strangers Within the Realm: Cultural Margins of the First British Empire*, eds. Bernard Bailyn and Philip D. Morgan, 314-362. Chapel Hill: University of North Carolina Press, 1991.

Hay, Douglas. "Property, Authority and the Criminal Law" in *Albion's Fatal Tree: Crime and Society in Eighteenth-Century England*, eds. Douglas Hay and Peter Linebaugh, 17-63. London, Pantheon: 2011.

Greene, Jack P. "Social and Cultural Capital in Colonial British America: A Case Study" in *Patterns of Social Capital: Stability and Change in Historical Perspectives*, eds. Robert I. Rothberg and Gene A. Bruckner, 153-171. Cambridge: Cambridge University Press, 2001.

Lemmings, David. "Introduction: Law and Order, Moral Panics, and Early Modern England" in *Moral Panics, the Media, and the Law in Early Modern England*, eds. David Lemmings and Claire Walker, 1-21. New York: Palgrave MacMillan, 2009.

Articles

Blackman, Paul H. and McLaughlin, Vance. "Mass Legal Executions in America up to 1865." *Crime, Histoire & Sociétés/Crime, History & Societies* 8, no. 2, (2004): 33-61.

Bond, Edward L. "England's Soteriology of Empire and Roots of Colonial Identity in Early Virginia." *Anglican and Episcopal History* 66, no. 4 (December, 1997): 471-499.

Greenberg, Douglas. "Crime, Law Enforcement, and Social Control in Colonial America." *The American Journal of Legal History* 26, no. 4 (October, 1982): 293-325.

Greene, Jack P. "Colonial South Carolina and the Caribbean Connection." *The South Carolina Historical Magazine* 88, no. 4 (October, 1987): 192-210.

Hay, Douglas. "Crime and Justice in Eighteenth- and Nineteenth-Century England." *Crime and Justice* 2 (1980): 45-84.

Klein, Lawrence. "Politeness and the Interpretation of the British Eighteenth Century." *The Historical Journal* 45, no. 4 (2002): 869-898.

Magra, Christopher P. "Faith at Sea: Exploring Maritime Religiosity in the Eighteenth Century." *International Journal of Maritime History* 19, no. 1 (June, 2007): 87-106.

McGowan, Randall. "Civilizing Punishment: The End of the Public Execution in England." *Journal of British Studies* 33, no. 3 (July, 1994), 257-282.

Rediker, Marcus. "Under the Banner of King Death: The Social World of Anglo-American Pirates, 1716 to 1726." *The William and Mary Quarterly* 38, no. 2 (April 1981): 203-227.

Sharpe, J.A. "Last Dying Speeches:' Religion, Ideology, and Public Executions in Seventeenth-Century England." *Past and Present* 107 (May, 1985): 144-167.

Shoemaker, Robert B. "The Old Bailey Proceedings and the Representations of Crime and Criminal Justice in the Eighteenth Century." *Journal of British Studies* 47, no. 3 (July, 2008): 559-580.

Simon, Rebecca. "The Many Deaths of Captain Kidd." *History Today* 65, no. 7 (July, 2015): 7.

Williams, Daniel E. "Puritans and Pirates: A Confrontation Between Cotton Mather and William Fly in 1726." *Early American Literature* 22, no. 3 (1987): 233-251.

——— "Of Providence and Pirates: Philip Ashton's Narrative Struggle for Salvation," *Early American Literature* 24, no. 3 (1989): 169-195.

Witte Jr., John E. and Arthur, Thomas C. "Three Uses of the Law: A Protestant Source of the Purpose of Criminal Punishment?" *Journal of Law and Religion* 10, no. 2 (1993-1994): 433-465.

Web Sources

Andrews, Evan. "Did Pirates Really Make People Walk the Plank?" History. August 31, 2018. https://www.history.com/news/did-pirates-really-make-people-walk-the-plank Accessed July 1, 2020.

Barnes, Tom. "The Definitive History of Pirate Metal." *Thrillist*. April 18, 2019. https://www.thrillist.com/entertainment/nation/the-definitive-oral-history-of-pirate-metal Accessed February 24, 2020.

Cronin, Cat. "Plagued by Piracy: Are West African Waters Safe?" *American Security Project*. July 16, 2019. https://www.americansecurityproject.org/plagued-by-piracy-are-west-african-waters-safe/ accessed July 5, 2020.

Donnelly, Sally B. "Horror on the High Seas." *Time Magazine*. November 14, 2005. Reprinted in the *Jerusalem Center for Public Affairs*, February 8, 2009. https://jcpa.org/article/piracy-and-international-law/ Accessed February 24, 2020.

Fleming Jr., Mike. "Truly*Adventurous Sets Sail With Digital IP Journalism Formula That Is Generating Flurry Of Film." *Deadline*. February 19, 2020. https://deadline.com/2020/02/trulyadventurous-digital-journalism-film-tv-deals-greg-nichols-matthew-pearl-1202862932/ accessed July 5, 2020.

Galuppo, Mia. "Margot Robbie, Christina Hodson Reteam for New 'Pirates of the Caribbean' Movie for Disney (Exclusive)." *The Hollywood Reporter*. June 26, 2020. https://www.hollywoodreporter.com/heat-vision/margot-robbie-christina-hodson-team-new-pirates-caribbean-movie-1298722 accessed July 5, 2020.

George, Richard. "The Dawn of Assassin's Creed IV: Black Flag." *IGN*. March 4, 2013. https://www.ign.com/articles/2013/03/04/the-dawn-of-assassins-creed-iv-black-flag Accessed February 24, 2020.

Just, Martin. "Interviews: Rolf Kasparek." *Webcitation*. February, 1996. https://www.webcitation.org/query?url=http%3A%2F%2Fwww.runningld.net%2Fhtml%2Frk021996.html&date=2011-05-14. Accessed February 24, 2020.

Moriarty, Colin. "Examining the History Behind Assassin's Creed IV: Black Flag." *IGN*. March 12, 2013. https://www.ign.com/articles/2013/03/12/examining-the-history-behind-assassins-creed-iv-black-flag. Accessed February 24, 2020.

Roche, Jason. "Alestorm Plays Metal Inspired by Pirates: 'Other Metal Bands Don't Get Drink Any More.'" *LAWeekly*. November 16, 2012. https://www.laweekly.com/alestorm-plays-metal-inspired-by-pirates-other-metal-bands-dont-get-drunk-any-more/ Accessed February 24, 2020.

Silva, Marty. "Assassin's Creed 4: Black Flag Review." *IGN*. October 29, 2013. https://www.ign.com/articles/2013/10/29/assassins-creed-4-black-flag-review Accessed February 24, 2020.

——— "The Remarkable World of Assassin's Creed IV: Black Flag." *IGN*. July 13, 2016. https://www.ign.com/articles/2013/08/23/the-remarkable-world-of-assassins-creed-iv-black-flag. Accessed February 24, 2020.

Simon, Rebecca. "The Princess Bride and How Image Shaped the Pirate." *Raiders of the Lost Archives: A Film and History Blog*, October 25, 2016. https://raidersofthelostarchivessite.wordpress.com/2016/10/25/the-princess-bride-and-how-image-shaped-the-pirate/ Accessed March 8, 2020.

Simon, Rebecca. "The Revenge of Anne and Mary." *Truly*Adventurous*. October 8, 2019. https://medium.com/truly-adventurous/the-revenge-of-anne-and-mary-477143d7bf4d accessed July 5, 2020.

Thardor, Ishaan. "As Patrols Increase, Somali Pirates Widen Their Reach." *Time Magazine*. April 27, 2010. http://content.time.com/time/world/article/0,8599,1984473,00.html Accessed February 24, 2020.

Thomas, Leah Marilla. "Is 'Black Sails' Based on History or Just 'Treasure Island?' The Starz Series Draws From Fact & Fiction." *Bustle*. January 24, 2015. https://www.bustle.com/articles/60206-is-black-sails-based-on-history-or-just-treasure-island-the-starz-series-draws-from-fact Accessed April 8, 2020.

"About Us," Town of Ramsgate. 2016–2020. http://townoframsgate.pub/?page_id=9 accessed July 5, 2020.

National Archives. "Currency Converter 1270–2017." https://www.nationalarchives.gov.uk/currencyconverter/.

"UN Dismisses Captain Kidd 'Treasure' Find in Madagascar." BBC News. July 14, 2015. https://www.bbc.com/news/world-africa-33524216. Accessed January 26, 2020.

"The History of & Changes to Pirates of the Caribbean," *Park Ride History*, YouTube, August 13, 2018. https://www.youtube.com/watch?v=BEC0wsXkx1o&feature=youtu.be Accessed April 8, 2020.

"Prospect of Whitby." Londonist. February, 2020. https://londonist.com/pubs/pubs/pubs/prospect-of-whitby accessed July 5, 2020

"Pirate Festivals List, Pirate Faires List," *Pirate Festivals.* http://piratefestivals. com/Pirate-Festivals-By-Area.html accessed August 18, 2020.

Talk Like a Pirate. www.talklikeapirate.com Accessed August 21, 2020.

Other Media

Alestorm. "Over the Seas." *Captain Morgan's Revenge.* Napalm Records, 2008.

The Princess Bride. Directed by Rob Reiner. 1987; Act III Communications; Twentieth Century Fox.

ACKNOWLEDGMENTS

This book has been over a decade in the making. I could not have created this alone.

My first thanks goes to the wonderful people at Mango Publishing who trusted me to bring this project to life. Thank you to my editors Natasha Vera, Yaddyra Peralta, Lisa McGuiness, and Diana Valcarcel for your suggestions, corrections, and pointing me in the right direction to make this a better project than I could have imagined.

Many, many thanks goes to my PhD supervisors, Professor Richard Drayton and Professor Laura Gowing. Over the years, Richard served as a mentor and often knew how to articulate what I could not say. His knowledge of archival material and historical theory served me to craft this project. Not to mention, his excellent guidance through the trees helped me see the forest. Likewise, Laura guided me into early modern legal and public history to help me develop my arguments into something comprehensible. More thanks for those at King's who offered help and support goes to Anne Goldgar, Vincent Hiribarren, Anna Maeker, and Adam Sutcliffe. I must also thank Dr. Simon Layton and Professor Diana Paton for their guidance.

I am particularly grateful to the staff at the British Library, National Archives in Kew, Royal Maritime Museum, and the Jamaica National Library. These institutions had myriads of material that helped me develop this project from a simple three-thousand-word paper to jumpstart my doctorate up to publication. The librarians and archivists at these institutions were kind, informative, and gave me special access to materials I might not have been able to look at otherwise.

Academic communities allowed me to share my arguments and expand on my research. I need to thank those who attended conferences and workshops such as The Problem of Piracy: An Interdisciplinary Conference on Plunder by Sea Across the World From the Ancient to the Modern; the British Group of Early American Historians workshop; British Society of Eighteenth-Century Studies; The Emergence of a Maritime Nation: Britain in the Tudor and Stuart Age, 1485–1714 conference at the Royal Maritime Museum in London; and Society for Early Americanists, among many others. Thank you to those who chose me to present, invited me to speak, watched my presentations, gave me valuable insight and suggestions, and bought me one too many rounds.

Others have helped me along the way. I must, in particular, give thanks to Dr. Mark Hanna at the University of California, San Diego. Over lunch, he gave me excellent advice about how to interpret the fascinating and complicated source, A General History of the Pyrates. Gratitude goes to Margarette Lincoln at the Royal Maritime Museum for giving me helpful advice in the early stage of my research, along with Dr. Josh Newton, who showed me some awesome artwork available in the collections.

I need to take a quick step back in time to thank those who gave me the grand jumpstart to my career as a historian, teacher, and a writer. Thank you to Dr. Benjamin Klein for your myriad of history classes that helped me find my way and for keeping in touch all these years. Special thank-yous go to Professors Richard Horowitz, Erik Goldner, and Frank Vatai for steering me through my master's thesis with endless support and kindness. I also need to thank Dr. Christopher Magra for introducing me to pirates in the first place.

I have also received professional support surrounding this project. For that I need to thank my colleagues at Wildwood School, who supported me from day one as I dove into the early writings of this

bank. A humongous thank-you to Steve Bayes, Alex Cussen, Becca
Hedgepath, Emily Johnson, Megan O'Keefe, Sarah Pease-Kerr,
Rebecca Rollinson, and Paul Waked. Thank you all for the laughter
and support needed over the years. I also need to thank public
historians and figures who gave me advice and chances along the
way: Piers Alexander, Levy Chambers, Moshe Kasher, Greg Jenner,
Jonathan Van Ness, and Dr. Sam Willis.

They say it takes a village to raise a child, but it also takes one to help
create a book. My personal friendships and support networks were
instrumental for my motivation to write this book. My fellow PhDers
(and friends) offered much respite and support over the years as we
all poured blood, sweat, and tears into our work. To the Crow's Nest:
Drs. Philip Abraham, Tom Colville, James Fisher, Philippa Hellawell,
Alice Marples, and Will Tullett–I cannot thank you all enough for
the feedback, your undying friendship, endless rounds, and loads
of laughter.

Other forms of refuge were also instrumental for light-hearted fun.
Thank you to Dr. Stephanie Hutchinson and the Concert Singers
for helping me make music that was needed during the writing of
this book.

My closest friends also lent their support and took the time to read
this manuscript to offer their insights in too-short a period of time.
Thank you to Keli Kittinger for pointing out what was fun and
what was boring. Thank you, Elizabeth Wright, for going over the
chapters with a fine-tooth comb to help point out mechanical errors
and for your suggestions about how to help certain passages make
more sense. Thank you to Laura Smith for letting me rant about
this whenever I wanted. Special thanks also belongs to Dr. James
Roffee for endless support and always keeping his door open for
me in the Southern Hemisphere. Finally, I have to thank the best

bitches for films, drinks, and laughter: Alison Caffrey and Gerry and David Hersey.

Last but not least, I need to thank my loving family. First my parents, Gayle and Mitch, my brothers Fred, Sherwood and my sister-in-law Ashton, Matt, Ari, and sister, Kat and my sister-in-law Meghann. And I cannot leave out my dog, Pippin, who often sat on my lap for moral support during the editing process.

ENDNOTES

1 Marcus Rediker, Villains of All Nations: Atlantic Pirates in the Golden Age (Boston: Beacon Press, 2004), 9.

2 Rediker), 8.

3 In the meantime, I can recommend a book called *Black Jacks: African American Seamen Men in the Age of Sail* by W. Jeffrey Bolster. If you are interested in a book about the experience of the slave ship from the enslaved peoples' perspectives, I direct your attention to Sowande M. Mustakeem's powerful book, *Slavery at Sea: Terror, Sex, and Sickness in the Middle Passage.*

4 *A Discourse of the Laws Relating to Pirates and Piracies, and the Marine Affairs of Great Britain* (London, 1726), 4.

5 Robert C. Ritchie, *Captain Kidd and the War Against the Pirates* (Cambridge, 1986), 141; 28 Henry 8, c. 15. "Offences of the Sea Act, 1536," *Statutes of the Realm*, III, 671.

6 OBO (www.oldbaileyonline.org, version 7.0, accessed November 12, 2014), February 1737, trial of Robert Coyle (t17370224-1).

7 OBO (www.oldbailey.org, version 7.0, accessed November 12, 2014), February 1752, trial of James Lowrey (t17520218-1).

8 See Amadeo Policante, *The Pirate Myth: Genealogies of an Imperial Concept* (London: Routledge, 2015), 12–13.

9 Douglas Hay, "Property Authority and the Criminal Law," in *Albion's Fatal Tree: Crime and Society in Eighteenth-Century England,* eds. Douglas Hay and Peter Linebaugh (London: Pantheon, 2011), 17–63. See also Douglas Hay, "Crime and Justice in Eighteenth- and Nineteenth-Century England," *Crime and Justice* 2 (1980), 45–84.

10 See Michael Foucault, *Discipline and Punish: The Birth of the Prison*, trans. Alan Sheridan (New York: Vintage Books, 1995).

11 Cynthia B. Herrup, *The Common Peace: Participation and the Criminal Law in Seventeenth-Century England* (Cambridge: Cambridge University Press, 1987).

12 Foucault, *Discipline and Punish*, 48–49. See also J.A. Sharpe, "'Last Dying Speeches:' Religion, Ideology, and Public Executions in Seventeenth-Century England," in *Past and Present* 107 (May, 1985), 161; Sharpe, "Last Dying Speeches," 161.

13 Edward L. Bond, "England's Soteriology of Empire and Roots of Colonial Identity in Early Virginia" in *Anglican and Episcopal History* 66, no. 45 (December, 1997), 495.

14 "The Lamentations…" *Public Ledger*, April 7, 1774; "Political Speculation," *Public Ledger*, July 11, 1774.

15 As of 2017, this would be between $50,000 and $90,000 (as of 2017). See Currency Converter 1270–2017, National Archives, Kew, UK. https://www.nationalarchives. gov.uk/currency-converter/ This site only converts up until 2017 values. I am using monetary values from 1720, as that was the height of the Golden Age of Piracy. From here on out I will simply list today's currency in the footnotes.

16 $30,000 or $45,000.

17 $15,000.

18   W. Jeffrey Bolster, *Black Jacks: African American Seamen in the Age of Sail* (Cambridge, Harvard University Press: 1997), 13.

19   Ibid, 14.

20   David Cordingly, *Under the Black Flag: The Romance and Reality of Life Among the Pirates* (New York: Random House, 2006), 16.

21   Peter T. Leeson, *The Invisible Hook: Hidden Economics of Pirates* (Princeton: Princeton University Press, 2009), 156–157.

22   For more discussion about different religions on pirate ships, see Edward Kritzler, *Jewish Pirates of the Caribbean: How a Generation of Swashbuckling Jews Carved Out an Empire in the New World in Their Quest for Treasure, Religious Freedom, and Revenge* (London: Anchor, 2009).

23   Cristina Bacchilega and Marie Alohalani Brown, eds. *The Penguin Book of Mermaids* (New York: Penguin Classics, 2019), xx.

24   David Cordingly, *Seafaring Women: Adventures of Pirate Queens, Female Stowaways, and Sailors' Wives* (New York: Random House, 2001), 154–170.

25   Suzanne Stark, *Female Tars: Women Aboard Ship in the Age of Sail* (Annapolis: Naval Institute Press, 1996), 14.

26   Cordingly, *Seafaring Women*, 154–155.

27   Robert Louis Stevenson, *Treasure Island* (London: Alma Classics, Reprint Edition, 2015 edition), 11.

28   Stevenson, *Treasure Island*, 64, 70, 102, 172–180.

29   Rediker, *Villains of All Nations*, 73.

30   Cordingly, *Under the Black Flag*, 9.

31   Cordingly, *Under the Black Flag*, 130. Francis Grose, Dictionary of the Vulgar Tongue (London, 1788), 258. See also, Evan Andrews, "Did Pirates Really Make People Walk the Plank?" August 31, 2018. https://www.history.com/news/did-pirates-really-make-people-walk-the-plank Accessed July 1, 2020.

32   Rediker, *Villains of All Nations*, 8.

33   Colin Woodard, *The Republic of Pirates: Being the True and Surprising Story of the Caribbean Pirates and the Man Who Brought Them Down* (Boston: Mariner Books, 2008), 30–31, 264, 272, 309–310, 319–320.

34   "London," *London Journal*, June 20, 1724.

35   *The American Weekly Mercury*, June 6–13, 1723.

36   Captain Charles Johnson, *A General History of the Pyrates*, ed. Manuel Schoenhorn (Dover, 1999), 318–336.

37   Alexander Exquemelin, *The History of the Buccaneers of America* (London, 1771 edition), 3–4.

38   Peter Earle, *The Pirate Wars: Pirates vs. the Legitimate Navies of the World* (London: Thomas Dunne Books, 2004), 135.

39   *Calendar of State Papers Colonial, America and West Indies* (hereafter *CSPC*)18, Item 318, "Gov. Read Edling to Mr. Secretary Vernon," April 12, 1700.

40   *CSPC* 33, Item 142, "Governor Sir N. Lawes to the Council of Trade and Plantations, May 18, 1722.

41 NLJ MS 60, *Jamaica Council Minutes*, Vol. I, "An Act declaring the Laws of England in force in this Island passed to the Council," November 10, 1664; NLJ MS 60, *Jamaica Council Minutes*, Vol. III, "At a Council Held at St Jago de la Vega," March 14, 1674.

42 *CSPC* 29, Item 331, "Council of Trade and Plantations to Mr. Secretary Methuen," September 13, 1716.

43 Woodard, *The Republic of Pirates*, 86–114.

44 *A General History of the Pirates, Vol. II*, Chapter 3, "Of Captain William Kidd."

45 See Chapter 4 in Richard Zacks, *The Pirate Hunter: The True Story of Captain Kidd* (New York: Hatchett Books, 2003).

46 Close to $115 million as of 2020.

47 Captain Charles Johnson, *A General History of the Pyrates*, ed. Manuel Shonhorn (Mineola, 1999), 53.

48 For a full description of the life of Captain Henry Avery, see Johnson, *A General History of the Pyrates*, 49–62.

49 *CSPC* 15, Item 1187, "Jeremiah Basse to William Popple," July 18, 1697.

50 *CSPC* 16, Item, 434, "Governor Cranston to Council of Trade and Plantations," May 8, 1698; CSPC 16, Item 446, "Draft of a bill for the more easy and speedy trial of pirates," May 12, 1698; CSPC 16, Item 451, "Edward Randolph to William Popple," May 12, 1698.

51 *CSPC* 15, Item 1178, "Information of Thomas Robinson," July 13, 1697.

52 *CSPC* 16, Item 451, "Narrative of Captain Robert Snead," May 12, 1698.

53 *CSPC* 15, Item 1203, "Jeremiah Basse to William Popple," July 26, 1697.

54 *CSPC* 15, Item 604, "Council of Trade and Plantations to Lieutenant Stoughton," January 20, 1697.

55 *The Tryals of Joseph Dawson, Edward Forseith, William May, William Bishop, James Lewis, and John Sparkes for several Piracy and Robberies by them committed, in the Company of Every, the Grand Pirate, near the Coasts of the East-Indies; and several other Places on the Seas* (London, 1696), 28.

56 *The Tryals of Joseph Dawson...*, 28.

57 *The Tryals of Joseph Dawson...*, 28.

58 Currency Converter, 1270–2017, The National Archives, Kew, United Kingdom. https://www.nationalarchives.gov.uk/currency-converter/ accessed June 29, 2020.

59 Johnson, *A General History of the Pyrates*, 440–451.

60 Henry Wilder Foote, *Annals of King's Chapel from the Puritan age of New England to the present day*, Vol. I (Boston, 1900), 86.

61 Thomas Andrew Green, *Verdict According to Conscience: Perspectives of the English Criminal Trial Jury, 1200–1800* (Chicago: University of Chicago Press, 1985), 106–111; GR Elton, "Introduction: Crime and the Historians," in *Crime in England, 1550–1800*, ed. JS Cockburn (Princeton: Princeton University Press, 1977), 4; J.M Beattie, *Crime and the Courts in England, 1660–1800* (Oxford: Oxford University Press, 1986), 433–434.

62 *The Arraignment, Tryal, and Condemnation of Captain William Kidd for Murther and Piracy, upon Six several Indictments* (London, 1701), 3–5.

63 *The Arraignment, Tryal, and Condemnation of Captain William Kidd*, 5.

64 *The Arraignment, Tryal, and Condemnation of Captain William Kidd,* 6.

65 *The Arraignment, Tryal, and Condemnation of Captain William Kidd,* 22.

66 *The Arraignment, Tryal and Condemnation of Captain William Kidd,* 184.

67 BL, IOR/H/36, "Extract of an Eminent Indian Merchant at Suratt Viz. Agapery," April 16, 1698.

68 Kevin Williams, *Read All About It! A History of the British Newspaper* (London: Routledge, 2010), 33.

69 Joel H. Baer, *British Piracy in the Golden Age: History and Interpretation 1660–1740,* Vol. IV (London: Routledge, 2007), 365.

70 "An Elegy of Captain Kidd, who was Executed at Execution-Dock, on Friday the 23rd of this Instant May, 1701," Maggs Brothers, *Proclamations Against Piracy 1603–1701* (London, No Date). The original copy is in the National Library of Jamaica in Kingston, Jamaica.

71 "Captain Kidd: A Noted Pirate, who Hanged at Execution Dock in England," Boston, between 1775 and 1810.

72 *CSPC* 17, Item 621, "Governor Lord Bellomont to the Council of Trade and Plantations," July 8, 1699.

73 BL, RP.8780, "Autograph Letter Signed to Jonathan Dickinson, discussing trading matters including an account of the remnants of Captain Kidd's crew and tales of buried treasure," Philadelphia, July 9, 1699.

74 BL, IOR/H/36, "To Their Excellencies The Lords Justices of England The Humble Petition of the Governour & Company of Merchants of London trading into the East Indies," September 21, 1699.

75 *CSPC* 18, Item 14, "Letter from Lord Bellomont," January 5, 1700.

76 "[No Title]," *Post Boy,* September 7–9, 1699. See also Ritchie, *Captain Kidd and the War Against the Pirates,* 194.

77 *CSPC* 18, Item 156, "William Penn to Mr. Secretary Vernon," February 26, 1700.

78 £7.5 million as of 2017, which amounts to $9.5 million in today's currency.

79 "Execution Dock," *The Speaker: The Liberal Review* 19 (January 21, 1899), 77.

80 Samuel Sewall, *The Diary of Samuel Sewall, 1674–1729,* Vol. II (Boston, 1878), 6.

81 Today, £32 million/$40 million.

82 *CSPC* 17, Item 680, "Governor the Earl of Bellomont to the Council of Trade and Plantations," July 26, 1699; "London, August 23rd," *London Post with Intelligence Foreign and Domestick,* August 21–23, 1699. Currency: £2.2 million/$2.8 million

83 £107,000/$136,000

84 Between £5.4 million/$6.8 million and £6.4 million/$8.1 million.

85 Sewall, *The Diary of Samuel Sewall,* 6n.

86 Dion Clayton Calthrop, "Captain William Kyd," *The Idler* 16 (1900), 341.

87 "Captain Kidd," *Salem Gazette,* August 15, 1823; also in *Haverhill Gazette,* August 23, 1823. Kiddenhooghten was the location of a trading post meant to smooth relations between colonists and Native Americans during the seventeenth century,

88 "Captain Kidd," *National Magazine* 10, no. 55 (May, 1861), 14.

89 "Philadelphia, Nov. 30," *The Morning Chronicle,* December 17, 1844.

90   [No Title], *Semi-Weekly Eagle*, February 12, 1849; "From the Springfield Republican," *Semi-Weekly Eagle*, February 15, 1849.

91   Graham Harris, *Treasure and Intrigue: The Legacy of Captain Kidd* (Toronto: Dundurn, 2002), 23, 169.

92   TNA, MEPO 2/9166, "Attempts to raise money to finance expeditions to search for Captain Kidd's Treasure in the South China Seas."

93   As of 2020 that is approximately £47,000/$60,000

94   TNA, MEPO 2/9166/12.

95   Rebecca Simon, "The Many Deaths of Captain Kidd," *History Today* (July 2015), 7.

96   "UN Dismisses Captain Kidd 'Treasure' Find in Madagascar," *BBC News*, July 14, 2015. https://www.bbc.com/news/world-africa-33524216 (accessed January 26, 2020).

97   T, "A Cruise with Kidd," *Belgravia: A London Magazine* (October, 1874), in British Periodicals, 473, 478–479.

98   TNA, HO 45/19503, "Pardons: Questions of free pardon to Captain Kidd (executed in 1701)," 1936–1944.

99   Lauren Benton, *A Search for Sovereignty: Law and Geography in European Empires, 1400–1900* (Cambridge: Cambridge University Press, 2009), 116, 120.

100 David Armitage and Michael J. Braddick, *The British Atlantic World, 1500–1800* (Basingstoke: Red Globe Press, 2009), 3.

101 *CSPC* 19, Item 1039, "Minutes from the Council of Maryland," November 29, 1701.

102 *CSPC* 18, Item 15, "Governor Sir William Beeston to the Council of Trade and Plantations, January 5, 1700.

103 *CSPC*, Item 468, "The present State of British Sugar Colonys in South America and of the Trade of the Northern Colonys on the Continent to and from the French Sugar Islands and Suriname considered," October 3, 1730.

104 Douglas Burgess, Jr., *The Politics of Piracy: Crime and Civil Disobedience in Colonial America* (Lebanon: ForeEdge, 2014), 27–28.

105 Douglas Burgess, Jr., *The Pirates' Pact: The Secret Alliances Between History's Most Notorious Buccaneers and Colonial America* (New York, 2009), 17.

106 *CSPC* 19, Item 180, "Edward Randolph to the Council of Trade and Plantations, February 19, 1701.

107 *CSPC* 18, Item 300, "Col. Quary to Mr. Secretary Vernon," March 6, 1700.

108 *CSPC* 15, Item 698, "Council of Trade and Plantations to the Lords Proprietors of Carolina," February 9, 1697; Lane, *Pillaging the Empire*, 168.

109 William E. Nelson, *The Common Law in Colonial America, Volume II: The Middle Colonies and the Carolinas, 1660–1730* (Oxford: Oxford University Press, 2013), 74–75.

110 *CSPC* 15, Item 1203, "Jeremiah Basse to William Popple," July 26, 1697.

111 *Executive Journals of the Council of Virginia*, Vol. II, August 3, 1699–April 27, 1705 (Richmond, 1925), 69.

112 Peter Hoffer, *Law and People in Colonial America* (Baltimore: Johns Hopkins University Press, 1992), 19.

113 Peter Hoffer, *Law and People*, 22.

114   Hoffer, *Law and People*, 12–17.

115   Benton, *A Search for Sovereignty*, 147; Ritchie, *Captain Kidd,* 144.

116   Kris E. Lane, *Pillaging the Empire: Piracy in the Americas, 1500–1750* (New York: Routledge, 1998), 125.

117   *CSPC* 19, Item 180, "Edward Randolph to the Council of Trade and Plantations, February 19, 1701.

118   *CSPC* 29, Item 203, "Governor Lord A. Hamilton to the Council of Trade and Plantations," June 12, 1716.

119   *Calendar of State Papers Domestic* [hereafter *CSPD*] 243, "By the king, a proclamation." March 6, 1701.

120   National Library of Jamaica, Kingston, Jamaica, MS 60/101, "At a Council Holden at St Jago de la Vega on Thursday May 3rd 1688," Jamaica Council Minutes, Vol. 5, 1683–1688.

121   K.J. Kesselring, *Mercy and Authority in the Tudor State* (Cambridge: Cambridge University Press, 2003), 3.

122   Beattie, *Crime and the Courts*, 431.

123   *CSPC* 13, Item 703, "Recommendation as to reducing pirates and privateers in America," January 9, 1690.

124   TNA SP 44/347 f.474, "Warrant to insert Robert Seely in the next general pardon for the poor convicts of Newgate for piracy, without condition for transportation, in compassion for his tender years," 1699.

125   TNA, SP 44/350 f.143, "Warrants to Dr. Geo. Oxenden," May 26, 1701.

126   Beattie, *Crime and the Courts in England*, 440.

127   £11,000/$14,000; £2,100/$2,700.

128   *CSPD* 243, "By the king, a proclamation," March 6, 1701.

129   TNA Sp. 44/350 f. 98, "Warrant to Chief Justice Holt and Sir Char. Hedges, judge of the Admiralty Court," July 4, 1700.

130   CSPC 17, Item 15, "Council of Trade and Plantations to Gov. The Earl of Bellomont," January 5, 1699.

131   *CSPC* 19, Item 71, "Copy of a Commission for the trying of pirates in the Massachusetts
      Bay, New Hampshire, and Rhode Island," January 24, 1701; *CSPC* 19, Item 73,
      "Memorandum of Commission for trying Pirates at Newfoundland," January 24,
      1701; *CSPC* 19, Item 74, "Memorandum of Commission for trying pirates in Jamaica,
      January 24, 1701; *CSPC* 19, Item 75, "Memorandum of Commission for trying pirates
      in Maryland," January 24, 1701; *CSPC* 19, Item 76, "Memorandum of a copy of a
      Commission for trying pirates at Bermudas," January 24, 1701; *CSPC* 19, Item 77,
      "Memorandum of a copy of a Commission for trying pirates in the Leeward Islands,"
      January 24, 1701. See also, *CSPC* 19, Item 84, 'William Popple to Governor Sir Wm.
      Beeston, enclosing Commission for trying pirates at Jamaica, the Bahamas, or at
      sea', 27 January 1701; *CSPC* 19, Item 86, 'William Popple to Governor Nicholson,
      enclosing a Commission for trying pirates at Virginia, or North and South Carolina, or
      at sea', 27 January 1701; *CSPC* 19, Item 87, 'William Popple to Governor Codrington,
      enclosing Commission for trying pirates in the Leeward Islands or at sea', 27 January
      1701; *CSPC* 19, Item 89, 'William Popple to Governor Grey, enclosing a Commission
      for trying pirates in Barbados or at sea', 27 January 1701; *CSPC* 19, Item 90, 'William
      Popple to Governor Earl of Bellomont [for trying pirates in Massachusetts Bay, New
      Hampshire, Rhode Island or at sea]', 27 January 1701; *CSPC* 19, Item 91, 'Same
      to same [commission for trying pirates in New York, East and West New Jersey,
      Connecticut or at sea]', 27 January 1701.

132   Angus Konstam, *Blackbeard: America's Most Notorious Pirate* (Hoboken, 2006), 259.

133   Konstam, *Blackbeard*, 184–187, 190–196.

134   BL, Add. MS 61620/155b–156, "Petition of Pirate Wives," 1701.

135   OBO (www.oldbaileyonline.org, version 6.0, 10 January 2014), *Ordinary of Newgate's
      Account*, February 1750 (OA17600211).

136   "The Confession of Walter Kennedy, who was condemn'd at the Sessions of the
      Admiralty for that he with other Pirates, had robb'd and plunder'd the Ship called the
      Loyal Rover, etc.," *A Select and Impartial Account of the Lives, Behavior, and the Dying
      Words of the most Remarkable Convicts from the Year 1700, to the present Time* I
      (London, 1760), 232–237.

137   "The Behavior, Confession, and Dying Words of Capt. John Massey, who was Executed
      at Execution-Dock, on Friday the 26th of July 1723, for Piracy on the High-Seas, near
      St. James's Island on the Coast of North Africa," *A Select and Impartial Account of the
      Lives, Behavior, and the Dying Words of the most Remarkable Convicts from the Year
      1700, to the present Time* I (London, 1760), 269–275.

138   *The Ordinary of Newgate's Account of the Behavior, Confession, and Dying Words of
      Capt. Joseph Halsey, Who was executed at Execution-Dock on Wednesday the 14th of
      March, 1759, For the murder of Daniel Davidson* (London, 1759), 6–7.

139   "The Second Edition with Additions, of The General History of the Pirates," *American
      Weekly Mercury*, December 22–29, 1724; December 29–January 5, 1724, January
      5–12, 1725.

140   "Advertisements," *London Journal*, July 31, 1725.

141   £225,000/$285,000

142   "London, April 3," *American Weekly Mercury*, July 1–8, 1725.

143   Sollom, Emyln, *A Complete Collection of State-Trials and Proceedings for High-
      Treason, and Other Misdemeanours; The Fourth Edition: Commencing with the
      Eleventh Year of the Reign of King George III* (London, 1730).
      Charles Leslie, *A New History of Jamaica, from the Earliest Accounts to the Taking of
      Porto Bello by Vice-Admiral Vernon* (London, 1740).

144   *London Post and General Advertiser* on May 28. 1740; May 30, 1740; June 26, 1740;
      and July 11, 1740.

145   Eve Taylor Bannet, *Transatlantic Stories and the History of Reading, 1720–1810*
      (Cambridge: Cambridge University Press, 2011), 2–3.

146   Joad Raymond, *Pamphlets and Pamphleteering in Early Modern Britain* (Cambridge:
      Cambridge University Press, 2006), 5.

147   Raymond, *Pamphlets and Pamphleteering*, 12, 108.

148   Raymond, *Pamphlets and Pamphleteering*, 118.

149   *An Extract Abridgement of all the Tryals, Not omitting and Material Passage therein,
      relating to High Treasons, Piracies, &c. in the reigns of the Late King William III of
      Glorious Memory, and of our Present Gracious Sovereign Queen Anne* (London, 1703);
      *A Compleat Collection of Remarkable Tryals, of the most Notorious Malefactors, at
      the Sessions-House in the Old-Bailey, from the Year 1706, to the last Sessions, 1720*
      (London, 1721); *A Complete Collection of State-Trials and Proceedings upon High-
      Treason, and other Crimes and Misdemeanours; from the Reign of King Richard II
      to the End of the Reign of King George I* (London, 1730); *A Collection of the Most
      Remarkable Trials of Persons for High-Treason, Murder, Rapes, Heresy, Bigamy,
      Burglary, and other Crimes and Misdemeanours* (London, 1734).

150   A Person of Quality, *A Full Account of the Proceedings in Relation to Capt. Kidd in
      Two Letters* (London, 1701); *Remarks upon the Tryal of Capt. Thomas Green and his
      Crew* (London, 1705); *A Full and Exact Account of the Tryal of Pyrates, Lately Taken
      by Captain Ogle, on Board the Swallow Man of War, on the Coast of Guinea* (London,
      1723); *An Account of the Conduct and Proceedings of the late John Gow, alias Smith,
      Captain of the late Pirates, Executed for Murther and Piracy Committed on Board the
      George Gally, afterwards call'd the Revenge; with A Relation of all the horrid Murthers
      they committed in Cold Blood* (London, 1725). One and three pence is equivalent to
      50 pence—£1.40/63 cents—$1.77.

151   Baer, *British Piracy* I, xviii.

152   Leeson, *The Invisible Hook*, 117.

153   "Execution of the Pirates," *Diary or Woodfall's Register*, January 6, 1790.

154   Benton, *A Search for Sovereignty*, 34.

155   Known as the "it factor." Joseph Roach, *It*, (Ann Arbor: University of Michigan Press,
      2007), 1–4.

156   "Musical Pirates," *Times*, Iss. 37214 (London, October 17, 1903), 13.

157   Johnson, *A General History of the Pyrates*, 211–212.

158   Rediker, *Villains of All Nations*, 72; Cordingly, *Under the Black Flag*, 94.

159   Pieces of eight were Spanish pesos minted out of gold and silver in modern-day
      Mexico City in 1536. These coins were transported back to Spain and by the 1600s
      they were the standard trading currency in the Caribbean. Cordingly, *Under the
      Black Flag*, 35.

160   Johnson, *A General History of the Pyrates*, 342–343.

161   Cordingly, *Seafaring Women*, 6–7.

162   As quoted in Cordingly, *Seafaring Women*, 12.

163   Cordingly, *Seafaring Women*, 7–8.

164   Their individual gender identities were not known. I have chosen to use she/her pronouns to keep descriptions consistent with the primary documents.

165   Johnson, *A General History of the Pyrates*, 148–165.

166   Cordingly, *Seafaring Women*, 54–55. See also Stark, *Female Tars*.

167   Bayus B. Brooks, *Quest for Blackbeard: The True Story of Edward Thache and His World*, Lulu.com, 2020. Kindle.

168   B.R. Burg, *Sodomy and the Pirate Tradition: English Sea Rovers in the Seventeenth-Century Caribbean* (New York: New York University Press, 1995), 128.

169   *CSPC* Vol. 17, 530.VI., "Copy of Deposition of Theophilus Turner."

170   John Franklin Jameson, *Privateering and Piracy in the Colonial Period* (New York: MacMillan & Co., 1923), 199. Retrieved on *Project Gutenberg* February 9, 2020.

171   Aaron Skirboll, *The Thief-Taker Hangings: How Daniel Defoe, Jonathan Wild and Jack Sheppard Captivated London and Created the Celebrity Criminal* (Guilford: Lyons Press, 2020), xv.

172   Peter Linebaugh, *The London Hanged: Crime and Civil Society in the Eighteenth Century*, 2nd ed. (London: Verso, 2003), xvii; Martha Grace Duncan, *Romantic Outlaws, Beloved Prisons: The Unconscious Meanings of Crime and Punishment* (New York: New York University Press, 1996), 82, 85.

173   Walter Thornbury, "The Thames Tunnel, Ratcliffe Highway, and Wapping," *Old and New London: Volume 2* (London, 1878), 128–137.

174   Madge Darby, *Waeppa's People: History of Wapping* (Colchester: Connor & Butler, 1988), 28, 32, 37.

175   Daniel Vickers, *Young Men and the Sea: Yankee Seafarers in the Age of Sail* (New Haven, Yale University Press, 2005), 132.

176   OBO, May 1722, trial of Roger Mead, John Russell, Edward Tankard (t17220510-19).

177   TNA, HCA 1/112, Execution Dock Papers, "Menu Respecting Execution Dock," July 18, 1806. See also Thornbury, "The Thames Tunnel," 128–137.

178   "Prospect of Whitby," Londonist, February 2020, https://londonist.com/pubs/pubs/pubs/prospect-of-whitby accessed July 5, 2020; "About Us," Town Of Ramsgate, 2016–2020. http://townoframsgate.pub/?page_id=9 accessed July 5, 2020.

179   Foucault, *Discipline and Punish*, 33–34.

180   Margarette Lincoln, *British Pirates and Society, 1680–1730* (London: Routledge, 2014), 37.

181   "London, June 11," *Daily Post*, June 11, 1725; Cordingly, *Under the Black Flag*, 223–224.

182   The mentions appear as footnotes in the following cases: Old Bailey Online (Ch. 1, p. 59 in thesis)

183   *English Post Giving an Authentick Account of the Transactions of the World Foreign and Domestick*, November 11–13, 1700.

184   Paul H. Blackman and Vance McLaughlin, "Mass Legal Executions in America up to 1865," *Crime, Histoire & Sociétés/Crime, History & Societies* 8, no. 2 (2004), 40–41.

185   Mark G. Hanna, *Pirate Nests and the Rise of the British Empire, 1570–1730* (Chapel Hill: University of North Carolina Press, 2015), 332–333.

186   Sewall, *The Diary of Samuel Sewall*, 109–110.

187   NMM, PAD1370, "A Perspective View of the River Thames," March 1782.

188   "The Ordinary of Newgate," *Post Boy*, May 22–24, 1701; "On Wednesday," *Original Weekly Journal*, April 12–19, 1718; "Yesterday," *Daily Journal*, June 12, 1725; "London, July 2," *Daily Journal*, July 2, 1725; "Yesterday at Noon," *General Evening Post*, October 14–16, 1784.

189   "Yesterday a board of Admiralty…" *Boston Gazette*, April 24–May 1, 1732; *American Weekly Mercury*, May 11–18, 1732.

190   "London, November 7," *Pennsylvania Chronicle*, January 6–13, 1772; *New-York Journal*, January 23, 1772; *Boston News-Letter*, January 23, 1772; *New-York Gazette*, January 27, 1772; *Essex Gazette*, January 21–28, 1772.

191   Randall McGowan, "Civilizing Punishment: The End of the Public Execution in England," *Journal of British Studies*, 33, no. 3 (July, 1994), 259.

192   McGowan, "Civilizing Punishment," 274.

193   McGowan, "Civilizing Punishment," 273.

194   "Execution Dock," *The Speaker: The Liberal Review* 19 (January 21, 1899), 77.

195   John Brewer, *The Pleasures of the Imagination: English Culture in the Eighteenth Century* (London: Farrar, Straus, and Giroux, 1997), 106.

196   Lawrence Klein, ed., *Anthony Asher Cooper Third Earl of the Shaftesbury: Characteristics of Men, Manners, Opinions, Times* (Cambridge, 1999); See also Lawrence E. Klein, "Politeness and the Interpretation of the British Eighteenth Century," *The Historical Journal*, 45, no. 4 (2002), 869–898.

197   See Daniel E. Williams, "Puritans and Pirates: A Confrontation Between Cotton Mather and William Fly in 1726," *Early American Literature*, 22, no. 3 (1987), 233–251; Sharon V. Salinger, *Taverns and Drinking in Early America* (Baltimore: Johns Hopkins University Press, 2002); James Nicholls, *The Politics of Alcohol: A History of the Drink Question in England* (Manchester: Manchester University Press, 2009); Susanne Schmid and Barbara Schmidt-Haberkamp, Eds., *Drink in the Eighteenth and Nineteenth Centuries* (London: Routledge, 2015).

198   Duncan, *Romantic Outlaws*, 59.

199   Sharpe, "Last Dying Speeches," 150, 152.

200   Douglas Greenberg, "Crime, Law Enforcement, and Social Control in Colonial America" *The American Journal of Legal History* 26, no. 4 (October, 1982), 297.

201   Jack P. Greene, "South Carolina and the Caribbean Connection," *The South Carolina Historical Magazine* 88, no. 4 (October, 1987), 193.

202   Greene, "South Carolina and the Caribbean Connection," 194.

203   Jack P. Green, "Social and Cultural Capital in Colonial British America: A Case Study," *Patterns of Social Capital: Stability and Change in Historical Perspectives,* eds. Robert I. Rotberg and Gene A. Brucker (Cambridge: Cambridge University Press, 2001), 163–163.

204   Michael Craton, "Reluctant Creoles: Planters' World in the British West Indies," *Strangers Within the Realm: Cultural Margins of the First British Empire,* eds. Bernard Bailyn and Philip D. Morgan (Chapel Hill: University of North Carolina Press, 1991), 353.

205 TNA HCA 1/112, "Execution Dock Papers: Menu Respecting Execution Dock," May 20, 1811. Although this is dated in the 19th century, this is the only detailed list of duties and operations of hangings at Execution Dock. The ritual of public executions remained, for the most part, the same until the early nineteenth century. Therefore, we can assume that this order of operations can be applied here.

206 "Edinburgh, April 12," *Boston News-Letter*, September 17–24, 1705.

207 Anonymous, *The liues, apprehensions, arraignments, and executions, the 19 late pyrates Namely: Capt. Harris, Jennings, Loncastle, Downes, Haulsey, and their companies. As they were severely indited on St. Margarets Hill in Southwarke, on the 22 of December last, and executed Fryday the following* (London, 1609), 26.

208 [No Title], *Morning Herald*, January 14, 1788.

209 Sharpe, "Last Dying Speeches," 150, 152.

210 *A Select and Impartial Account of the Lives, Behaviour, and Dying Words of the most remarkable Convicts from the Year 1700 down to the present Time,* Vol. 1 (London, 1760), 2–3.

211 [No Title], *Boston News-Letter*, May 28–April 4, 1724.

212 [No Title], *Boston News-Letter*, May 28–August 4, 1724.

213 Anna Bryson, *Courtesy to Civility: Changing Codes of Conduct in Early Modern England (Oxford: Oxford University Press, 1998)*, 3, 96.

214 Salinger, *Taverns and Drinking*, 39.

215 Nicholls, *The Politics of Alcohol*, 1.

216 "Bermudas, July 30," *London Gazette*, September 21–24, 1717; "Boston, May 3," Boston News-Letter, April 29–May 6, 1718.

217 Peter Linbaugh and Marcus Rediker, *The Many-Headed Hydra: Sailors, Slaves, Commoners, and the Hidden History of the Revolutionary Atlantic* (Boston: Beacon Press, 2013), 158.

218 NLJ MS 60, Jamaica Council Minutes 1, "An Act against tipling, cursing, and swearing," November 8, 1664.

219 Lane, *Pillaging the Empire*, 195.

220 There is a theory that due to the lack of women in Jamaica, many men were engaging in same-sex sexual relations. As a result, British officials deliberately sent prostitutes to the island to stop this behavior.

221 NLJ MS 60, Jamaica Council Minutes 3, "The Deposition of John Yardley Master to the Ketch John's Adventure, July 5, 1676.

222 TNA, CO 139/8/8–9, *Act of Assembly Passed in the Island of Jamaica from 1681–1737 Inclusive*, London, 1738. At the turn of the eighteenth century, £20 was worth £2,200/$2,775 in today's currency.

223 TNA, CO 138/3/16, *Entry books of commissions, instructions, correspondence, etc.: Jamaica*.

224 Christopher P. Magra, "Faith at Sea: Exploring Maritime Religiosity in the Eighteenth Century," International Journal of Maritime History 19, no. 1 (June, 2007) 5, 20.

225 Michael J. Crawford, ed. *The Autobiography of a Yankee Mariner: Christopher Prince and the American Revolution* (Washington DC: Brassey's Inc., 2002), 151.

226 Hugh Jones, *The Present State of Virginia, Giving a particular and short Account of the Indian, English and Negroe Inhabitants of that Colony* (London, 1724), 149.

227 [No Title], *Boston News-Letter*, June 26–July 3, 1704.

228 John E. Witte Jr., and Thomas C. Arthur, "Three Uses of the Law: A Protestant Source of the Purpose of Criminal Punishment?" *Journal of Law and Religion* 10, no. 2 (1993–1994), 436.

229 Jones, *The Present State of Virginia*, 95–97.

230 Alison Games, *Migrations and Origins of the English Atlantic World* (Cambridge: Harvard University Press, 2001), 134.

231 David Lemmings, "Introduction: Law and Order, Moral Panics, and Early Modern England," in *Moral Panics, the Media, and the Law in Early Modern England*, eds. David Lemmings and Claire Walker (New York: Palgrave MacMillan, 2009), 7.

232 "The Account which the Captain of the Cassandra gives to the India Company…" *Weekly Journal or British Gazetteer*, April 22, 1721.

233 "Capt. Massey…" *London Journal*, August 3, 1724.

234 "London," *London Journal*, June 20, 1724.

235 Merrall Llewelyn Price, *Consuming Passions: The Uses of Cannibalism in Late Medieval and Early Modern Europe* (New York: Routledge, 2003), 7.

236 "6," *Monthly Chronicle*, May 1729.

237 "On this day…" *Monthly Chronicle*, May 1729.

238 This information comes from a survey and analysis of the Early American Newspapers Series I (1690–1876), which was accessed remotely at the British Library, London, between 2013 and 2016.

239 "The following Account of the Murder of Capt. Christopher Brooks, Commander of the Ship Haswell, of London, with his first and second Mate, we have extracted from the Barbados Gazette, of the 17th of April past, written by James Hill, a Passenger on board the said Ship," *Weekly Rehearsal*, June 9, 1735.

240 "We received…" *Weekly Journal or Saturday's Post*, August 31, 1723.

241 "7 April 1719 at St Jago de la Vega," *Jamaica Weekly Courant*, April 15, 1719.

242 Roderick Cave, *Printing and the Book Trade in the West Indies* (London: Prindar Press, 1987), 1–6, 17.

243 "American News, New York, October 15," *Bermuda Gazette*, November 13, 1784.

244 "Letters from Jamaica," *Compleat Set of St. James's Journals*, October 4, 1722; *British Journal*, October 6, 1722; *London Journal*, October 6, 1722.

245 "By our last Letters from New England," *The Post Boy*, September 7–9, 1699; "We have a malicious Report…" *The Post Boy*, November 14–16, 1699; "We Have Advice from Boston," *The Post Boy*, November 30–December 2, 1699.

246 Robert B. Shoemaker, "The Old Bailey Proceedings and the Representations of Crime and Criminal Justice in the Eighteenth Century," *Journal of British Studies* 47, no. 3 (July, 2008), 563–565. Money conversion as of 2019.

247 "Ordinary of Newgate's Accounts," The Proceedings of the Old Bailey: London's Central Criminal Court, 1674–1913, 2018. https://www.oldbaileyonline.org/static/Ordinarys-accounts.jsp# Accessed August 19, 2020.

248 "Philip Roche, Executed on the 5th of August 1723, for many Murders on the High Seas and Piracy," *Newgate Calendar*, http://www.exclassics.com/newgate/ng168.htm, accessed October 20, 2019. NOTE: Although the date of his executed was stated as August 22, 1723, the actual date in documents appears differently in several sources.

249   "The Behaviour, Confession, and Last Dying Words of Philip Roche, who was executed
       at Execution-Dock at Wapping the 14th of August, 1723, for Piracy on the High Seas,"
       *A Select and Impartial Account of the Lives, Behaviour and the Dying Words of the
       most Remarkable Convicts from the Year 1700, to the present Time*, Vol. 1 (London,
       1760), 276–284. NOTE: The dates in the account differ then that of the title.

250   "The Confession of Walter Kennedy, who was condemn'd at the Sessions of the
       Admiralty, for that he with other Pirates, had robb'd and plunder'd the Ship called the
       Loyal Rover, etc." *A Select and Impartial Account of the Lives, Behaviour and the Dying
       Words of the most Remarkable Convicts from the Year 1700, to the present Time*, Vol. 1
       (London, 1760), 232–237.

251   *The Tryals of Major Stede Bonnet and Other Pirates...Who were all condemn'd for
       Piracy* (London, 1719), 11.

252   Ordinary of Newgate, "Ordinary's Accounts: Biographies of Executed Criminals,"
       London Lives, http://www.londonlives.org/browse.jsp?div=OA172312232312230005,
       accessed October 28, 2019.

253   Richie, *Captain Kidd and the War Against the Pirates*, 229.

254   Cotton Mather, *The Diary of Cotton Mather, 1681–1708* (Boston, 1911), 122.

255   Kenneth Silverman, *The Life and Times of Cotton Mather*, (New York: Welcome Rain
       Publishers, 2001), 47–48.

256   Daniel A. Cohen, *Pillars of Salt, Monuments of Grace: New England Crime Literature
       and the Origins of American Popular Culture, 1674–1860* (Oxford: Oxford University
       Press, 1993), 14.

257   Sharpe, "Last Dying Speeches," 161.

258   Mather, *Useful Remarks*, 23–24.

259   Mather, *Useful Remarks*, 26.

260   Mather, *Useful Remarks*, 27–28.

261   As quoted in Daniel E. Williams, "Of Providence and Pirates: Philip Ashton's Narrative
       Struggle for Salvation," *Early American Literature* 24, no. 3 (1989), 176.

262   Philip Ashton, *Ashton's Memorial: Or an Authentick Account of the Strange Adventures
       and Signal Deliverances of Mr. Philip Ashton* (London, 1722), 21.

263   Ashton, *Ashton's Memorial*, 27–28.

264   Reverend John Adams, *The Flowers of Modern History* (Dublin, 1789), 22.

265   Marcus Rediker, "Under the Banner of King Death: The Social World of Anglo-
       American Pirates, 1716 to 1726," *The William and Mary Quarterly* 38, no. 2 (April
       1981), 221–222, 277.

266   "A Letter from Portsmouth, Dated Feburary 1," *The New York Gazette*, March 28,
       1757; "Further Advices by the Packet, London, June 1," *The New York Gazette*,
       August 14, 1769.

267   [No Title], *The Boston News-Letter*, June 26–July 3, 1704.

268   *CSPC* 16, Item 1077, "Benjamin Fletcher to the Council of Trade and Plantations,"
       December 24, 1698; *CSPC* 17, Item 26, "T. Weaver to the Council of Trade and
       Plantations, January 9, 1699; *CSPC* 17, Item 167, "Council of Trade and Plantations to
       the King," March 9, 1699.

269   Hanna, 394.

270   Roach, *It*, 208.

271   Hannah, 404.

272   Cordingly, *Under the Black Flag*, 19.

273   See JM Barrie, Chapter XIV, *Peter Pan in The Complete Works of JM Barrie* (Sussex: Delphi Classics, 2015).

274   "The History of & Changes to Pirates of the Caribbean," *Park Ride History* via YouTube, August 13, 2018.https://www.youtube.com/watch?v=BEC0wsXkx1o&feature=youtu.be Accessed April 8, 2020.

275   Cordingly, *Under the Black Flag*, 172–173.

276   *The Princess Bride* (1987).

277   Rebecca Simon, "The Princess Bride and How Image Shaped the Pirate," *Raiders of the Lost Archives: A Film and History Blog*, October 25, 2016. https://raidersofthelostarchivessite.wordpress.com/2016/10/25/the-princess-bride-and-how-image-shaped-the-pirate/ Accessed March 8, 2020.

278   "Urca de Lima Shipwreck," *National Park Service*, September 19, 2019. https://www.nps.gov/articles/urcadelima.htm Accessed April 8, 2020.

279   Leah Marilla Thomas, "Is 'Black Sails' Based on History or Just 'Treasure Island?' The Starz Series Draws From Fact & Fiction," *Bustle*, January 24, 2015. https://www.bustle.com/articles/60206-is-black-sails-based-on-history-or-just-treasure-island-the-starz-series-draws-from-fact Accessed April 8, 2020.

280   John MacDonald, *Travels in Various Parts of Europe, Asia, and Africa During a Series of Thirty Years and Upward* (London, 1790), 276.

281   Francis Grose, *1811 Dictionary of the Vulgar Tongue*, extracted from *Project Gutenberg*. https://archive.org/details/1811dictionaryof05402gut accessed April 5 2020.

282   Linebaugh, *The London Hanged*, xvii; Duncan, *Romantic Outlaws*, 82, 85.

283   John Stephen Farmer, *Slang and Its Analogues Past and Present*, Vol.II (1891), 258.

284   Daniel Defoe, *The Four Years Voyages of Capt. George Roberts* (London, 1726), 89.

285   "Kingston, Jamaica; May 29. 1819," *St. George's Chronicle and Grenada Gazette*, September 18, 1819.

286   Benerson Little, *The Sea Rover's Practice: Pirate Tactics and Techniques, 1630–1730* (Lincoln: Potomac Books, 2007), 91

287   Richard George, "The Dawn of Assassin's Creed IV: Black Flag," *IGN*, March 4, 2013. https://www.ign.com/articles/2013/03/04/the-dawn-of-assassins-creed-iv-black-flag Accessed February 24, 2020.

288   Colin Moriarty, "Examining the History Behind Assassin's Creed IV: Black Flag," *IGN*, March 12, 2013. https://www.ign.com/articles/2013/03/12/examining-the-history-behind-assassins-creed-iv-black-flag Accessed February 24, 2020.

289   Marty Silva, "The Remarkable World of Assassin's Creed IV: Black Flag," *IGN*, July 13, 2016. https://www.ign.com/articles/2013/08/23/the-remarkable-world-of-assassins-creed-iv-black-flag Accessed February 24, 2020.

290   Marty Silva, "Assassin's Creed 4: Black Flag Review," *IGN*, October 29, 2013. https://www.ign.com/articles/2013/10/29/assassins-creed-4-black-flag-review Accessed February 24, 2020.

291   Tom Barnes, "The Definitive History of Pirate Metal," *Thrillist*, April 18, 2019. https://www.thrillist.com/entertainment/nation/the-definitive-oral-history-of-pirate-metal Accessed February 24, 2020.

292   Martin Just, "Interviews: Rolf Kasparek," *Webcitation*, February, 1996. https://www.webcitation.org/query?url=http%3A%2F%2Fwww.running-wild.net%2Fhtml%2Frk021996.html&date=2011-05-14 Accessed February 24, 2020.

293   Jason Roche, "Alestorm Plays Metal Inspired by Pirates: 'Other Metal Bands Don't Get Drink Any More,'" *LAWeekly*, November 16, 2012. https://www.laweekly.com/alestorm-plays-metal-inspired-by-pirates-other-metal-bands-dont-get-drunk-any-more/ Accessed February 24, 2020.

294   Barnes, "The Definitive History of Pirate Metal".

295   Alestorm, "Over The Seas," *Captain Morgan's Revenge* (Napalm Records, 2008).

296   Jason Roche, "Alestorm Plays Metal Inspired by Pirates."

297   For a full list see "Pirate Festivals List, Pirate Faires List," *Pirate Festivals* http://piratefestivals.com/Pirate-Festivals-By-Area.html accessed August 18, 2020.

298   Pirate Invasion Long Beach http://www.pirateinvasionlongbeach.com/ accessed April 5, 2020.

299   All information is from John Baur and Mark Summer's website, www.talklikeapirate.com

300   Sally B. Donnelly, "Horror on the High Seas" from *Time Magazine*, November 14, 2005. Reprinted in the *Jerusalem Center for Public Affairs*, February 8, 2009. https://jcpa.org/article/piracy-and-international-law/ Accessed February 24, 2020.

301   Ishaan Thardor, "As Patrols Increase, Somali Pirates Widen Their Reach," *Time Magazine*, April 27, 2010. http://content.time.com/time/world/article/0,8599,1984473,00.html Accessed February 24, 2020.

302   Cordingly, Under the Black Flag, 20–21.

303   Hanna, *Pirate Nests*, 420.

304   Rediker, *Villains of All Nations*, 171.

305   Hamilton W. Mabie, "Should the Young Read Novels?" *Ladies Home Journal*, Vol. XXIV, No. 10, September 1907, 28.

306   Cat Cronin, "Plagued by Piracy: Are West African Waters Safe?" *American Security Project*, July 16, 2019. https://www.americansecurityproject.org/plagued-by-piracy-are-west-african-waters-safe/ accessed July 5, 2020.

307   Rediker, *Villains of All Nations*, 54.

308   Mike Fleming Jr., "Truly*Adventurous Sets Sail With Digital IP Journalism Formula That Is Generating Flurry Of Film," *Deadline*, February 19, 2020 https://deadline.com/2020/02/trulyadventurous-digital-journalism-film-tv-deals-greg-nichols-matthew-pearl-1202862932/ accessed July 5, 2020.
See Rebecca Simon, "The Revenge of Anne and Mary," *Truly*Adventurous*, October 8, 2019. https://medium.com/truly-adventurous/the-revenge-of-anne-and-mary-477143d7bf4d accessed July 5, 2020.

309   Mia Galuppo, "Margot Robbie, Christina Hodson Reteam for New 'Pirates of the Caribbean' Movie for Disney (Exclusive)," *The Hollywood Reporter*, June 26, 2020. https://www.hollywoodreporter.com/heat-vision/margot-robbie-christina-hodson-team-new-pirates-caribbean-movie-1298722 accessed July 5, 2020.

ABOUT THE AUTHOR

Dr. Rebecca Simon completed her doctorate in history about eighteenth-century public executions of pirates at King's College London in 2017. She has presented her research around the world and has published in academic journals and popular productions such as *History Today* and *Medium*. She has been featured on podcasts such as Getting Curious with Jonathan Van Ness and You're Dead to Me to talk all things pirate. Rebecca is currently working on projects about female pirates, the pirates' code, and life on the pirate ships. When she's not writing, she is likely in an airplane on her next adventure. Rebecca lives in Los Angeles, California, with her dog, Pippin, and teaches history at Santa Monica College.

Mango Publishing, established in 2014, publishes an eclectic list of books by diverse authors—both new and established voices— on topics ranging from business, personal growth, women's empowerment, LGBTQ studies, health, and spirituality to history, popular culture, time management, decluttering, lifestyle, mental wellness, aging, and sustainable living. We were recently named 2019 *and* 2020's #1 fastest growing independent publisher by *Publishers Weekly*. Our success is driven by our main goal, which is to publish high quality books that will entertain readers as well as make a positive difference in their lives.

Our readers are our most important resource; we value your input, suggestions, and ideas. We'd love to hear from you—after all, we are publishing books for you!

Please stay in touch with us and follow us at:

Facebook: Mango Publishing
Twitter: @MangoPublishing
Instagram: @MangoPublishing
LinkedIn: Mango Publishing
Pinterest: Mango Publishing

Newsletter: mangopublishinggroup.com/newsletter

Join us on Mango's journey to reinvent publishing, one book at a time.